Nestled behind a leafy courtyard in San Francisco's Mission Dis[trict], with the warm glow of lanterns illuminating well-worn wood[en] counters, Rintaro is a beautiful escape; familiar and unexpect[ed], bold and restrained. And its food is straightforwardly delicious: dashimaki tamago, juicy and piping hot; pork gyoza, each dumpling held together by a web of crispy batter; udon with hand-rolled noodles and a hot-spring egg; and a towering melon parfait with bright melon jellies that all but burst in your mouth. This is food that tastes both like Japan and California—not fusion food—but the food that you'd expect if the Bay Area were a region of Japan.

Rintaro, the debut cookbook from this groundbreaking restaurant, translates the experience of a Tokyo izakaya to the home kitchen. Beautiful and idiosyncratic, *Rintaro* is both a master class in making homemade udon noodles, and plumbs the depths of true comfort in food, with recipes like its curry rice. With over 70 recipes showcasing inspiration and detailed instruction in equal measure, *Rintaro* is a book for anyone who loves Japanese food, from the curious novice to expats craving the tastes of home. It is a book that blends careful mastery with the pure delight of making the tastiest food, it encourages you to find the beauty in your own terroir and the heart in your own cooking.

For my father

RINTARO

RINTARO

JAPANESE FOOD FROM AN IZAKAYA IN CALIFORNIA

SYLVAN MISHIMA BRACKETT

WITH JESSICA BATTILANA

PHOTOGRAPHS BY AYA MISHIMA BRACKETT

Hardie Grant
NORTH AMERICA

CONTENTS

RECIPES

Maguro no Yukke Don
まぐろのユッケ丼
Marinated Tuna over Rice
213

Katsudon
かつ丼
Pork Katsu and Egg over Rice
216

Oyakodon
親子丼
Chicken and Egg over Rice
217

Mabodofu Don
マーボー豆腐丼
Spicy Tofu and Pork over Rice
218

Bifu Kare Raisu
ビーフカレーライス
Beef Curry Rice
221

Kakiage Don
かきあげ丼
Mixed Tempura over Rice
224

UDON
うどん

Udon Men
うどん 麺
Udon Noodles
230

Udon Dashi
うどんだし
Udon Broth
238

Udon Kaeshi
うどんかえし
Udon Seasoning Base
239

Kake Udon
かけうどん
Udon in Hot Broth
240

Kamo Nanban Udon
鴨南蛮うどん
Duck and Mushroom Udon
243

Kama Tama Udon
釜玉うどん
Udon "Carbonara"
244

Bukkake Udon
ぶっかけうどん
Chilled Udon with Daikon and Ginger
247

Hiyashi Udon
冷やしうどん
Chilled Udon with Sesame Sauce
250

Kaisen Nabeyaki Udon
海鮮鍋焼きうどん
Seafood Udon Clay Pot
253

DEZATO
デザート
DESSERTS

Hojicha Panna Cotta
ほうじ茶パンナコッタ
Roasted Green Tea Panna Cotta
260

Almond Cookies
アーモンドクッキー
263

Gurepufurutsu Zeri
グレープフルーツゼリー
Ruby Grapefruit Kanten Jelly
264

Melon Parfait
メロンパフェ
Green Melon Ice Cream Parfait
267

Ichigo Daifuku
いちご大福
Mochi-Wrapped Strawberries
270

Roll Cake
ロールケーキ
275

Soufflé Cheesecake
スフレチーズケーキ
277

Mont Blanc
モンブラン
281

Umeshu
梅酒
Plum Brandy
283

INTRO-DUCTION

IN 2007, I BOUGHT A one-way ticket from San Francisco to Japan. I was thirty-one years old and had just finished a six-year stint at Chez Panisse, where I worked as Alice Waters's assistant. My plan was to stay in Japan for six months. A friend whom I had met in college offered to put me up at his place in Yokohama, just south of Tokyo, while I looked for restaurant work. I knew I wanted to eat and cook as much as possible, but beyond that, I had no real idea what I was doing.

Luckily another friend of mine, Nancy Hachisu, had a better plan. She suggested I meet Kanji Nakatani, the chef/owner of a restaurant called Soba Ro. Soba Ro is in Saitama, a prefecture about an hour north of Tokyo, and Nancy lived nearby, where she ran an English-immersion preschool. If things worked out, she offered to let me live in one of the small rooms she rented to teachers in her preschool.

Nancy took me to meet Kanji-san at his restaurant, and we hit it off. He had (and has) an extremely big personality: He drives fancy cars (think Mercedes G-class and Range Rovers), is really into jazz, smokes like crazy, drinks a lot, and runs a fantastic soba restaurant in a pretty sleepy agricultural region. I'm from Northern California, so I like to describe Saitama as the Central Valley of Japan.

When I visited Soba Ro, I was struck by how beautiful it was. The restaurant is surrounded on three sides by rice paddies, with a weathered bamboo fence at the entrance. Once inside, guests remove their shoes in a stone foyer that, in the summer, the staff douses in water, leaving the entrance cool and refreshing. The restaurant has several homey dining rooms—quite different from many of the sterile, upscale restaurants I'd encountered in Tokyo—with stained glass, vintage Windsor chairs, and a woodstove that make the place feel as if it had been transported from the 1940s.

Kanji-san was generous with his time. I worked at Soba Ro four days a week with three other cooks. We arrived for work at 8:30 each morning and lunch would start at 11:30. At 3:00 p.m. lunch would end, after which we'd clean up and Kanji-san would prepare a meal for the four of us. What I remember most was a dish he'd make us called Neapolitan: pasta with bacon, ketchup, and mayonnaise. It's classic post-war Japanese food, now made for kids but originating from a time when Japan was a truly poor country. It was something he never would have served at the restaurant, but it was delicious, and I loved that he cooked it for us, since he figured it was something the younger cooks would enjoy. After our lunch, the four of us would curl up and take a quick nap on zabuton cushions laid out on the floor of one of the dining rooms, while Chef hand wrote the night's menu or tinkered in the garden. Dinner service went until 10:00 p.m., which meant we worked until 11:00 each night. Since there wasn't a dedicated dishwasher on staff, the cooks serviced everything. We swept, took out the garbage, washed the giant soba pot, and scrubbed the copper tenpura pot until it gleamed. Finally, we got on our hands and knees with towels to wipe the floor clean with hand towels.

After work, once or twice a week, Kanji-san took me out on the town. On an average night, we would visit three restaurants and two bars; this is called hashigo, which translates to "ladder." First you go somewhere for a snack, then somewhere for dinner, then somewhere else for another snack ... or another dinner. Kanji-san took me to all the best tiny restaurants, ones I never would have found on my own. For example, we visited a fish-based izakaya, which was run exclusively by women—something that is uncommon in Japan. The husband of one of the owners had opened the restaurant, but when he died, she and her sister took it over. There, I ate perfect sashimi, half-dried grilled fish, and Japanese sea snails with sake and soy sauce, grilled in their own shells over a small brazier set on the table. Kanji-san's English is, well, almost nonexistent, and, if I'm being honest, my Japanese is poor. But even though a lot of our communication was through excited, drunken hand gestures, I still learned so much from him on those late nights out.

Beyond the techniques and recipes, he taught me—how to roll udon, roll-cut daikon, shave katsuobushi for dashi, and make kaeshi seasoning base for soba broth—Kanji-san taught what it means to cook with heart. He showed me the foods he thought were delicious, and why. And he taught me about the subtle work of taking care of your guests. The perfect representation of this is the way he would cook soba for his senior diners. Typically, he'd cook it al dente, but for older people, he'd cook it for a moment or two longer, just a small gesture to make the eating experience easier and more pleasurable.

During this time, I was also commuting back to Tokyo to work two nights a week at a high-end kaiseki restaurant in Aoyama, a tony neighborhood known for its fashion boutiques. The restaurant was very expensive. It was also very beautiful, but not warm like Soba Ro. All the employees wore pure white: jacket, pants, and tabi (toe socks). I was impressed by the skill of the cooks there. We were sometimes served katsu for our staff meal, and I remember watching as one of the cooks used a razor-sharp knife instead of a mandoline to shave the cabbage into a snowy mound. Only an insane person would do that, I thought. One of my tasks was to boil and shell edamame. I'd take each bean and remove the paper-thin inner skin and then grind the edamame into a super smooth paste. It was a time-consuming, monotonous task, but it gave me a real sense of the precision involved in this style of high-end cooking.

But to me, Saitama was heaven. Every couple of days, Kanji-san would take me to the tiny regional fish market that was no bigger than my current restaurant, Rintaro, but it was packed with the freshest, most vibrant seafood imaginable. It was like Tokyo's famous Tsukiji Market but in miniature. We would visit the farms of Kanji-san's friends and pick up daikon, negi (large Japanese scallions), and sesame seeds that the farmers had harvested and painstakingly winnowed. Then we would toast them to use as a garnish or grind them to make goma dofu.

When my six-month stay was over, I was sad to leave, but I was ready. I was also exhausted. I had been working six days a week and commuting three hours twice weekly between Yokohama and Saitama on the Hachikō Line, famous for its frequent stops and maddeningly slow pace. (Of course, there was a faster, forty-five-minute bullet train, but I didn't have much money and couldn't afford it.) Despite eating and drinking constantly, I had lost twenty pounds, just from the stress and intensity of it all. And, too, I missed my wife, Jenny, who was home in San Francisco, and I hadn't seen her since I left.

But I returned home with a notebook, filled with ideas: notes on every dish and ingredient I had encountered and inspiration for things I wanted to make back home in California. I had beautiful pieces of pottery—soba dipping cups, small plates—that Nancy had helped me find at local flea markets and junk shops. And at last, I had the

confidence I needed to launch my own business. When I got back to San Francisco, I returned to Chez Panisse and worked part-time as the restaurant's creative director, in charge of graphic design, special dinners, and events. The rest of the week, I focused on building a catering company, which I named Peko Peko—a Japanese onomatopoeia for the sound an empty, hungry stomach makes.

At Peko Peko, I cooked many of the dishes I had learned during my time in Japan and others I picked up on subsequent trips. Every year, I went back to Japan for a month or two, often with my wife. Japanese friends took us to all kinds of izakaya and yakitori shops crowded with sloppy, drunk salarymen. We spent hours in a five-seat oden restaurant in old-town Yokohama. The master was in his seventies and his mother worked by his side, frying up fish cakes. In Matsumoto, up in the mountains, we were taken to a restaurant in an old farmhouse at the edge of town. It was packed, and the music was loud, and we ate freshly made udon and horse sashimi with garlic.

I loved these places. The food was direct and delicious, and you could drink and eat for hours with friends. At the time, there was nothing even remotely like them in California. During one visit, I realized that it was time for me to open an izakaya of my own. I would call it Rintaro, my name in Japanese, which, like Sylvan, roughly translates to "boy of the woods." Rintaro would be my first brick-and-mortar restaurant, and the first izakaya of its kind in the Bay Area. My hope was that at Rintaro I would be able to synthesize everything I'd learned and tasted and experienced, not only on those recent research trips but throughout my life—at Soba Ro, at Chez Panisse, and even as a kid growing up in Northern California and Japan.

I was born in a municipal hospital in Kyoto, Japan, in the swinging '70s. My mother, who had grown up in a tiny village outside Kyoto, met my American father at the jazz café where she worked. He was in Japan working as a temple carpentry apprentice and was something of a novelty as one of the first non-Japanese people to learn this craft. Growing up, my father often told me how he had learned to do good work: brutal seventeen-hour shifts, six days a week. These stories made an impression on me.

When I was a year old, we left Japan for Northern California. My parents bought forty wild acres, an hour's drive outside of Nevada City in the Sierra Foothills on winding roads. It was profoundly rural: way beyond the reach of the regional utility company PG&E; there were no sewers, no streetlights, no streets, no neighbors—just a creek and lots of birds and trees. My father cut timber from the land to build our house, a traditional Japanese building with narrow hallways called engawas, fitted with sliding doors that opened onto the woods, woven tatami mats, shoji screens, and a bath heated by a wood-fired stove. We had kerosene for light, wood for heat, and a garden that supplied lots of what we ate.

My mother was and still is a great cook. I grew up picking peas in her garden, helping her fold gyoza, and taking out the compost. Every third year she took me and my sister back to her home village outside Kyoto for the summer to visit my grandmother. I loved these trips. There was exciting Japanese candy, video games, and toys that had not yet made it to America, and, of course, the food. We ate grilled fish and miso soup for breakfast, snacked on fried croquettes called korokke from the grocery store and, on special occasions, ate futomaki, fancy thick sushi filled with simmered vegetables, egg, and shiitake.

When I was eight years old, on a trip to Japan, my family was treated to dinner by my father's former boss, and I ate raw and twitching shrimp and absurdly tender and fatty beef in a penthouse restaurant in Kyoto. I still remember the sensation of the shrimp moving in my mouth: I was freaked out but also fascinated. When I reflect on all my most powerful childhood memories, food is almost always at the center.

In high school, I opened a pop-up restaurant behind the English building. The first dish I served my classmates was Japanese curry. My physics teacher was supportive and let me use the burners in the science lab as a heat source. The only real hiccup was when I tried to serve fondue and got in trouble with the vice principal for bringing white wine, kirsch, and a butane camp stove onto the school grounds.

Back then, cooking was just something I enjoyed; I had no real thoughts of turning it into a career, at least not until I got a bit older. I went to Reed College in Portland, Oregon. During the summers, I took kitchen jobs in San Francisco, Portland, and finally on the Cote d'Azur in France. After graduating, I continued to cook, mostly in Italian and "New American" restaurants in Portland before returning to California, where I started working at Chez Panisse in Berkeley, initially as Alice Waters's assistant. As with so many others who have worked at Chez Panisse, it was a formative experience for me. The whole world came though Alice's office. Every chef and food writer I'd ever heard of would call or visit. I'd arrange discreet tables for famous actors, musicians, and writers. Alice was exacting, occasionally unreasonable, unflinching once she'd set her mind to something—but always generous. One of my jobs was to type up drafts of menus from her scribbled notes for special dinners. She and I did this dozens of times: drafting ideas for a meal that took advantage of the ingredients that were best at that moment, reviewing the menu, revising it, and then revising it again. I didn't realize it at the time, but this process of thinking critically about how to put together a menu was an important education for me.

When people asked me what kind of restaurant Rintaro would be, I'd tell them that I wanted Rintaro to translate the experience of a Tokyo izakaya to San Francisco. I wanted it to be a place with exciting but simple food that tasted both like Japan and California—not fusion food, but the kind of food you'd expect if the Bay Area were a region of Japan. The build-out of the restaurant was intense and stressful, but in the end, we had a space

that met all my requirements. There was a beautiful hinoki (cypress) counter facing an open yakitori grill, booths with a slight step up to give a sense of privacy, outdoor seating in a garden courtyard and a private dining room in the back. My father did the carpentry work, using some of the most beautiful wood from his lumber decks.

We stocked the shelves with dishes from Yuko Sato, my longtime cook and ceramicist. And my friend Eugene Whang bought us a vintage Sansui amp and huge speakers from the 1970s to fill the room with music and provided a twenty-four-hour-long playlist. And I signed up my friend and collaborator, Louesa Roebuck, to install her dreamy foraged arrangements of wild flowers and branches.

Nothing was more intense than my hunt for ingredients, which I had begun years before I even found a space for Rintaro. I hunted down uncommon but vital Japanese ingredients from around the West Coast: I dug bamboo shoots in Livermore, a sub-urban town deep in the East Bay; picked ume plums in Winters, not too far from Sacramento; befriended the makers of America's best soy milk in Gardena in southern L.A. County; and bought beautiful fresh wasabi root grown on the coast of Half Moon Bay. I also continued my regular trips back to Japan to work in kitchens, visit with other chefs, and find new ideas and recipes. The trips gave me a chance to develop relationships with Japanese producers who still send me top-quality staples like whole katsuobushi from a generations-old factory in Kagoshima (see page 13), good kombu from Hokkaido, and handmade soy sauce from Saitama.

It's been eight years since we first opened the doors at Rintaro, and during that time, many people have asked me when I would write a Rintaro cookbook. Finally, I feel the time is right. This book isn't exhaustive, but it does show a cross section of Japanese food that isn't usually found in American cookbooks. Basic foods like curry rice, tonkatsu, and yakitori that are eaten most often at lunch counters and in home kitchens live alongside fresh bamboo shoots, and other dishes that are usually considered part of a more elevated Japanese cooking tradition. What these foods have in common are direct and robust flavors, an approach that guides all our cooking at Rintaro.

Food doesn't exist in a bubble. It is and should be in conversation with its surroundings. We are a Japanese izakaya, but even in Japan, a country often considered homogeneous, Japanese food is highly regional and varied and has been shaped by immigrants and would-be invaders. Curry came from India via the British, mabodofu and gyoza from China, and nanbanzuke and panko-fried foods from Portugal and other European traders. These are now regular fixtures of the cuisine, if still recognized as Yoshuku, or non-Japanese. And so, in California, with its own long tail of immigration from Japan, we are a Japanese restaurant with California roots and California influences. Pain de mie from Berkeley-based Acme Bread Company is the basis for our panko. Koda Farms' Kokuho Rose rice, grown in the Central Valley, is our brand of choice. This cultural cross-pollination, a continuum across the oceans and back through time, is the context for our food.

My hope with this book is to teach readers how to adapt traditional Japanese dishes in a way that stays true to their original ideas yet respects the special vibrant ingredients that are native to whatever region they live. The ingredients in California are wonderful, but they are different from what you would find in Japan. This means

I must find ways to honor both the Japanese traditions that mean so much to me and ingredients such as perfectly ripe Violette de Bordeaux figs from a friend in Sonoma, giant spot prawns that are still jumping from Eureka in far-northern California, and fragrant passionfruit picked off my own vine. It's a very Chez Panisse-ian approach, but it is also very Japanese. I always say that the food we serve at Rintaro is neither fusion nor strictly traditional. It's food that imagines California as the farthest western prefecture of Japan. With this book, I hope to show you how to adapt this approach to your own place in the world.

Above all, I want readers of this book to use these recipes and for them to work. Many of these recipes grew from home cooking and only later were adapted for the restaurant. In writing this book, I returned to my roots and made sure that every recipe will work in any kitchen. Most ingredients can be found in Japanese and Asian grocery stores or online from The Japanese Pantry, Umami Mart, or online.

EVEN BEFORE I ENTERED THE city limits of Makurazaki, I could smell the katsuobushi—a light, pervasive scent of smoke and fish. It had been a long drive, winding through the countryside to get here from Kagoshima. My traveling companions and I had passed the time chatting and eating mikan (mandarin oranges), and I was excited to have arrived. The dozen or so katsuobushi that I always keep stocked in my kitchen in California are my most precious ingredients, and the dashi I make with them finds its way into almost everything I cook. I had often explained to my American friends that this woodlike piece of bonito was the foundation of the Japanese taste, but I struggled to explain just how it was produced.

The katsuobushi-ya we visited, Maruhisa Katsuobushi Shop, seemed from another era. The building was large and dark, made of wood and tin with large open doors, and smelled strongly of bonito and wood smoke. Although the floors were washed clean, flies buzzed around. In uncovered cement pools by the front entrance, dozens of enormous fish lay thawing in icy water. A low fence around the periphery kept out the neighborhood cats. The master of the shop, a compact, friendly man, enthusiastically explained the process. He has been making katsuobushi for four decades, and the particularities were endless. Although I didn't follow every detail, I gathered that the bonito were caught and frozen out at sea in a ship's hold—the ones thawing here had been caught near Thailand. Once thawed, the fish are cleaned, and the heads and guts removed on a cutting table worn down by decades of fishy disembowelments. The process is now partially mechanized, since many of the younger workers aren't able to cleanly and quickly remove the large bonito heads with a deba bocho (a heavy, single-bevel fish knife). Once cleaned, the katsuo are then filleted (san-mai oroshi) and simmered, dozens at a time in a huge underground cauldron. The fillets are then arranged onto racks and brought to the next, unexpected step in the process.

Sitting in a circle in the middle of the gloomy workspace, four young women, each wearing a colorful bandana over her hair, carefully but quickly smeared bonito surimi over the fillets, smoothing the surface. Made with the meat from between the bones, the dark gray surimi looked positively pastelike. Although labor-intensive, this procedure both made good use of the fish scraps and filled any gaps that would later have to be sanded away. While this work qualifies as both kitsui and kitanai (difficult and dirty), it's important in the production of high-quality katsuobushi, though it's often skipped to save time and money. The workers then brought racks of prepped fillets to an oversized oven, several stories high and as large as a room, where they were smoked and dried slowly over a wood fire. The master was always in charge of this delicate step, lighting small piles of logs on the floor of the oven, and then moving the racks progressively up and away from the heat.

After about a month, workers remove the racks; the fillets are now hard as wood and rough with creosote and smoke and ready to be smoothed and polished by electric sanders. It was this smoky dust from this and neighboring katsuobushi factories that we must have smelled as we entered town.

The final step is a stay in the warm and humid koji room, where the flavor develops further and much of the remaining moisture is sapped out by a light coat of mold. The final product is beautiful: hard and clean, with a dusting of koji. It struck me as so amazing that this product, the basis for dashi—one of the most delicate and elegant foods I know—is produced in such medieval conditions. At the end of our tour, we gathered at a long worktable, where we ate what I imagined to be the grandfather of modern miso soup: a pinch of shiny, light katsuobushi flakes in a bowl, with a dab of miso and hot water. I tasted the katsuobushi in a new way. It tasted exactly of the careful procedure used to make it and just like the smell of the place: smoky, slightly musty, and deeply delicious.

KATSUOBUSHI ICHIBAN DASHI

BASIC KONBU AND KATSUOBUSHI DASHI

かつおぶし 一番だし

4¼ cups / 1L water
1 (2-inch / 5 cm) square piece konbu
2½ cups / 40 g shaved katsuobushi

MAKES ABOUT 3½ CUPS / 826ML

A fine katsuobushi konbu dashi is one of the wonders of the edible world and forms the basis for much of Japanese cooking. It is simultaneously light and rich, with a distinctly smoky depth. There are a handful of dashi (best translated as clear stocks) in Japanese cooking: shiitake and konbu dashi, iriko or dried anchovy dashi, dried and cured mackerel and tuna dashi, and even a very fancy dried shrimp dashi. But katsuobushi konbu dashi is the king of them all.

Given that outside of Japan it's almost impossible to find blocks of katsuobushi to shave yourself (also requiring a special katsuobushi shaver), seek out the best shaved katsuobushi you can find. You're looking for shavings made with *honkarebushi*, that is, katsuobushi that has been cured with koji (see page 13, chapter intro). I recommend checking out the Japanese Pantry online. As katsuobushi is shaved into extremely thin flakes, only a fraction of the thickness of paper, it oxidizes quickly and loses its fragrance. Although the sealed bags you can find at Japanese markets are pumped with nitrogen to slow the oxidation process, look for ones that are a bright rusty red rather than the dim brown, which indicates oxidation. This recipe uses *hana katsuobushi*, very thinly shaved katsuobushi, which is the type most commonly sold in the west. You can also use a thicker shaved version called *atsukezuri bushi*, which because of its thickness, holds its flavor better, but doesn't make as delicate a dashi. If you are using the thicker shaved katsuobushi, increase the simmering time to 10 minutes.

Another important consideration when making dashi is the temperature of the water and the length of the cooking time. When brought to a full boil, konbu develops an iodine flavor, so it should always be heated gently. And katsuobushi's rich flavor is likewise best coaxed out gently. If it over boils, some of the bitter and fishy qualities of the flakes will compromise your dashi.

Combine the water and konbu in a large saucepan over low heat. Slowly, over the course of at least 15 minutes, heat until the water registers 150°F / 66°C on an instant-read thermometer, then remove and discard the konbu (or reserve for niban dashi; page 19). Increase the heat to high and bring the water to a boil. Add the katsuobushi, stir with chopsticks to submerge, and immediately reduce the heat to a low simmer. Cook for 2 minutes, then remove from the heat and let stand for 5 minutes more, or until the katsuobushi sinks to the bottom of the pot.

Pour through a strainer lined with a layer of damp heavy-duty paper towels into a bowl and allow to drip through. Discard the katsuobushi or reserve for niban dashi (page opposite). The dashi is best used the same day, although it will keep covered and refrigerated for a day before losing its best flavor.

KATSUOBUSHI NIBAN DASHI

SECOND KONBU AND KATSUOBUSHI DASHI

かつおぶし 二番だし

2½ cups / 590ml [based on 1 cup / 236ml] water

Konbu and katsuobushi left over from one recipe of katsuobushi dashi (page 18)

MAKES ABOUT 2 CUPS / 472ML

Niban, or second, dashi is made with katsuobushi and konbu that has already been used to make the first (ichiban) batch of dashi. Think of it as the second steep, as with tea. The fragrance and color is not nearly as strong and the cooking time is increased to draw out the last bits of flavor from the used konbu and katsuobushi. Japan is only recently a wealthy country and has a well-developed ethos around not wasting food. Given the incredible work that goes into making katsuobushi and harvesting and drying konbu, it's a shame to throw them away when they've still got some life left in them. Although the fragrant ichiban dashi is required for dashimaki tamago (page 100) and ohitashi (page 89), niban dashi is a good substitute in many of the simmered dishes, where the dashi plays only a small supporting role, such as in the kare raisu (page 221), gyusuji nikomi (page 189), or mabodofu (page 218).

Combine the water with the used konbu and katsuobushi. Bring to a low simmer and cook for 20 minutes. Pour through a strainer lined with a layer of damp heavy-duty paper towels into a bowl. The dashi is best used the same day, although it will keep covered and refrigerated for a day before losing its best flavor.

SASHIMI
刺身

IN JAPAN, YOU ARE SURROUNDED by incredibly beautiful fish everywhere you go. You can find perfect fillets of tai (sea bream) at the grocery store, piles of knife-shaped silver-skinned sanma (mackerel) in front of markets at the train station, and glassy-eyed kinmedai (snapper) as you walk into department store food courts. And, at the Tsukiji wholesale fish market (relocated by the Tokyo Olympics to Toyosu), I found what seemed to be the entire contents of the world's ocean under one roof.

I've wondered why we don't seem to have this same abundance of perfect fish here in the United States. It's true that Japan is an island nation, surrounded by the sea. But California shares the same Pacific Ocean. Japan, however, is also an old nation, with a long heritage of eating fish. Your average non-foodie office worker in Japan knows the difference between four kinds of mackerel. Fishermen know which of them is best in which season, how to catch them without damaging their flesh, and how to store them when they are landed. The wholesalers who buy from the fishermen know how to ice them properly, and the distribution system is set up to get the fish to market within a day of being caught. The fishmonger knows how to separate the good ones from the mediocre and how to clean and display them immediately. And it is there where your average non-foodie office worker, who knows the difference between four kinds of mackerel, will choose a few of the best looking to take home for dinner, rewarding all those people who did a good job keeping the fish beautiful on their trip from the ocean.

When I came back to California, it was a challenge to find a good variety of sashimi to include on the menu. I could have imported all the fish from Japan (as do all the high-end sushi restaurants in San Francisco), but the entire point of Rintaro was to take a Japanese approach to seasonality and locality and apply it here in California. The first local fish that we used with regularity was halibut. Caught with a hook and line (rather than in a net that is dragged along the seafloor), they were consistently beautiful. Then came the local Pacific mackerel, much leaner than most you find in Japan, but with a fresh, clean flavor. After some trial and error, we started getting Pacific bigeye and bluefin tuna, mostly caught off the coast of Southern California. Then came the uni from Fort Bragg, north of San Francisco, and the kanpachi from Baja. The longer I looked, the more great fish I found: live spot prawns, herring, sardines, spiny lobsters, and even on occasion, bonito. Once, we even got a couple of local barracuda—one of my very favorites.

There are half a dozen fishermen and suppliers that I call throughout the year, but we source most of our fish from two wholesalers down near Fisherman's Wharf: Monterey Fish and Water2Table. Now, when I wake up, usually still in bed, I call Carlos Trujillo, our guy at Monterey Fish, to check on the previous night's order. Apart from my wife, I probably spend more time on the phone with Carlos than anyone else. This relationship has allowed me to serve the best fish available. I know that Carlos will choose the brightest loin of bigeye and let me know about a surprise delivery of spot prawns or perfect sardines. But just as importantly, he'll tell me when the fish isn't good enough: if the bluefin is too dark or the mackerel bellies have gone soft.

Monterey Fish sells mostly West Coast fish, with imports from the East Coast and farther afield, with a particular eye to sustainability. They buy their fish from fishermen they know, who use sustainable methods (no factory trawlers, no pirate tuna boats, no antibiotic-laden farmed fish). And Monterey Fish takes the issue seriously. In fact, the owner of the company, Paul Johnson, wrote the book on sustainable fisheries called Fish Forever, and he is one of the great champions of small-scale sustainable fisheries.

Now that I have a stable supply of consistently excellent West Coast fish, I will occasionally bring in a few special fish from Japan. I think of this like truffles—the ones from Italy and France are the best—and sometimes you want to put something exotic on the menu.

The quality of the sashimi you make at home is absolutely dependent on the quality of the fish you buy, so it's important to spend some time looking for the best you can find. Talk to your fishermen friends, chat up the people down at the pier, and befriend the fishmonger at the best market in town. Also, since the pandemic, individual fishermen who once sold only to restaurants have also started to offer their catch direct to consumers at farmers' markets, via CSA boxes, or through special pickups at the wharf.

When it comes to sashimi, freshness is just the first step. In fact, most of the fish that we serve raw has been cured in some way to improve the texture and flavor. Some cures are minimal, just a sprinkle of salt and a few hours in the refrigerator, while others are more intense, like the halibut, which is cured for two days on konbu. In this chapter, I describe how to break down each of the five basic types of fish for sashimi and how to cure, slice, and arrange them attractively on a plate. I also provide some suggestions for garnishes (tsuma), condiments (yakumi), and sauces (tare).

The standard knife used for breaking down a fish is called a deba, a thick single-bevel knife with a very sharp tip and heavy base for cutting through bones. I prefer to use a finer honesuki, a poultry-boning knife, while some of my cooks like to use a standard santoku, an all-purpose double-beveled kitchen knife. Whichever one you use, it's important that your knife be extremely sharp. It's nearly impossible to make clean, precise cuts with a dull knife. I also keep two moist, clean kitchen towels folded by my cutting board. I use one to wipe up any blood or splatter. The second is reserved only for wiping the blade of my knife while I'm filleting. Keep the towels separate; you don't want to contaminate the flesh with any bacteria from the innards of the fish. Also, take care to wash your cutting board well after cutting off the head and removing the guts.

Don't despair if you don't find beautiful fish on your first trip to the seafood market. Good sashimi fish can be difficult to find, especially at the resale level, but a genuine show of interest and kindness goes a long way when it comes to developing a relationship with your fishmonger.

MEBACHI TO HONMAGURO NO SASHIMI

めばちと本まぐろの刺身

BIGEYE AND BLUEFIN TUNA SASHIMI

Tuna saku ready for
   slicing, totaling 3 lb /
   1.3kg
Sea salt

FOR SERVING:
Roll-Cut Daikon Tsuma
   (page 51)
Shiso
Wasabi
Shoyu or Tosajoyu
   (page 39)

**MAKES 6 TO 8
SERVINGS**

A decade ago, Yuri Nomura, a good friend, took me on an early morning visit to Mr. Nojiri, the proprietor of Ishimiya, a top tuna wholesaler in Tokyo's Tsukiji Market. Amid the controlled chaos of the market, his stall stood out with its pristine wooden-framed glass display boxes. He sold only two items: bluefin tuna and swordfish, and each, I would venture to say, were the best of their kind in the world. There is a lot of drama in the tuna business at Tsukiji, from the auctions where whole fish are sold for thousands (and occasionally millions) of dollars, to the enormous swordlike knives that highly skilled fishmongers use to cut whole fish into loins. But Mr. Nojiri himself was quiet and understated. He offered me a little slice, cut from an enormous back loin. Maybe it was the early morning or the disorienting frenzy of the market, but it is a piece of tuna that I still remember to this day; it was a beautiful ruby red with a soft electric texture. Not to be melodramatic, but for a while, when I got back to California, I thought I could never eat tuna again.

For the first year, we didn't serve tuna at Rintaro. And then, slowly, I started to open my eyes to the huge, beautiful bigeye tuna that were being landed in San Diego. Although leaner than bluefin, bigeye can have a similarly deeply flavored, ruby red back loin, called *akami* or "red meat," but without the soft, luxurious fat of a bluefin. And in the last couple of years, maybe due to the changing climate, we have also started to see increasing numbers of bluefin tuna in California waters. Most of them are nowhere near the quality of tuna sold by Ishimiya, but some of them, with their dark red loins that brighten to ruby as they oxidize and their buttery belly loins, certainly give me the same butterflies.

I buy my tuna from Monterey Fish, who, in turn, buy directly from individual fishermen running their own small boats. That said, tuna is a huge international business. Factory trawlers, which go out for weeks at a time, harvest the fish by the ton, processing them onboard and freezing them with liquid nitrogen for storage and transport. Given the efficiency of these operations and the seemingly endless appetite for tuna worldwide, it's not surprising that many stocks of tuna—bluefin, in particular—are threatened and top the do-not-eat lists of sustainable fish organizations. But I trust Monterey Fish's judgment. They pointed me to NOAA Fisheries, the agency responsible for the nation's fisheries. The Pacific bluefin, according to their website, "is a smart seafood choice because it is sustainably managed under rebuilding measures that limit harvest by U.S. fishermen." This is deeply happy news.

MEBACHI TO HONMAGURO NO SASHIMI, CONTINUED

While freshness is no doubt important for delicious sashimi, tuna is a good example of a fish that requires significant aging to bring out its best attributes. Ideally, a tuna should age between four and ten days from the time it is caught before being served as sashimi. During this time, if cared for properly, the enzymes in the fish will start to improve the flavor, the muscles and sinews will relax and become more tender, and the blood and excess water will be leached from the fish.

Unless you are dealing with a wholesaler or the fishermen themselves, it's hard to know exactly when the fish was landed. That said, if the *saku*, the Japanese word for "blocks ready to be cut into slices," are firm and bright, it's going to be delicious, and you can enhance the flavor and texture by simply salting the fish and drawing out the extra moisture with paper towels.

If you're lucky enough to live near a good Japanese market, you should be able to purchase tuna cut into saku. If you have access to sashimi-grade tuna from a non-Japanese fish market, you will likely need to buy a larger chunk and cut the saku yourself, see page 30.

Place the tuna saku on a clean cutting board, and very lightly sprinkle the top, bottom, and sides with a small pinch of salt. Wrap tightly in a paper towel and then wrap tightly in plastic wrap and place in the coldest part of the refrigerator. The salt will draw out the excess water and blood. Check after an hour to see if the paper towel is saturated. If it is, rewrap the tuna with fresh paper towels and again with plastic. Let rest in the refrigerator for at least another 3 hours or overnight.

To slice the tuna: Place the saku on the cutting board with the most attractive side facing up. With a razor-sharp knife, start your cut at the base of the knife and draw your blade through the fish, cutting through the fish in a single stroke. Depending on the thickness of the saku, you can make your slices between ¼ to ½ inch / 6 to 12 mm thick; thinner for larger saku and thicker for the smaller ones. As you finish one slice, use the blade of your knife to push it on your cutting board a few inches to the right and continue with the next, stacking one next to the other. In this way your slices are arranged nicely and ready to be transferred to a chilled plate. Serve the tuna with the daikon tsuma, shiso, wasabi, and shoyu. Like beef, different parts of the loin will have different characteristics. I like to include three different cuts on each plate for a diversity of textures.

RINTARO 28

HOW TO BREAK DOWN A TUNA LOIN

If this is your first time breaking down a loin of tuna, I recommend starting with a 5-lb / 2.3kg skin-on section of the back loin: any less and your *saku*, the Japanese word for "blocks ready to be cut into slices," will be very small; any larger and you'll have more fish than you can handle. The process for cutting the back loin is less complicated than that of the belly loin. Unless you are buying bluefin tuna with its buttery otoro section, the quality of the fat in the belly sections of the bigeye (and yellowtail) is less desirable than the *akami*, "red meat," and I prefer the back loins of the bigeye (and yellowtail).

The quality and yield of usable saku also depend upon the portion of the loin that you choose. The tail section of a tuna, as with all fish, is finely tapered with a concentration of sinew. The top of the loin by the head and the middle section, on the other hand, are more evenly proportioned and will yield the most evenly shaped, sinew-free sashimi.

Once you've chosen your section, check the color of the fish. It should be a deep ruby red without any brown or gray oxidation. If you are lucky enough to find a fish that has been caught within the previous three days, you may find that the loin will be a darker brick red. The color will brighten to ruby over the next day or two. However, once a fresh tuna has finished brightening, as it ages, it will continue to oxidize and become darker again. Avoid any loins with bruising or gashes. Small holes in the loin are evidence of parasites.

The process of breaking down a loin of tuna is called *sakudori*. Typically, I use a long-bladed yanagi sashimi knife to break down a tuna loin, although many cooks use an all-purpose double-beveled kitchen knife. Whichever you use, it's important that your knife be extremely sharp. It's nearly impossible to make clean, precise cuts with a dull knife.

I also keep two moist, clean kitchen towels folded by my cutting board. I use one to wipe up any blood or splatter. The second is reserved only for wiping the blade of my knife. Keep them separate. You don't want to contaminate the flesh with any bacteria from the skin of the fish.

Once you've cut the tuna loin into saku for sashimi, you will be left with a lot of trim. These edible bits can be chopped and used for the Maguro no Yukke Don (page 213) or seasoned with minced scallions and salt and served alongside the tuna sashimi (page 26). To prepare the trim, scrape the flesh from the larger sinew-y section with a soup spoon and discard the sinew. Then, scrape any fat and meat from the skin and discard the skin. Coarsely chop the rest of the trimmings, removing and discarding any thick pieces of sinew and residual blood line. Spoon into a paper towel–lined bowl, cover, and refrigerate until ready to use.

Removing the bloodline: Turn the loin so the thicker, head side is facing toward you. Using long, shallow strokes, remove the chi-ae, the dark red blood line. You'll notice that it is separated from the muscles of the fish by a thin membrane. Discard.

Removing the top section: Measure 2 inches /5 cm up from the skin and score the end of the loin with your knife. Holding the knife perfectly level and using the score as a guide, with a subtle sawing motion, cut off the top of the loin and set aside.

Cutting saku from the bottom section: Measure approximately 1-inch / 2.5 cm in from the side where you removed the blood line, cut through to the skin with a single stroke. Remove the first saku by cutting it from the skin, set aside on the baking sheet. Repeat with the next two saku.

Cutting the triangular saku: Facing the end of the loin, you will see a diagonal line of sinew. Cutting at a 45-degree angle, remove a triangular saku, leaving the sinew attached to the loin.

Removing the sinew and final saku: Following the underside of the sinew, remove the sinewy section from the loin and set aside. Remove the final saku from the skin. Trim the sinew on the bottom, skin-side of the saku.

Bisecting the top section: Return the top section of the loin to the cutting board. Measure 1.5-inch /3.8 cm up from the bottom edge and score the loin with your knife. Holding the knife perfectly level and using the score as a guide, cut the loin with subtle sawing motion. Repeat with the final top piece. You should have two 1.5-inch / 3.8 cm thick blocks.

Cutting saku from the top sections: Cut the larger block into four or five saku, about 2 inches/ 5 cm wide. Cut the smaller of the blocks into two saku. Trim the saku into tidy rectangular, triangular, or rounded pieces. Reserve the trimmings.

Final trim for all saku: Depending on the shape, the saku should be trimmed to tidy round, triangular, or rectangular blocks. Remove any residual bloodline and sections with heavy sinew.

HIRAME NO KOBUJIME

KONBU-CURED HALIBUT

ひらめの昆布締め

---

4 (¾ lb / 340 g) skinless sashimi-grade halibut or fluke fillets

Sea salt

¼ cup / 60ml rice vinegar

¼ cup / 60ml cooking sake

5 (4 by 11-inch / 10 by 28 cm) pieces konbu (see Note below)

FOR SERVING:

Shoyu

Wasabi

Roll-Cut Daikon Tsuma (page 51)

Lemon or yuzu slices (optional)

MAKES 6 TO 8 SERVINGS

Note: You will need enough konbu for 5 layers, approximately the same dimensions as your fillets. If you don't have long sheets of konbu, piece together smaller ones.

The halibut here in the Bay Area are sublime, with fine, nearly translucent flesh. They are also a perfect example of the importance of curing a fish to bring out its best characteristics. Halibut, and their East Coast cousin, fluke, are quite watery and soft when you first cut them. One of the basic methods for curing white fish is to use salt and then konbu to draw out excess moisture. This method concentrates the flavor of the fish and imbues it with a subtle konbu flavor. Konbu is also a powerful preservative, and raw halibut cured between layers of konbu will last for four or five days, although we usually limit the curing time to two or three days.

If you'd like to break down your own halibut into fillets, see page 34.

To cure the halibut: Line a baking sheet with a layer of heavy-duty paper towels and sprinkle with ¼ teaspoon of salt.

Lay two fillets side by side on the prepared baking sheet and sprinkle them with another ¼ teaspoon salt. Cover with a second layer of paper towels and repeat with the remaining fillets. Cover with a final layer of paper towels and refrigerate for 2 hours.

Combine the vinegar and sake in a small bowl. Moisten a paper towel with some of the mixture and wipe both sides of the konbu. Let the konbu stand for a few minutes until it's pliable.

Layer the fillets between the konbu. If you've cut your own fish and have the engawa strips (see page 34), lay them on top of the final layer of konbu, flesh-side down, and wrap the entire package tightly with plastic wrap. Store in the coldest part of the refrigerator for at least 24 hours and up to 3 days. I find the cure is at its best after 48 hours.

To slice the fillets: Gently remove the fillets from the konbu, being careful not to tear the flesh as you remove the

konbu, then wrap them individually in plastic wrap. Reserve half of the konbu and cut it into 2½ by 3-inch / 6 by 7.5 cm rectangles. Discard the rest.

If you have the engawa (see page 34), place it, skin-side down, on the cutting board with the head side facing the right. Holding the tail side with your left hand, insert the knife between the flesh and the skin and remove the skin. Set aside.

Lay one of the fillets, skin-side up, with the head side facing to the left. Starting at the wide end of the fillet, using a razor-sharp knife, start your cut at the base of the knife and draw your blade through the fish, cutting through the fish in a single stroke. Cut ⅛-inch / 4 mm slices at a 45-degree angle against the grain. Arrange four slices to a piece of konbu, slightly overlapping. If using, cut the engawa into 1-inch / 2.5 cm -long segments.

To serve, place the halibut on the konbu slices on a platter and, if using, add the engawa on the side. Garnish with the shiso, daikon tsuma, wasabi, and lemon slices (if using).

HOW TO BREAK DOWN A WHOLE HALIBUT

When choosing a whole halibut (or fluke), look for one that's between 4 and 6 lb /1.8 to 2.7kg. If it's available, ask for one that has been caught by hook and line rather than in a net, which badly bruises a fish. Clear eyes and a clean ocean smell are the first signs of freshness. Look for evidence of bruising such as missing scales and blood under the skin near the fins. Bruised fish will often have blood in the fillet, making them unusable for sashimi. Press your finger gently into the side of the fish. It should be firm, and if you're lucky, it might even still be in rigor mortis and hard as a board—a sign that it was caught very recently.

The process for breaking down a halibut and other flat fish is called *gomai oroshi*, or "five section fillet," because you end up with two back fillets, two belly fillets, and the skeleton. A skilled chef will preserve a ribbon of muscle that controls the fins and lines the top and bottom fins on both sides of the fish. This ribbon of muscle is called the *engawa* and is prized for its distinctive grain and chewy texture.

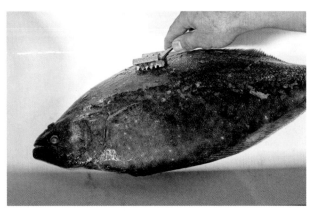

Washing and removing the scales: Place the halibut in the sink. Using a fish scaler, remove the scales, starting at the tail and moving towards the head. Pay particular care in removing the scales along the back fins and belly. Rinse with cold water and dry well with paper towels.

Removing the head and guts: With the head facing left, cut from just behind the pectoral fin through to just below the pelvic fin. Then cut from the pectoral fin up to the forehead of the fish. Use the thicker bottom portion of your knife to cut through the backbone. Turn the halibut over and repeat. Remove the head and guts.

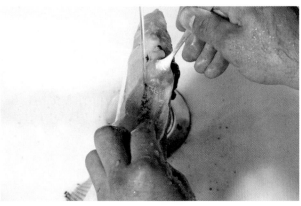

Cleaning the blood line: There is a blood line along the inner side of the backbone. Use the tip of your knife to slice the blood line and, with a teaspoon, scrape it out, scrubbing away any residual blood with a towel or old toothbrush. Rinse with cold water and dry well with paper towels.

Cutting the lateral line: With the head of the halibut facing left and using the lateral line that runs along the skin down the middle of the fish as a guide, slice the length of the fish down to the spine, separating the back loin from the belly loin.

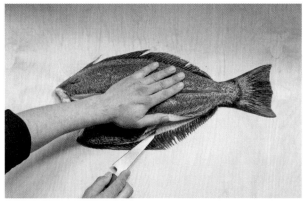

Cutting the belly side: To separate the belly fillet, run your knife along the top of the belly fins, using long, shallow strokes to cut first through the skin and then, using the fin bones as a guide, cut another ¾ inch / 2 cm deep.

Removing the belly fillet: Starting at the center-line incision, using long, shallow strokes, separate the top of the belly fillet from the backbone and ribs. Use the ribs as a guide as you cut. You should feel a distinctive clicking as your blade passes over each rib. Continue cutting in long, shallow strokes, holding the knife in your right hand, while you gently fold the fillet away from the bones with your left hand. When you have cut through to the fin side, lift out the fillet.

Removing the back fillet: Turn the fish and repeat the same procedure on the other side, starting by cutting along the back fins, and then cutting from the center-line incision, using long shallow strokes to separate the back fillet from the backbone and ribs.

Repeat: Turn the halibut over, cut along the lateral line, then cut along the belly fins, cut from the central line to remove the fillet. Repeat with the back fillet. Discard the skeleton or save for fish stock.

Remove the engawa fin meat: Run your finger between the engawa fin meat and the fillet to separate the engawa. Gently folding back the fillet with your left hand, use your right hand to slice the engawa. Remove and set aside. Repeat with the rest of the fillets. Leave the skin on the engawa.

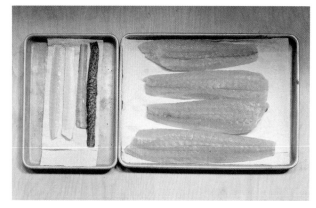

Final trim and skinning: To remove the skin, lay a fillet, skin-side down on your board. Cut near the end of the fillet to insert your blade between the meat and the skin. Hold the blade angled a few degrees downward, and using a towel for grip, reach around with your left hand to hold the tail firmly in place. With a slight sawing motion, move your blade toward the head, cutting as closely to the skin as possible.

KANPACHI NO SASHIMI

YELLOWTAIL AMBERJACK SASHIMI かんぱちの刺身

---

4 skin-on sashimi-grade kanpachi fillets: 2 back loins and 2 belly loins (about ¾ lb / 340 g each)

Sea salt

FOR SERVING:

Roll-Cut Daikon Tsuma (page 51)

Shiso

Wasabi or yuzu kosho (optional)

Shoyu or Meyer Lemon Ponzu (page 39)

MAKES 6 TO 8 SERVINGS

Kanpachi has a mild flavor, beautiful silver skin with a vivid red blood line, and a significant quantity of fat that gives it a smooth, almost creamy texture. Kanpachi is related to hamachi, buri, and hiramasa, and the method for slicing them for sashimi is similar.

The vast majority of yellowtail served around the world are farm raised. For a long time, I was leery of farmed yellowtail. To my taste, much of the farmed hamachi can be too oily and soft, with a sour quality I don't like. This is the result of the fish being crammed together in their pens, fed an oil-rich diet, and, due to poor water quality, often needing to be treated with antibiotics.

But, as with any kind of agriculture, there are big differences among different methods of fish farming. The kanpachi that we serve at the restaurant are farmed, but they are raised in deepwater pens in the Sea of Cortez, just south of San Diego. The fish are fed a marine diet of algae and fish meal, and because they swim where the currents are cold and strong, they stay healthy and relatively lean, without the addition of antibiotics or growth hormones. They arrive at the restaurant in perfect condition, with bright eyes and smelling of the sea.

Much of the beauty of kanpachi lies just under the skin. On the back loin, there is a layer of vivid red, and on the belly loin, there is a layer of metallic silver under the skin. Since kanpachi oxidize relatively quickly, I recommend keeping the skin on the fillets until a few hours before you plan to serve the fish.

If you'd like to break down your own kanpachi, see page 40.

To prepare the fillets: Remove the skin by laying each fillet, skin-side down, with the head side facing to the left. Cut into the tail section 1-inch / 2.5 cm up from the end and insert your blade between the flesh and the skin. Using the middle of your blade, angle it just a few degrees downward from flat. Reach your left hand around and hold the tail firmly to keep it from moving, using a kitchen towel for grip. With a slight sawing motion, move your blade toward the head, cutting as closely to the skin as possible.

Kanpachi is a fairly firm fish and needs only a bit of salt to draw off excess moisture. Line a rimmed sheet pan with a layer of heavy-duty paper towels and sprinkle it with a scant ¼ teaspoon salt.

Lay the four fillets side by side on the prepared pan and sprinkle each with another ¼ teaspoon salt. Cover the fillets with a layer of paper towels, wrap with plastic wrap, and refrigerate for 2 hours.

To slice the fillets: For the back fillets, place each fillet, skin-side up, with the head side facing to the right. Starting at the wide end of the fillet and using a razor-sharp knife, start your cut at the base of the knife and draw your blade through the fish, cutting straight down and through the fish in a single stroke. Depending on the thickness of the fillet, you can make your slices between ¼ to ½ inch / 6 to 12 mm thick—thinner for larger fillets and thinner for smaller

ones. As you finish one slice, use the blade of your knife to push it on your cutting board a few inches to the right and continue with the next, stacking one next to the other. This way, your slices are arranged nicely and can be easily transferred to a plate.

For the belly fillets, place them, skin-side up, with the head side facing to the right. Starting at the tail end of the fillet, angle your knife so that it's perpendicular to the grain of the fish.

Remove the first inch of the tail and discard. Cutting at a 30-degree angle, slice the fillet into ¼-inch / 6 mm-thick slices. After you finish five slices, use the blade of your knife to move them a few inches to the left and continue with the next set of five.

To serve, transfer the sliced fish to a chilled plate and serve with the daikon tsuma, shiso, wasabi or yuzu kosho (if using), and shoyu.

MEYER LEMON PONZU

½ cup / 118ml shoyu

Zest of 1 yuzu or Meyer lemon

½ cup / 118ml yuzu or Meyer lemon juice (or a combination)

2 tablespoons mirin

½ cup / 8 g thinly shaved katsuobushi

1 (2-inch / 5 cm) piece konbu

MAKES ¾ CUP

If you are lucky enough to find yuzu at the market, their distinctive fragrance makes the most delicious ponzu sauce. Meyer lemons, once rarely seen outside of California, are now fairly ubiquitous and are a good substitute. It's important that you squeeze the juice fresh, though, since bottled juices (even yuzu) don't have the lovely bright aroma that makes ponzu special.

Combine the shoyu, yuzu zest, juice, mirin, katsuobushi, and konbu in a small bowl. Cover and refrigerate for at least 2 hours and up to 3 days.

Line a fine-mesh sieve with damp paper towels. Strain the ponzu through the paper towels into a bowl. Squeeze the last drops from the katsuobushi and konbu before discarding. Ponzu will keep, refrigerated, in an airtight container for a couple of weeks.

TOSAJOYU

KATSUOBUSHI SHOYU

¾ cup / 177ml shoyu

2 tablespoons mirin

¼ cup / 4 g finely shaved katsuobushi

MAKES ¾ CUP

Kanji Nakatani, my mentor and the chef at Soba Ro, introduced me to tosajoyu the first summer I worked in his kitchen. Its rich flavor works especially well in place of plain shoyu with densely flavored fish such as bonito and tuna.

Bring the shoyu and mirin to a boil in a small saucepan over medium-high heat. Skim and discard any foam that rises to the surface and then add the katsuobushi. Remove the pan from the heat and let the mixture steep for 30 minutes.

Line a fine-mesh sieve with damp paper towels. Strain the tosajoyu through the paper towels into a bowl. Squeeze the last drops from the katsuobushi and konbu before discarding. Tosajoyu will keep, refrigerated, in an airtight container for up to a month.

HOW TO BREAK DOWN A WHOLE KANPACHI

As with other fish, when choosing a whole yellowtail, bright eyes and a clean, ocean smell are the first signs of freshness. If you've found one that has already been cleaned, look at the cavity to make sure it hasn't started to oxidize. Choose a 5- to 6-lb / 2.3 to 2.7kg fish.

The process for breaking down a yellowtail and other round fish is called *sanmai oroshi*, or "three section fillet," since you end up with two fillets and the skeleton. The process is similar for smaller fish such as mackerel, but with a larger fish like yellowtail, it will also yield two collars that are excellent grilled.

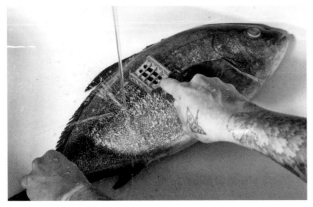

Removing the scales: Place the kanpachi in the sink. Starting at the tail and moving towards the head, remove the scales using a fish scaler. Pay particular care in removing the scales along the back fins and belly. Rinse with cold water and dry well with paper towels.

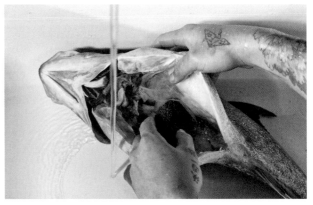

Removing the guts: Starting at the head side, slice towards the tail to the end of the intestinal cavity. Do your best to not puncture any organs as you cut the fish open. Remove and discard the organs. There is a bloodline along the inner side of the backbone. Use the tip of your knife to slice the bloodline and scrub away the residual blood. Wash the fish in the sink and dry well.

Removing the head: With the head facing left, cut from just in front of the pectoral fin up to the forehead, between the eyes. Use the thicker end of your knife to cut through the backbone. The backbone of a yellowtail is thick. You may need to reposition your blade to cut between the vertebrae. Turn the yellowtail over and repeat. Remove and discard the head.

Cutting the belly side: With the head facing the right, cut through the skin along the top of the belly fins starting at the tail, using a long shallow stroke. Once the skin has been cut, use the tip of your knife to locate the rib bones under your blade near the tail. In several long, shallow strokes, run your knife along the rib bones until your blade has reached the spine.

Cutting the back side: Rotate the fish so that the head side is facing to the left. In a long shallow stroke, cut through the skin along the top of the back fins, starting at the head end of the fish. Once the skin has been cut, use the tip of your knife to locate the rib bones under your blade. In several long, shallow strokes, run your knife along the rib bones until your blade has reached the spine.

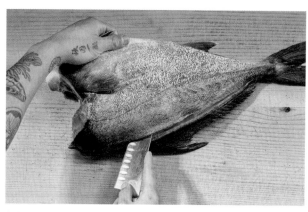

Splitting the fish: At the tail of the fish with the blade facing towards the head, insert your knife until it comes out the other side. The fillet should still be attached at the tail. Holding the tail firmly, with the knife very slightly angled downwards, run your blade down the spine, separating the fillet. Cut the fillet from the tail. Turn the fish over and repeat.

Separating the collar: Place your fillet skin-side up. Cutting at an angle, cut a triangle section of the belly up to the pectoral fin, and then straight up from the pectoral fin to the top of the fillet. Repeat on the other fillet; reserve the collars for grilling.

Removing the belly bones: The bones that line the belly cavity are connected to the pin bones that stick up from the center line of the fish. Turn your knife upside down, and using the very tip of your blade, sever the connection. Cutting as close to the belly bones as you can, remove them from the fillet.

Cutting the belly side: With the head facing the right, cut through the skin along the top of the belly fins starting at the tail, using a long shallow stroke. Once the skin has been cut, use the tip of your knife to locate the rib bones under your blade near the tail. In several long, shallow strokes, run your knife along the rib bones until your blade has reached the spine.

Two belly saku and two back saku: This is how the whole kanpachi should look after you've broken it down.

SASHIMI

SHIME SABA

VINEGAR-CURED MACKEREL

1 cup / 270 g sea salt

4 skin-on sashimi-grade
  mackerel fillets
  (about ¼ lb / 115 g
  each)

1 lemon, cut into
  ¼-inch / 6 mm rounds
  (optional)

1 cup / 236ml rice
  vinegar

FOR SERVING:

Roll-Cut Daikon Tsuma
  (page 51)

Shiso

Grated ginger

Sliced scallions

Shoyu or Goma Dare
  (page 250; optional)

MAKES 4 SERVINGS

Mackerel and other hikarimono, silver-skinned fish such as sardines and the elegant kohada (gizzard shad), make for some of my favorite sashimi. Although they tend to be the cheapest fish at the market, don't underestimate them. The esteemed chef Jiro Ono at Sukiyabashi Jiro includes vinegar-cured sardines as part of his omakase menu. Of all the perfect pieces of sushi on his menu, his fatty-cured sardine nigirizushi are my favorite.

Generally speaking, hikarimono are most prized in the fall and winter months, when they have put on a lot of fat. During spawning in the spring and early summer, they are the leanest. Their flavor is the strongest of all the fish eaten as sashimi, and traditionally, mackerel and its relatives are cured heavily with salt and then in vinegar. This curing process is said to help make the mackerel more digestible and to kill bacteria and parasites. I'm not sure about that, but there is no doubt that the salt and vinegar firm up the flesh, concentrate the taste, and balance the strong oily flavor of mackerel and its relations.

We often serve mackerel simply, with grated ginger, scallion, and shoyu. I also love a version popular in Fukuoka in southern Japan, where the mackerel are served with a sweet sesame sauce. They are strongly flavored and rich and pair especially well with crisp beer or a large glass of chilled sake—or both.

If you'd like to break down your own mackerel, see page 46.

To prepare the fillets: In a rimmed baking sheet, sprinkle ½ cup / 135 g of the salt to make a bed for the 4 fillets. Lay the fillets on top of the salt in a single layer, skin-side down, and coat with the remaining ½ cup / 135 g of the salt. Cover the dish with plastic wrap and refrigerate for 30 minutes, until the salt has pulled a significant amount of water from the fish and their flesh has firmed.

Wash the salted fillets in a bowl of cold water; discard the salt. Dry the fish well with paper towels and slip them into a large ziptop storage bag, arranging in a single layer. Arrange the lemon slices on top of the fillets, if using, and pour the vinegar into the bag with the fish. Squeeze as much air as you can from

the bag, seal, and return to the refrigerator for another 30 minutes.

Remove the fillets from the bag and dry them very well with paper towels but do not rinse them. Lay them skin-side down on a cutting board. Use your fingertip to locate the pin bones that run down the center of each fillet and, using tweezers, remove them one at a time. Don't forget the bones hiding on the head end and double-check your work by running your finger down the center of the fish to make sure you've removed all of them. Wrap each fillet in a paper towel and then in plastic wrap and refrigerate for at least 2 hours and up to 12 hours to allow the vinegar to penetrate the flesh. For smaller fillets,

I find they tend to overcure and lose their color if left overnight. Larger fillets are best after 4 hours.

To slice the fillets: Remove the skin by placing the fillet on the cutting board skin-side up with the thicker end of the fillet facing to the right. Starting at the thicker end, grasp the skin and gently peel it toward the tail, revealing the beautiful metallic blue under the skin. Trim the end of the thick side and set aside.

Make your first cut ¼-inch / 6 mm from the end, cutting a third of the way through the fillet and then completing the slice ½ inch / 12 mm from the end, cutting all the way through. This decorative shallow cut is called *mushi-kiri*, and is typical of mackerel sashimi. (My mentor at Soba Ra, Kanji Nakatani, told me that this was to demonstrate the care taken by the cook to make sure there were no parasites in the fish. In any case, it makes an attractive presentation.) Repeat this step with the rest of the fillets. As you finish one slice, use the blade of your knife to push it on your cutting board a few inches to the right and continue with the next, stacking one next to the other. In this way your slices are arranged nicely to be transferred to a plate.

To serve, transfer the slices to a chilled plate and serve with the daikon tsuma, shiso, ginger, and sliced scallions. You can also serve it as is commonly done in Fukuoka with goma dare, rather than shoyu, if you'd like.

Notes: If you are using smaller mackerel, plan to salt them for 10 minutes per 3½ oz /100 g of the weight of the fillet. If you are using very small fish, such as sardines, plan to salt them for no more than 10 to 15 minutes before rinsing them in cold water.

Similarly, if you are using smaller mackerel, plan to cure them in vinegar for 10 minutes per 3½ oz /100 g of the weight of the fillet. If you are using very small fish, such as sardines, plan to cure them in vinegar for no more than 10 to 15 minutes.

GOMA DARE

SESAME SAUCE

¼ cup / 60ml sake
¼ cup / 60ml mirin
1 tablespoon sugar

⅓ cup / 47 g golden
 sesame seeds
1½ teaspoons rice
 vinegar
¼ cup / 60ml shoyu
 (see page 239)

MAKES ¾ CUP

Shime Saba (page 42), served with Goma Dare, is a regional specialty of Fukuoka, one of my favorite food cities in Japan.

Bring the sake, mirin, and sugar to a boil in a small saucepan over medium-high heat. Turn down the heat and simmer until the alcohol has evaporated, about 5 minutes. The best way to see if the alcohol is burned off is to put your face over the pot. Alcohol vapor will curl your eyelashes and sting your nostrils.

Meanwhile, toast the sesame seeds in a dry skillet over medium heat, shaking constantly for several minutes until they're fragrant and can be crushed easily between your fingertips. Sesame seeds burn easily, so pay close attention and taste them often. When done, pour immediately into a suribachi grinding bowl or a mortar and pestle.

Grind the sesame seeds until completely smooth. They should start to release oil. Add the sake and mirin mixture, vinegar, and shoyu and mix until combined.

Store in an airtight container in the refrigerator for up to a week.

HOW TO BREAK DOWN A WHOLE MACKEREL

When choosing a whole mackerel, a clean, ocean smell is the first sign of freshness. Look to see that the belly is still intact without any splits. Mackerel and other hikarimono spoil quickly, and their bellies are the first to go. Press your finger gently into the side of the fish. It should be firm, and if you're lucky, it might even still be in rigor mortis, a sign that it was very recently caught. Mackerel sizing is highly variable. Choose larger 2-lb / 900 g fish if they are available.

The process for breaking down a mackerel and other round fish is called *sanmai oroshi*, or "three section fillet," since you end up with two fillets and the skeleton. The process for smaller fish like mackerel is similar to larger fish such as yellowtail jacks, with a few small differences.

Rinsing the fish: Rise the fish under cold water and dry well with paper towels.

Cutting the head: With the head facing to the left, position your knife just behind the pectoral fin. Then, cut from the pectoral fin up to the forehead of the fish. Use the thicker, bottom portion of your knife to cut through the backbone. Turn the mackerel over and repeat.

Removing the guts: Starting at the head, slice towards the tail to the end of the intestinal cavity. Do your best to not puncture any organs as you cut the fish open. Discard the head and organs. There is a bloodline along the inner side of the backbone. Use the tip of your knife to slice the bloodline and scrub away the residual blood. Wash the fish in the sink and dry well.

Cutting the belly side: With the head facing to the right, cut through the skin along the top of the belly fins starting at the belly cavity and running to the tail, in a long shallow stroke. Once the skin has been cut, use the tip of your knife to locate the rib bones near the tail. In several shallow strokes, run your knife along the rib bones until your blade reaches the spine.

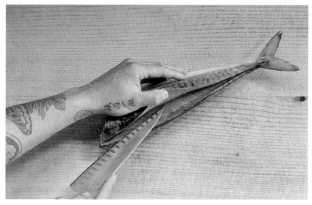

Cutting the back side: Rotate the fish so that the head is facing to the left on your cutting board. In a long shallow stroke, starting at the tail end of the fish, cut through the skin along the top of the back fins. Once the skin has been cut, use the tip of your knife to locate the rib bones. In several long, shallow strokes, run your knife along the rib bones until your blade has reached the spine.

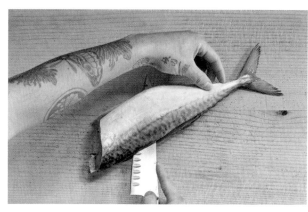

Splitting the fish: At the tail of the fish with the blade facing towards the head, insert your knife until it comes out the other side. The fillet should still be attached at the tail. Holding the tail firmly in your left hand, with the knife very slightly angled downwards, run your blade down the spine, separating the fillet. Cut the fillet from the tail.

Repeat on the other side: Repeat the same procedure on the other side: Turn the fish over, cut the skin on the belly side and then along the top of the bones to the spine. Turn the fish and cut the skin along the back fins and then in several long shallow strokes to the spine. Insert your knife at the tail and run your blade down the spine, separating the fillet. Cut the fillet from the tail. Place both fillets skin-side down on a baking sheet.

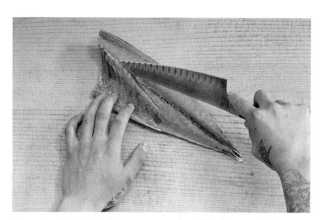

Severing the belly bone connection: The bones that line the belly cavity are connected to the pin bones that stick up from the center line of the mackerel. Turn your knife upside down, and using the very tip of your blade, gently sever the connection between the belly bones and the pin bones.

Removing the belly bones: Slide your blade under the tops of the belly bones, and cutting as close to the bones as you can, remove them from the fillet and discard. Repeat on the other half of the fish.

Two fillets: Your final two fillets should look like this.

KATSUO NO TATAKI

CHARRED BONITO

鰹のたたき

---

4 skin-on sashimi-grade bonito or albacore fillets: 2 back fillets and 2 belly fillets (about ¾ lb / 340 g each)

4 (10 to 14-inch / 25 to 36 cm) metal skewers and some rice straw, fir or redwood needles, or dry wheat straw (aka straw), for smoking and searing the fish

FOR SERVING:

Roll-Cut Daikon Tsuma (page 51)

Shiso leaves

Grated garlic

Grated ginger

Sliced scallions

Shoyu or Meyer Lemon Ponzu (page 39)

MAKES 6 TO 8 SERVINGS

Most of the katsuo consumed in Japan is eaten in the form of katsuobushi. These smoked, dried, and fermented blocks of skipjack tuna are shaved into flakes to make the dashi, which appears in almost every traditional Japanese meal. Served fresh, katsuo is also one of my favorite sashimi. Like mackerel, the best season for katsuo is the late fall and early winter, when the fish have put on a bit more fat. The spring and early summer katsuo, in contrast, are quite lean and prized for katsuobushi, where the fat isn't desirable, since it makes for a cloudy dashi.

Because of their small size, bonito is one of the few tuna species that is practical for us to regularly buy whole. It's a torpedo of a fish, sleek and muscular, with a beautiful blue-metallic skin. Like other tuna, it is a warm-blooded fish, and when you cut into one, the flesh looks almost beefy. Although sometimes served simply as sashimi with minimal curing, bonito is more commonly charred over a hot fire in a method called tataki. The skin is left on the fillets during this process and is charred to a smoky black, while the interior remains raw. Traditionally, this searing is done over rice straw (which is ubiquitous in Japan), and the process firms the flesh and gives the meat a lovely smoky flavor. Rice straw is hard to source in California, so I've opted to use the dry redwood needles that pile under the redwood tree behind my house. The flavor of the redwood smoke is distinctly coniferous, a difference from the traditional that I accept happily. In the last several years, Pacific bonito have been caught off the coast of Monterey. They are relatively uncommon in our waters, though, and I'll sometimes substitute a small albacore tuna. Albacore have lighter-colored flesh that is softer than that of bonito—and that makes them all the more suitable for charring. Albacore's fat content is often very high, making it delicious raw.

A boldly flavored fish requires strong condiments, and we serve the katsuo with thinly sliced onions, grated garlic, scallions, and ginger.

If you'd like to break down your own bonito, see page 52.

To prepare the fillets: Wipe the fillets well (bonito are a bloody fish) and store them wrapped in paper towels and placed on a sheet pan in the coldest part of the refrigerator until you are ready to use them.

Place a fillet on a cutting board with the thicker head side facing you. Using long, shallow strokes, remove the chi-ae, the dark red blood line. You'll notice that

it is separated from the main muscles of the fish by a thin membrane. Discard and repeat with the remaining fillets.

Slice the fillets in half crosswise. Skewer each fillet crosswise, running the skewer close to the skin.

To prepare the fillets for smoking and searing: Light 3 or 4 charcoal briquettes in a grill chimney. Set a bag of dry straw or conifer needles near a grill along

with a bowl of ice water large enough to accommodate the fillets.

Put a handful of rice straw in the grill and add one briquette. You'll first smoke the fish and, at this point, you don't want the tinder to catch fire. Hold a skewered bonito in the thick white smoke, turning occasionally, for 3 to 4 minutes. Repeat with the remaining skewers. Add more tinder or adjust the charcoal or tinder, if needed, to generate sufficient smoke without igniting a full blaze.

Once the fish is smoked, add another large handful of rice straw and the rest of the briquettes. The tinder should catch fire. Hold a skewered bonito, skin-side down, a few inches from the fire, until the skin is thoroughly charred. At this point, oil should start to render from the skin. Cook over the flame for 1½ to 2 minutes, adding tinder as needed, and then turn the fish over and char the flesh side for another 30 seconds. Remove the fillet from the skewer and plunge it into the prepared ice water to stop the cooking. Repeat with the remaining skewers.

After the bonito are thoroughly chilled, remove them from the ice water and dry well with paper towels. Wrap them in paper towels until you are ready to serve.

To slice the fillets: Place a fillet, skin-side up, on a cutting board with the thicker side facing to the right. Starting at the thicker end of the fillet, with a razor-sharp knife, start your cut at the base of the knife and draw your blade through the fish, cutting straight down and through the fish in a single stroke. The slices should be a little more than ¼-inch / 6 mm thick. As you finish one slice, use the blade of your knife to push it on your cutting board a few inches to the right, and continue with the next, stacking one next to the other. This way, your slices are arranged nicely and can be easily transferred to a plate. Repeat with the rest of the fillets.

To serve, transfer the sliced fish to a chilled plate and serve with the daikon tsuma, shiso, garlic, ginger, scallions, and ponzu.

ROLL-CUT DAIKON TSUMA

The most time-consuming of the sashimi garnishes is the daikon *tsuma*, a word that means "wife," (an unsurprisingly sexist name, given Japan's traditional gender roles), which describes the very finely sliced daikon that play a supporting role on the finished plate. When a cook expresses interest in training on the sashimi station, I'll show them the basic daikon roll-cutting technique for making tsuma and will consider their request for training only after they present me with a perfectly cut bowl of tsuma. Although usually made with daikon, the same roll-cutting technique can be used with cucumbers, watermelon radishes, and carrots. I'll often mix in a bit of this color to the daikon tsuma for visual interest. There is no substitute for practice when it comes to roll cutting. When I first started working in Japan, after a fourteen-hour shift, I would return to the drafty little house where I was staying and practice with a section of daikon before bedtime. That said, if you'd rather not invest in developing this skill, feel free to cut the daikon thinly with a mandoline and then slice it finely with a knife.

Choose a daikon that's no more than 3 inches / 7.5 cm wide and cut it into 3-inch / 7.5 cm lengths. When you're getting started, it's easier to manage smaller pieces. As you gain experience, you can begin with thicker daikon and cut them into longer lengths. The knife that we use for roll cutting is called an usuba; its single-beveled blade is straight and well suited for the job.

Trim the ends of the daikon so the piece sits perfectly flat when stood on its end.

Holding the daikon in your left hand, grasp it with your fingers wrapped around the back and your thumb facing you and rotate it onto your blade.

Keep the blade stationary, only moving it up and down in a small sawing motion. Remove the skin and round off the daikon to make a perfect cylinder.

Continue rotating your daikon onto the blade, your two thumbs nearly touching and pulling the sheet of daikon over your blade.

Stack the sheets of daikon and cut very finely.

Rinse the sliced daikon in a bowl of cold water. Store in water until you are ready to use them. They should keep in a tightly sealed container in the refrigerator for two days.

HOW TO BREAK DOWN A WHOLE KATSUO (ALBACORE TUNA)

When choosing a katsuo, look for one that's between 6 to 8 lb / 2.7 to 3.6kg. If it's available, ask for one that has been caught by hook and line rather than in a net, which often bruises the fish badly. Bright eyes and a clean, ocean smell are the first signs of freshness. Check the gills to make sure they are bright red.

The process for breaking down a katsuo and other round fish is called *sanmai oroshi*, or "three section fillet," since you end up with two fillets and the skeleton.

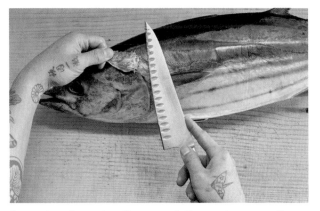

Removing the scales: Katsuo and albacore have a small section of scales near the pectoral fins and the back of the fish. Sliding your knife flush to the skin toward the head, slice them off in sheets; avoid slicing into the meat of the fish.

Cutting the head: With the head facing to the left, cut from just behind the pectoral fin through to just below the pelvic fin. Cut upward to the forehead, between the eyes. Use the thicker end of your knife to cut through the backbone. You may need to reposition your blade to cut between the vertebrae. Turn the fish over and repeat.

Removing the head and guts: Starting at the head, slice toward the tail to the end of the intestinal cavity. Do your best not to puncture any organs. Pull the head off and the guts out together and discard.

Cleaning the blood line: There is a blood line along the inner side of the backbone. Use the tip of your knife to slice the blood line and, using a kitchen towel or an old toothbrush, scrub away the residual blood. Wash the fish in the sink and dry well.

Cutting the belly side: With the head facing to the right, cut through the skin along the top of the belly fins, starting at the tail, using a long, shallow stroke. Once the skin has been cut, use the tip of your knife to locate the rib bones under your blade near the tail. In several long, shallow strokes, run your knife along the rib bones until your blade has reached the spine.

Cutting the back side: Flip the fish over so that the head is facing to the left. In a long, shallow stroke, cut through the skin along the top of the back fins. Once the skin has been cut, use the tip of your knife to locate the rib bones under your blade. In several long, shallow strokes, run your knife along the rib bones, until your blade has reached the spine.

Splitting the fish: At the tail of the fish with the blade facing towards the head, insert your knife until it comes out the other side. The fillet should still be attached at the tail. With the knife very slightly angled downwards, run your blade down the spine, separating the fillet. Cut the fillet from the tail. Place the fillet skin-side down on a baking sheet.

Repeat: Turn the fish over, cut the skin on the belly side and then along the top of the bones to the backbone. Turn the fish and cut the skin along the back fins and then in several long shallow strokes to the backbone. Insert your knife at the tail and run your blade down the spine, separating the fillet. Cut the fillet from the tail.

Removing the belly bones: The bones that line the belly cavity are connected to the pin bones that stick up from the center line of the fish. Turn your knife upside down, and using the very tip of your blade, gently sever the connection between the belly bones and the pin bones. Slide your blade under the tops of the belly bones, and cutting as close to the bones as you can, remove them from the fillet. Repeat with the other half of the fish.

Separating the back and belly fillets: Place the split fish skin-side down on your cutting board. Use your fingers to locate the pin bones that run down the center of the fillet. Cutting as close to the bones as possible, remove the back section. Cutting as close to the bones as possible, remove the belly section, leaving a strip of pin bones. Repeat with the other half of the fish.

SASHIMI

TSUMA TO YAKUMI

SASHIMI GARNISHES AND CONDIMENTS

つま　と　薬味

Fish butchery takes practice, as do the various curing techniques, and the work of slicing and arranging the fish beautifully is endlessly nuanced. Aside from the fish itself, the sashimi cook at Rintaro is also responsible for making the various condiments and garnishes.

TYPES OF TSUMA

THINLY SLICED DAIKON, CARROT, CUCUMBER, WATERMELON RADISH
Thinly sliced daikon tsuma is the classic sashimi garnish. It takes a lot of practice to make it using the katsuramuki roll-cutting technique (see page 51). You can also make a decent version with a sharp mandolin: Slice 2.5- 3-inch sheets along the length of the daikon and then cut as thinly as possible. Rinse in cold water. The same technique can be used with watermelon radish, carrot and cucumber.

CRISP ONIONS
Very finely sliced white onions crisped in ice water also make a lovely garnish for stronger-tasting sashimi such as mackerel and bonito.

SCALLIONS
Thinly sliced scallions are a classic addition to mackerel and other silver-skinned fish. Use the finely sliced white parts (see page 249) or the green tops, cut very thin on the bias. Be sure to rinse them well in cold water.

SHISO
While shiso is a seasonal herb available in the late summer, most shiso is now grown in greenhouses so it's available year-round. The covered growing environment protects the delicate leaves from direct sunlight; this helps the leaves to stay mild and tender.

MYOGA
The bud of the myoga plant has a distinctive cedar-y taste and a crunchy texture. In Japan, it's widely available in the summer and is sometimes available in Japanese markets.

MEYER LEMON AND YUZU
Aromatic lemon and yuzu peel sliced thinly are an appealing addition to a sashimi platter. Sliced rounds are another simple way to liven up the plate.

GRATED GINGER
Sometimes, to cut the heat of the ginger, we add grated daikon that's been washed of its flavor and smell and squeezed until very dry. The ratio is typically 2 parts ginger to 1 part daikon. The ginger juice rehydrates the squeezed daikon.

YUZU KOSHO
Made from the peel of the yuzu citrus, salt, and hot chile peppers, yuzu kosho can be used as an aromatic condiment for sashimi. We serve it most often with kanpachi and other fatty white fish. It's very salty, so should not be combined with shoyu.

WASABI
The most common sashimi condiment is also the hardest to find in its pure state. For special occasions, consider ordering it directly from Half Moon Bay Wasabi. See more on page 57.

PONZU
The katsuobushi enriched citrus and shoyu-based sauce is exceptionally delicious with lightly flavored white fish such as sea bream. I also like it with charred bonito sashimi. See page 39 for the recipe.

TOSAJOYU
Katsuobushi-enriched shoyu is most often served with heavier sashimi such as bonito and bluefin or bigeye tuna. See page 39 for the recipe.

GOMA DARE
While not typically served with sashimi, this sweet sesame sauce is incredibly tasty with vinegar-cured mackerel. *Gomasaba* is regional dish of Fukuoka. See page 45 for recipe.

SEASONAL COLOR
I'm usually not a fan of a nonedible garnish. The one exception I make is for the use of foraged leaves on sashimi platters. Not only do foraged leaves add color and beauty to the plate, they also help root the sashimi here in the Bay Area and in the season. I typically use green Japanese maple leaves in spring and summer, wild fennel fronds in summer, red maple leaves in fall, and white pine in winter, but you should choose whatever beautiful (non-poisonous!) seasonal leaves grow in your area.

WASABI

Fresh, real wasabi is quite rare. Even in Japan, the actual rhizome is usually served only at higher-end restaurants. The wasabi powder available at supermarkets here in the United States is made with powdered horseradish and a bit of green coloring. It packs a satisfying punch but tastes completely different from the real thing. If powdered wasabi is all that is available, use grated daikon in place of water to hydrate it and to give it a better texture. You can also buy tubes of wasabi at Japanese markets; these typically contain real wasabi, a bit of corn syrup, and citric acid. There are a few brands available online that have few additives, but if you're ordering online, consider buying what we serve at the restaurant: whole roots from Half Moon Bay Wasabi.

For nearly a decade now, I've been buying fresh wasabi from Jeff Roller, a farmer in Half Moon Bay, which is south of San Francisco. He is one of only a handful of wasabi farmers in America—not because there isn't demand for the real thing, but because wasabi is notoriously difficult to grow. It requires fresh, clear cold water and a lot of expertise and patience (a large root can take two to three years to grow). Jeff started growing wasabi as a side project to his real work as an electrician. He harvests every Monday morning, and every Monday evening, he delivers a bag to the restaurant. His wasabi is beautiful and tasty, with the distinctive sweetness and heat that only the real thing can deliver. Although he's done a bit of electrical work for us in the past, he's now far too busy growing and selling wasabi to bother with the errant bad outlet.

Traditionally, the best graters for wasabi were made with shark skin, which is abrasive yet fine enough to yield a very smooth paste. A metal ginger grater works as well.

To prepare fresh wasabi for grating, trim the stems off at an angle as though sharpening a pencil—you want to preserve the usable wasabi right under the stem; it's too precious to waste. Likewise, use the back of your knife to scrape off the skin so you don't remove too much of the flesh below. A vegetable peeler will take off too much of the usable root. Grate the wasabi in a circular motion, starting with the stem end until you reach the very tip, where the wasabi turns from a vivid green to a dull white and becomes bitter. Place your grated wasabi on a cutting board and give it a few passes with a knife to mince up any larger bits. The heat in wasabi is a gas, so store the wasabi in a small airtight container until ready to use. Freshly grated wasabi should be used within 4 hours of grating. Leftovers can be wrapped tightly in plastic wrap and frozen.

Whole wasabi roots are best stored wrapped in a moist paper towel and kept in a resealable plastic bag in the refrigerator. Kept like this, a fresh root should last up to 2 weeks.

SEASONAL SAKE

BY JOHN LEE, BEVERAGE DIRECTOR

Nihonshu (or sake) has always been an integral part of izakaya culture. Izakayas originated during the Edo period as spaces to drink within sake shops. At some point, proprietors began offering *otsumami* or finger foods to accompany the alcoholic beverages. While today's izakayas may offer the gamut from craft beer to shochu cocktails, our beverage program at Rintaro highlights sake.

Early in my career, I learned to be attentive and anticipate the seasonality of food while working at Bi-Rite Market, a renowned San Francisco grocer. This respect and appreciation for the seasons aligns with Japanese culture and traditions. Sake, like food, has seasons. While the majority of brewing takes place after the rice harvest in the fall, bottling occurs throughout the year. Our beverage menu is ever evolving but centers around seasonal sake releases.

Winter is marked by the release of *shiboritate* (freshly pressed) sake. Bottled right after pressing, this is *namazake* (unpasteurized) and full of youthful promise; raw, unrefined, and often with a slight effervescence. We pair *shiboritate* with simple winter fare like sashimi or heartier brothy soups like oden or nabes.

Spring *namazakes* arrive as the plum trees begin to bloom. Sometimes called *haruzake* (spring sake), these brews are aged for a couple months, which results in a refreshing, bright, and lively sake. Spring cuisine, like fresh bamboo shoots or green, herbaceous sprouts and flowers are wonderfully complemented by *haruzake*.

While San Francisco doesn't experience the hot and humid conditions of a Japanese summer, we still welcome the appearance of *natsuzake* (summer sake). Lighter, cleaner, and typically lower in alcohol, these sakes provide a chilling respite from the summer heat.

As the autumn harvest begins, preparations are made for the upcoming brewing season. World Sake Day is celebrated on October 1st with *hiyaoroshi* (fall "draft" sake). These sakes are pasteurized once right after pressing before aging for six months. Full and rich, they are fragrant, layered, and silky smooth. At Rintaro, *hiyaoroshi* make perfect accompaniments to fall dishes like duck udon and roasted mushrooms and squash.

We are very fortunate to have access to sake from almost all of the forty-seven Japanese prefectures. Our beverage menu highlights small family-owned breweries that utilize traditional brewing processes and often farm their own rice.

In addition to the sake that we source from Japan, we have wonderful sake on our menu from two local breweries: James Beard award–nominated Den Sake Brewery (Oakland, CA) and Sequoia Sake (San Francisco, CA).

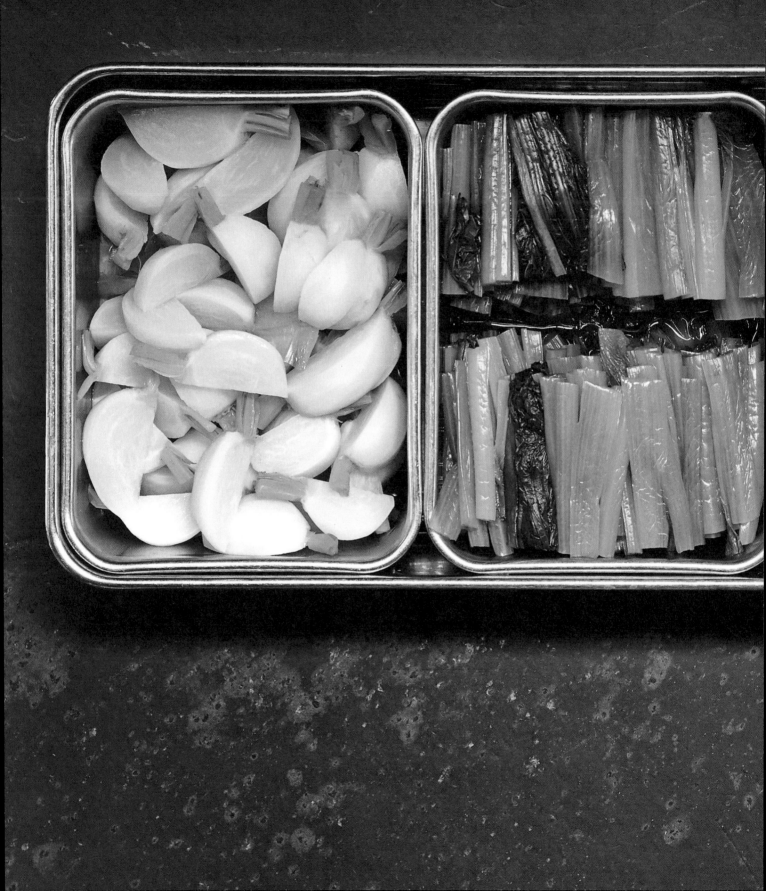

AEMONO,
OHITASHI
&
SARADA

和え物、酢の物、
おひたし、サラダ

DRESSED DISHES

BEFORE OPENING RINTARO, I SPENT seven years working at Chez Panisse, a restaurant known for its pristine produce. When I opened my restaurant, I felt a bit of pressure to do something miraculous with vegetables. California may be justly famous for its produce, but Japan is known for its "micro-seasonal" approach to using its vegetables and fruits. An ingredient might be available for only a week or two, during which time it will be swapped into a preparation that otherwise remains constant. I adopted this strategy at Rintaro, developing recipes that are in the Japanese tradition, using a handful of dressings and simple methods of preparation applied to a variety of vegetables in season.

Picking up on this seasonal mix-and-match approach, I've organized this chapter's recipes around their dressings, since it is the dressing—not the specific vegetables used—that really defines the dish. These "master" dressing recipes are versatile and can be used in myriad ways, across seasons.

Sunomono means "vinegared thing," and refers to a vegetable—typically cucumbers—dressed in rice vinegar and served in a variety of different ways, as a side dish or a component of a larger dish. Nuta is a mustardy white miso dressing, enriched with egg yolks and sesame paste and is typically used on vegetable dishes that also contain seafood. Shira-ae is a creamy dressing that is made from tofu and sesame. That, as well as the shoyu and onion that's used to dress the duck salad (page 90), is used in much the same way as a dressing is in Western cooking: to dress combinations of raw and blanched vegetables. The ohitashi and its variation, nibatashi, are a little different. Rather than being dressed with a sauce, the vegetables are soaked (or simmered) in seasoned dashi. What I love about all ohitashi and its variations is that a good dashi emphasizes the flavors of the vegetables without overpowering them, lending richness to what might otherwise be a one-note dish.

Although the recipes included here may seem specific, they are flexible. If you have a difficult time finding the exact vegetable that's listed, look to the best of what's available in your market. This spirit of micro-seasonality, of cooking with a vegetable at its peak, and then moving on, rather than seeking out a specific ingredient, is at the soul of Japanese cooking.

KYURI NO SUNOMONO

CUCUMBER SUNOMONO

きゅうりの酢の物

AMAZU

5 tablespoons / 75ml water

5 tablespoons / 75ml rice vinegar

1½ tablespoons sugar

SUNOMONO-SU

5 tablespoons / 75ml Katsuobushi Dashi (page 19), chilled

2 teaspoons sea salt, plus more as needed

1 lb / 450 g Japanese, Persian, or Armenian cucumbers

MAKES 4 SERVINGS

Sunomono translates to "vinegared thing" and, as the name implies, can take a million forms. The most common is cucumber sunomono, which is finely sliced and lightly salted cucumbers soaked in seasoned vinegar. The salt draws the water from the cucumbers, concentrating the flavor and giving them an excellent crunchy texture.

I don't think I understood how fine a sunomono could be until I visited Unagi Kuniyoshi, an eel restaurant near the famous hot spring town of Hakone, south of Tokyo. The restaurant has essentially been around forever—the current owner is seventeenth generation (!)—and apart from the beautiful lacquerware and insanely fresh grilled eel (killed to order), I was struck by the depth and delicacy of their grilled eel sunomono. The owner, Kunihiko Miyadai, is a friend of a friend, and when he visited San Francisco, he stopped in at Rintaro to show me his approach. He started with amazu, which is a combination of good rice wine vinegar, sugar, and water, to which he added fresh dashi and salt. The dashi plays a subtle but critical role, lending the dish an underpinning of smokiness and richness. I was also struck by how Miyadai-san handled the dressed cucumbers, squeezing the excess sunomono vinegar gently from the slices and then heaping them bit by bit into a small loose mound on the plate.

For Rintaro, I buy Japanese cucumbers from Hikari Farms in Watsonville, just south of San Francisco. It's a second-generation Japanese American farm that specializes in Japanese ingredients. Because of our mild climate and their greenhouses, I am able to keep their beautiful cucumbers on the menu year-round. If you can't find Japanese cucumbers, Persian cucumbers are a good substitute. You could also use the long, snakelike Armenian cucumbers, such as the variety called Painted Serpent, which can be found at some farmers' markets. I've given amounts for enough amazu for a single batch of cucumber sunomono, but it can be scaled up if you'd like to keep extra on hand.

To make the amazu: Bring the water, vinegar, and sugar to a boil in a small saucepan, stirring to dissolve the sugar. Remove the pan from the heat, let cool to room temperature, then transfer to a lidded jar and refrigerate until cold. The amazu will keep in the refrigerator for up to 2 months.

To make the sunomono-su: Combine the dashi with the chilled amazu. Add 1 teaspoon of the salt and stir to dissolve, then refrigerate until ready to use.

Peel the cucumbers so there are alternating strips of peeled and unpeeled. If your cucumbers are large, with a lot of seeds, cut the cucumbers lengthwise and scrape out the seeds with the tip of a teaspoon. Using a mandoline or a sharp knife, slice the cucumbers as thinly as you can and place them in a large bowl. Toss the sliced cucumbers with the remaining 1 teaspoon salt and let sit for 5 minutes. Massage the salted cucumbers gingerly until they are submerged in their own water. Gently squeeze handfuls of the cucumbers to remove the water, then place the squeezed cucumbers in a clean large bowl, discarding the water. Chill in the refrigerator until ready to serve, unless you are ready to use them immediately.

To serve, toss the salted and chilled cucumbers with the sunomono-su. Taste for seasoning, adding more salt if necessary. Gently squeeze out the excess sunomono-su from the cucumbers (they should remain quite wet) and pile them loosely on a serving dish.

VARIATIONS

I like to make a simple sunomono by combining the cucumbers with another seasonal fruit or vegetable. In spring, I might combine thinly sliced radishes with the cucumbers or with wakame (a type of seaweed). In summer, I add thin slices of ripe plums for a bit of sweetness, and in winter, when I have access to beautiful citrus, I'll often combine the cucumbers with thin slices of kumquat or pomelo segments. For other sunomono recipes, see pages 67 and 68.

TOMATO NO SUNOMONO トマトの酢の物

TOMATO SUNOMONO

---

4 medium Early Girl tomatoes, cored

1 cup / 236 ml Katsuobushi Dashi (page 19)

1½ teaspoons usukuchi (light-colored) shoyu

1 tablespoon mirin

1 recipe Kyuri no Sunomono (page 64)

2 teaspoons mayonnaise

10 shiso leaves

MAKES 4 SERVINGS

This is one of the more dramatic dishes we serve at Rintaro. I use Early Girl tomatoes, because I love their intense tomato-y flavor, but Momotaro or other heirloom varieties would work well, too. Obviously—at least to me—the success or failure of this dish depends on the quality of the tomato. Wait until they're ridiculously delicious. The poaching and removal of the skin may seem a bit tedious, but it makes a big difference in the texture, and removing the skin allows the seasoned dashi to penetrate the tomato, seasoning it fully. I usually pour the hot dashi over the chilled tomatoes to help speed up the seasoning process, although you could use chilled dashi and let them soak longer.

Cut a small × on the bottom of each tomato. Prepare a small ice water bath and bring a pot of unsalted water to a boil.

Drop the tomatoes in and count to 30. Quickly remove one of the tomatoes using a slotted spoon and test to see if the skin is peeling away at the ×. If not, return it to the boiling water for another 15 seconds. Remove all the tomatoes using the slotted spoon and plunge into the prepared ice water bath.

Carefully peel the skin off the tomatoes. (Note that if you overcook the tomatoes, the top layer of flesh will come off as well, and they won't be as pretty.) Stab the tomatoes all over with a skewer and place in a bowl just large enough to hold them one layer deep.

In a small saucepan over medium heat, combine the dashi, shoyu, and mirin and bring to a simmer. Reserve 2 tablespoons of the dashi mixture and set aside. Pour the remaining dashi mixture over the tomatoes. Transfer the bowl to the refrigerator and chill for at least 2 hours or overnight (if chilling overnight, transfer the reserved dashi mixture to a lidded jar and refrigerate as well).

When ready to serve, arrange the cucumbers around the perimeter of a shallow bowl. Remove the tomatoes from the dashi mixture with a slotted spoon and nestle them in the center of the cucumbers.

Put the mayonnaise in a small bowl and thin with some of the reserved dashi mixture (you may not need all of it; you just want to loosen the mayonnaise a bit). Dollop the mayonnaise over the tomatoes.

Stack the shiso leaves on top of one another and roll into a thin cigar. With a sharp knife, slice the cigar crosswise as thinly as possible so you have ribbons of shiso. Top each tomato with a little pile of shiso and serve immediately.

GINDARA NO SUNOMONO

銀だらの酢の物

MISO-CURED BLACK COD SUNOMONO

---

1 (1 lb / 450 g) skin-on
  black cod fillet

Sea salt

½ cup / 125 g saikyo
  (sweet white) miso

2 tablespoons sake

2 tablespoons mirin

1 recipe Kyuri no
  Sunomono (page 64)

Thinly sliced shiso, for
  serving

Wasabi, for serving

MAKES 4 SERVINGS

Gindara translates to "silver cod" (as in Ginkaguki, the "silver" temple complex in Kyoto known for its rock gardens), and it is highly prized in Japan. It's a common species here on the West Coast. Its flesh is very soft, with a high oil and water content and tiny fragile bones that are almost impossible to remove until the fish is cooked. I really only serve this fish cured; otherwise, the texture is too soft for my taste. The curing process happens in two steps: the fish is lightly salted and packed in absorbent paper towels to wick away the moisture, and it is then cured with saikyo miso for three days. Originating in Kyoto, saikyo miso was made for the imperial household. It's the most elegant of the misos—smooth, lightly sweet, and just a touch salty. The best versions are made only with soybeans, water, and koji, without added glucose or other sugars.

Once cured and grilled, the fish has a lovely buttery flavor and flaky texture. The cucumbers add crispiness and acidity that are a perfect counterpoint to the rich fish.

To prepare the fish: You will be making pieces that each weigh approximately 2 oz / 57 g and are ½ inch / 12 mm thick and 4 by 1½ inches / 10 by 4 cm wide. The most important dimension is the thickness; it needs to be consistent, so it cures and cooks evenly. Place the fillet, skin-side up, on a cutting board with the tail end facing to the right. You will be cutting the fish against the grain at a bias. Starting at the head side of the fillet, with your knife blade perpendicular to the fish and tilted to the right, start cutting pieces. You'll have to adjust the angle of the knife, depending on the shape of the fillet. You should get about eight nice pieces plus some scraps.

Line a rimmed sheet pan with a sheet of heavy-duty paper towels and sprinkle the paper towels lightly with salt.

Place the pieces of fish, skin-side up, on top of the paper towels in a single layer.

Salt the tops of the fish very lightly and cover with a second sheet of paper towels. (Since white miso has a very low salt content, salting the tops of the fish introduces a bit of salt as well as drawing excess moisture from the fillets to help firm the texture.) Cover the dish and refrigerate for at least an hour.

In a small bowl, whisk together the miso, sake, and mirin.

Remove the dish from the refrigerator and discard the paper towels. Smear the top and bottom of each slice of the fish with some of the miso mixture and return to the dish. Cover and refrigerate for 3 days.

Line a rimmed sheet pan with aluminum foil.

Remove the fish from the refrigerator, scrape the excess miso off with your finger, and wipe the fish clean with a

paper towel. Do not rinse the fish with water! Discard the miso marinade. Arrange the fish, skin-side up, in a single layer in the prepared pan.

Preheat the broiler to low. Place an oven rack 6 inches / 15 cm from the broiler element.

Set the pan on the rack and broil for 10 to 15 minutes, until the sugars from the miso begin to caramelize and the fish becomes a beautiful golden-brown color, rotating the pan as necessary.

Remove the pan from the broiler and, using tweezers, carefully remove the pin bones from each piece of fish.

To serve, divide the sunomono cucumbers evenly among four plates. Lean two pieces of fish atop the cucumbers. Garnish with a little pile of very finely sliced shiso and a dab of wasabi. This dish is especially tasty if you're able to serve the cold cucumbers with warm fish, but cooled to room temperature, the black cod is still delicious.

KANI NO SUNOMONO

CRAB SUNOMONO

かにの酢の物

1 (1 to 1½ lb /450 to 680 g) Dungeness crab (or another meaty crab variety)

1 recipe Kyuri no Sunomono (page 64)

Wasabi, for serving

MAKES 4 SERVINGS

If there is one ingredient that's emblematic of San Francisco, it is the Dungeness crab. Large, meaty, and sweet, their season begins each year around Thanksgiving, and steamed crabs are often served alongside turkey at California Thanksgiving feasts. Not only is the meat wonderful, Dungeness crabs also yield a significant amount of kani miso (crab butter, or tomalley). To the horror of my Japanese chef friends, in Western kitchens, the kani miso is usually discarded with the shells. But in Japan (and in most of Asia), it is considered a delicacy, and adding it brings the dish to another level.

Bring a large pot of salted water to a boil and prepare a large ice water bath. Drop in the crab headfirst and boil for 12 minutes, then remove it from the pot with tongs and immediately plunge it into the ice water bath. When it is cold, set it on a rimmed pan to drain in the refrigerator, head up and legs akimbo, for at least 10 minutes or overnight. This step will keep the kani miso from becoming watery.

Once drained, remove the carapace from the crab and pull out the gills and discard. Scrape and shake the yellowish crab fat and the orangish tomalley from inside the carapace into a bowl. Use a spoon to pass the tomalley through a fine-mesh sieve. Discard the solids and pass the tomalley through the

sieve a second time, so it's smooth and appetizing.

Crack the crab legs and claws and pick the crabmeat from the shell, doing your best to keep the large leg and claw segments intact.

Arrange the picked crabmeat on four plates, reserving the large leg and claw pieces. Top the crab with the sunomono cucumbers, dividing them evenly, then top with some of the reserved crab leg and claw pieces. Drizzle the crab pieces with a bit of the sunomono vinegar you squeezed from the cucumbers and top each serving with a teaspoon of the strained tomalley and a dot of wasabi. Serve immediately.

NUTA SUMISO

MUSTARDY WHITE MISO SAUCE

TAMAMISO

6 tablespoons /90ml sake

½ cup / 125 g saikyo (sweet white) miso

1 large egg yolk

1½ teaspoons sesame paste

2 teaspoons usukuchi (light-colored) shoyu

2 teaspoons sugar

1 tablespoon plus 1 teaspoon yuzu or lemon juice

2 teaspoons Japanese mustard powder

MAKES ABOUT ½ CUP / 120ML

Nuta is a very old recipe, dating back to the Muromachi Era (14th to 16th centuries), and is made by combining miso, vinegar, and sugar. Although nuta can be made with all sorts of miso, the version I prefer is made with mild white miso. To give the sauce a rounder flavor, rather than using straight miso, we cook the miso with sake, egg yolks, and sesame paste to make something called tamamiso (*tama* means "egg" plus miso). This recipe makes more tamamiso than you need for the nuta, but it's difficult to make a smaller batch, and it keeps in the refrigerator for two weeks. To make the nuta, the tamamiso is seasoned with yuzu or lemon juice (in place of the traditional vinegar), shoyu, sugar, and Japanese mustard powder.

Unlike most Western salads, those dressed with nuta are made with blanched vegetables. There are many variations, but to be a nuta, it must include tender, cooked green onions and often includes shellfish or fish.

To make the tamamiso: Bring the sake to a boil in a medium saucepan over high heat. Reduce to a simmer and cook until it no longer smells of alcohol, about 4 minutes. Keep an eye on it as it cooks so it doesn't reduce down to nothing; you should end up with about 2 tablespoons.

Meanwhile, in a small bowl, combine the miso, egg yolk, and sesame paste. Add the still-hot sake and whisk together. Transfer to a double boiler (or a heatproof bowl set over a saucepan of simmering water) and cook, scraping the bottoms and sides of the bowl constantly with a rubber spatula, until

the mixture registers 160°F / 71°C on an instant-read thermometer. Strain through a fine-mesh strainer into a clean bowl. Let cool to room temperature, then cover and chill for at least 1 hour.

To finish the nuta: Whisk together 5 tablespoons / 80 g of the tamamiso, the shoyu, sugar, yuzu juice, and hot mustard. The nuta will keep in an airtight container in the refrigerator for up to 1 day, but it will get spicier as it sits.

IKA NO NUTA

SQUID WITH MUSTARDY WHITE MISO SAUCE

いかのぬた

1 bunch (about 8 oz / 226 g) komatsuna

1 bunch (about 8 oz / 226 g) Tokyo turnips

1 bunch scallions

2 cups / 472ml seasoned Udon Tsuyu (page 248), optional

10 oz / 285 g fresh squid (bodies and tentacles), cleaned and cut into ¼-inch / 6 mm-thick rings

Sea salt

1 (2-inch / 5 cm) piece konbu

½ cup / 120ml vegetable or other neutral oil

¼ Fuji apple

1 recipe Nuta (page 72)

MAKES 4 SERVINGS

The squid most often available in the waters around San Francisco is the Pacific squid. It's relatively small, extremely abundant, and is almost always on our menu in the form of squid nuta. We blanch the squid until it's just cooked through, chill it in an ice water bath, salt it lightly, and store it in vegetable oil. The oil bath is one of the many tricks I learned from Kanji Nakatani, a mentor and the chef of Soba Ro—it transforms the squid's texture, making it lush and tender. And although you drain the oil from the squid before using it, the residual oil adds richness to the final dish. If you can't find fresh squid, frozen can be substituted; thaw it, rinse it well, and cook as instructed in the recipe.

Given all the vegetables that need to be peeled, blanched, squeezed, and cut when cooking for a crowd, this is a time-consuming dish to prepare. But at home, it's manageable and worth the effort. Along with the squid, this version includes the requisite blanched scallions as well as komatsuna (Japanese mustard greens), sweet Tokyo turnips, and Fuji apples. It's texturally terrific. If you can't find komatsuna, you can substitute rapini, hearty spinach, or even tender green beans.

To prepare the vegetables: Rinse and trim the komatsuna and bundle the greens with a rubber band. Trim the turnip greens to ½-inch / 12 mm. If the turnips are very young with tender skin, simply scrub them clean with a brush. If they are larger with coarser skin, peel them. For tiny turnips, cut them in half lengthwise; for larger ones, quarter or cut them into sixths. Trim the root end of the scallions and remove any discolored leaves or dry outer layers.

Bring a large pot of salted water to a boil and prepare an ice water bath.

Starting with the komatsuna, hold the greens by the tops with the stems in the water for 45 seconds before dropping in the entire bunch. Cook for 2 minutes, just until tender. Remove with a spider strainer and transfer to the prepared ice water bath. Repeat with the scallions,

holding them by their green tops with the bottom white section in the boiling water for 45 seconds before dropping in the bunch. Cook for 2 more minutes. Using a spider, transfer them to the ice water bath. When they are cold, transfer them to a paper towel–lined plate.

Add more ice to the ice water bath. Return the water to a boil, add the turnips, turn down the heat to a low boil, and cook for 3 to 7 minutes (depending on the size of the turnips), tasting them occasionally. They should be tender with no crunch; they will quickly overcook and become mushy if you're not paying attention. Using a spider, transfer them to the ice water bath; when cold, transfer to the paper towel–lined plate.

Squeeze the water from the komatsuna and cut into 1-inch / 2.5 cm pieces.

With the scallions, starting at the middle, squeeze them upward; the "gel" within will be pushed out of the tops and bottoms. Discard the gel and cut the scallions into 1-inch / 2.5 cm pieces. At this point you can store the vegetables in the refrigerator for a few hours or up to a day.

If you happen to have seasoned udon tsuyu on hand, you can soak your vegetables in that for at least 15 minutes or up to 4 hours, otherwise omit this step.

To prepare the squid: Bring a fresh pot of salted water to a boil. Prepare an ice water bath and set a fine-mesh strainer in the ice bath.

Add the squid to the boiling water and boil for 1½ minutes, just until cooked through. Using a spider, transfer the squid to the strainer. Repeat with the tentacles. Once cold, drain and transfer the squid to a small bowl. Lightly salt them to taste, add the konbu, and then pour the oil over them. You can hold the squid, refrigerated, for up to 2 days. Let them come to room temperature before using.

When ready to serve, core the apple quarter and cut crosswise into small pie-shaped slices about ¼-inch / 6 mm thick.

To assemble: Put the blanched vegetables in a large bowl (if you soaked them in tsuyu, strain, then squeeze the vegetables to remove excess liquid) and add the apple. Strain the squid, discarding the oil, and add to the bowl. Add the nuta sauce, mix, and serve. For individual portions, I like to mound the vegetables, apple, and squid rings and then top with one or two squid legs.

MAGURO NO NUTA

RAW TUNA WITH MUSTARDY WHITE MISO SAUCE　　まぐろのぬた

**8 oz / 226 g bigeye or
yellowfin tuna**

1 bunch scallions

**¼ cup / 60ml Nuta
(page 72)**

MAKES 4 SERVINGS

Although the squid and vegetable nuta (page 73) is by far the most common way
we use nuta sauce at Rintaro, it is also delicious on all sorts of raw and cooked fish
and shellfish. Feel free to add other blanched vegetables, but blanched scallions
are nonnegotiable. Individual small servings of bright red tuna and green blanched
scallions with a bit of the bright yellow nuta sauce is a striking first course.

Cut the tuna into ½-inch / 12 mm
cubes, salt lightly, and store in the
refrigerator between two sheets of
heavy-duty paper towels to remove
excess moisture and blood until ready
to serve.

Prepare an ice water bath and bring
a large pot of salted water to a boil.
Trim the root end of the scallions and
remove any discolored leaves or dry
outer layers. Hold the scallions by their
green tops with the bottom white sections in the boiling water for 45 seconds
before dropping in the whole bunch and

cooking for 2 minutes. Using a spider,
transfer the scallions to the prepared
ice water bath. When cool, starting at
the middle, squeeze the "gel" within
upwards out of the green tops and then
downwards out of the white bottoms,
then cut the scallions into ½-inch /
12 mm pieces.

Divide the tuna among four dishes,
arranging it in a little mound in each
dish and layering in slices of blanched
scallions. Top each with 1 tablespoon of
the nuta sauce.

VARIATIONS

Try the nuta sauce with shellfish such as mirugai sashimi (geoduck clams) or
steamed Manila clams.

SHIRA-AE GOROMO

RICH TOFU AND SESAME SAUCE

白和え衣

---

12 oz / 340 g firm tofu

2 tablespoons plus 1 teaspoon sesame seeds

2 tablespoons plus 1 teaspoon saikyo (sweet white) miso

2 teaspoons sugar

3 tablespoons / 45ml unsweetened soy milk

1 teaspoon lemon juice

¼ teaspoon sea salt

MAKES ABOUT 1½ CUPS / 354 ML

Cookbook author Nancy Hachisu gave me my first taste of shira-ae, when she made it for a gathering of farmers at her farmhouse in the countryside north of Tokyo. Using a ceramic suribachi mortar and wooden pestle, she ground toasted sesame seeds, tofu and miso, and rice wine vinegar together into a rough paste. She used this to dress komatsuna greens from her husband's garden, accented by slivers of yuzu peel grown from his trees. It was delicious and, like many of the recipes she champions, her version was true to the old style, before sugar was commonly used in Japanese food.

My second revelatory shira-ae was made by Daisuke Nomura, chef of Sougo Shojin restaurant in Tokyo. Equally delicious, it couldn't have been more different. Although his version also contained sesame and tofu, he didn't add vinegar, and he processed the sauce until it was completely smooth. It was sweetened with sugar and enriched with soy cream, the highest-fat soy milk. Rather than using it to dress simple komatsuna and yuzu, his shira-ae was used on summer fruits and greens.

The one we serve at Rintaro is a blend of these two approaches. We process it until it's smooth, and serve it both simply with the blanched leafy greens and in a more complex version that includes fruit.

The soy milk should be rich; this can be a tricky thing to source, but try asking at Asian grocery stores (and make sure to buy unsweetened soy milk). Don't be tempted to use grocery store soy milk, since it lacks body and flavor.

To press the excess water from the tofu, wrap it in paper towels, place it in a strainer over a bowl, and set a heavy weight on top. We use a 7-lb / 3.2kg stone mortar, but a bowl of water or a stack of heavy skillets would work well, too. Let the tofu drain for an hour or until it has lost 30 percent of its weight in water; after pressing, the tofu should weigh about 8 oz / 226 g.

Toast the sesame seeds in a small dry skillet over medium heat, shaking constantly for several minutes until they're fragrant and can be crushed easily between your fingertips. Sesame seeds burn easily, so pay close attention and taste them often. When they're done,

pour them immediately into a suribachi grinding bowl or a mortar and pestle.

Grind the sesame seeds until completely smooth. They should start to release oil. Add the miso and sugar and continue to grind until smooth.

At this point, transfer the sesame mixture to the bowl of a food processor, taking care to scrape out every last bit from the suribachi with a rubber spatula, and add the pressed tofu.

Add the soy milk to the food processor and process until smooth. Add the lemon juice and salt. Use right away or transfer to a lidded jar and store for up to 2 days in the refrigerator.

KOMATSUNA TO KAKI NO SHIRA-AE

KOMATSUNA AND PERSIMMON WITH SHIRA-AE

小松菜と柿の白和え

I bunch (about 8 oz /
226 g) komatsuna

I Fuyu persimmon

I cup / 200 g Shira-ae
(page 77)

MAKES 4 SERVINGS

I love the combination of persimmon with blanched greens. We use komatsuna (Japanese mustard greens), but you could substitute tender Chinese mustard greens or Taiwanese spinach.

Bring a large pot of salted water to a boil and prepare an ice water bath.

Rinse and trim the komatsuna and bundle the greens with a rubber band. Hold the komatsuna by the tops with the stems in the water for 45 seconds before dropping in the entire bunch. Cook for 2 minutes, until just tender. Using a spider strainer, transfer the komatsuna to the ice water bath. When cool, remove the komatsuna from the ice bath and squeeze well to remove all the water from the greens. Trim and discard the root ends and cut the komatsuna into 1-inch / 2.5 cm pieces.

Transfer to a medium bowl.

Core, peel, and quarter the persimmon. Then, cut each quarter crosswise into small pie-shaped pieces, about ¼-inch / 6 mm thick, reserving a few slices for garnish.

Add the persimmon to the bowl with the komatsuna. Add the shira-ae and toss well to coat. Arrange in small mounds on four plates, dividing evenly, and garnish each serving with a couple of slices of persimmon. Serve right away.

INGEN FURUTSU NO SHIRA-AE

いんげんとフルーツ
の白和え

ROMANO BEANS, FIGS, AND PEACH WITH SHIRA-AE

1 lb / 450 g Romano beans

1 ripe yellow peach

4 ripe figs, Black Mission, Adriatic, or other variety

1 cup / 200 g Shira-ae (page 78)

MAKES 4 SERVINGS

This is a version of shira-ae that we made as part of an all-vegetarian shojin menu. *Shojin*, or temple cuisine, dates back to the 13th-century Zen Buddhist monasteries, where meat, fish, and even eggs were forbidden foods. It's a wholly vegan style of cooking. Over the centuries, shojin has developed into one of the most sophisticated and technically strenuous genres of Japanese cooking.

This dish, however, is completely approachable. I love Romano beans, but any good green bean will do. Resist the urge to undercook your beans—they should keep their bright green color, but taste them often to make sure they're cooked until tender. Only use figs if they're soft and burstingly ripe; otherwise, simply omit them.

Bring a medium pot of salted water to a boil and prepare an ice water bath.

Blanch the Romano beans until tender, about 5 minutes. Using a spider strainer, transfer the beans to the ice water bath (do not discard the boiling water). When the beans are cold, remove them from the ice bath and slice each bean on the bias, about ½ inch / 12 mm wide and 2 inches / 5 cm long, discarding the stems. Transfer to a medium bowl.

Add the peach to the boiling water and blanch for 30 seconds, until the skin is loose. Transfer to the ice water bath

(adding more ice if necessary). Peel the peach, discarding the skin, cut into eight wedges, and then cut each wedge crosswise into thirds.

Slice the figs lengthwise into quarters or sixths. Add the figs and the peach to the bowl with the beans, reserving a few pieces of fig and peach for garnish. Add the shira-ae and toss well to coat. Arrange in mounds on four plates, dividing evenly, and garnish each serving with a couple of fig and peach slices. Serve right away.

OHITASHI AND NIBITASHI TSUKEJI

おひたしと煮びたしの漬け地

BLANCHED AND SIMMERED VEGETABLES IN SEASONED DASHI

2 cups / 472ml Katsuobushi Dashi (page 19)

2 tablespoons mirin

1 tablespoon usukuchi (light-colored) shoyu

½ teaspoon sea salt

1 bunch spinach

1 cup / 16 g shaved katsuobushi, for serving

MAKES ABOUT 2¼ CUPS / 532 ML

Ohitashi is one of the most basic building blocks of Japanese cooking. In its simplest form, it is blanched vegetables soaked in cold seasoned dashi and garnished with shaved katsuobushi. But there are variations, such as nibitashi, in which vegetables are simmered in the seasoned dashi and served either warm or cold, like the bamboo shoot recipe on page 85.

Whether you are making ohitashi or nibitashi, the master recipe is the same: a combination of dashi, mirin, and light soy sauce. But the strength of the seasoning varies, depending on the vegetable and the preparation: lighter for delicate vegetables that are soaked in the seasoning liquid versus a more heavily seasoned liquid for more robustly flavored and textured vegetables.

In a saucepan, stir together the dashi, mirin, shoyu, and salt. Bring to a boil. Skim off any foam and let the mixture cool to the temperature of a warm bath.

Trim the roots and wash the spinach thoroughly to remove any dirt.

Bring a medium pot of salted water to a boil and prepare an ice water bath. Add the spinach to the boiling water and blanch for 1 minute. Using tongs, transfer the spinach to the ice water bath to cool, then drain in a colander. Squeeze out the water from the spinach and cut into 1-inch / 2.5 cm pieces. Pour the warm ohitashi over the spinach and chill for at least an hour in the refrigerator.

To serve, squeeze the dashi from the spinach and discard, mound on a serving plate, and garnish with the katsuobushi.

TAKENOKO NIBITASHI

DASHI-SIMMERED BAMBOO SHOOTS

筍の煮びたし

2 freshly picked bamboo shoots, or store-bought vacuum-sealed whole bamboo shoots, approximately 1 lb / 450 g

1 cup / 236ml Katsuobushi Dashi (page 18)

1½ teaspoons usukuchi (light-colored) shoyu

1 tablespoon mirin

½ teaspoon sea salt

MAKES 4 SERVINGS

Before I opened Rintaro, I had a catering company, Peko Peko, which I ran out of my home garage. It was a fully unlicensed operation—breaking every possible zoning, health, and fire code in the county. But it was a functional kitchen with proper refrigeration and sinks, propane burners, and even a commercial dishwasher. During the Peko Peko years, I spent an incredible amount of time in the car looking for good Japanese fruits and vegetables. Every May, I would drive two hours round trip to pick bamboo shoots in the huge backyard of a retired firefighter in Livermore. He was a bamboo enthusiast and was always happy to have me wander around his bamboo groves, eyes down, looking for the shoots that were just poking out of the ground. Bamboo grows so fast, you can almost see the shoots creeping up out of the ground, and you have to catch them at just the right moment. The shoots are good only before the tiny green leaves begin to sprout from the top of the shoot. They need to be processed almost immediately to reduce the tannins.

I no longer have the time to drive several hours to pick bamboo shoots myself, but I've found a wonderful farm, Penryn Orchards Specialties, that now supplies the restaurant. Since they're grown specifically for the shoots, the farmer carefully tends to his bamboo grove, watering and mulching as necessary. I look forward to bamboo shoot season every year, and we use them in as many dishes as I can during the month in which they're available. They are precious, so I make sure to use every edible bit of the shoot.

Cut the bamboo shoots in half lengthwise. If using freshly picked shoots, remove the dark outer husk and discard. Peel away the white inner husks, revealing the shoots themselves. Give the shoots a quick rinse. The inner husks are also delicious. Taste the inner husks for tenderness and trim away any tough bits. Cut them into ½-inch / 12 mm squares. Trim the root end of the shoots and if they are tender (cut a bit to taste), cut them into ½-inch / 12 mm cubes. Cut the shoots into ¼ to ½-inch / 6 mm to 12 mm-thick wedges.

In a saucepan, stir together the dashi, shoyu, mirin, and salt. Bring to a boil. Using a slotted spoon, skim off any foam. Add the shoots and simmer for 10 minutes. Remove the pan from the heat and let the shoots cool in the liquid. Serve warm or cold or as part of a bigger dish, such as the Takenoko Okowa (page 207) or to garnish the Kinki no Nitsuke (page 183).

VARIATIONS

This method of simmering in seasoned dashi can be used with many other vegetables. The basic concept is the same: you first quickly cook the vegetable in plain water to remove the tannins and then simmer in the seasoned dashi. Try it with wedges of kabocha squash, batons of carrot, cardoon, or gobo (burdock root), or even trimmed artichokes. The simmering time will vary depending on the vegetable. The blanched kabocha and carrots need only a few minutes, but the gobo might take up to twenty minutes. The best way to assess doneness is by tasting a piece; it should be tender and have absorbed the flavor of the dashi.

NA NO HANA OHITASHI

菜の花のおひたし

FLOWERING RAPINI IN WARM MUSTARDY DASHI

2 bunches (about 1 lb / 450 g) flowering rapini or broccoli rabe

1 cup / 236 ml Katsuobushi Dashi (page 18)

1½ teaspoons usukuchi (light-colored) shoyu

1 tablespoon mirin

½ teaspoon sea salt

1½ teaspoons Japanese mustard powder

1 cup / 16 g finely shaved katsuobushi, for serving

MAKES 4 SERVINGS

Early spring brings a whole world of wild and cultivated vegetables to market in Japan, including sansai—wild foraged mountain vegetables, like fiddlehead ferns, spikenard, butterbur flowers, and a dozen other crisp and often bitter shoots and buds. With the exception of the occasional fiddlehead fern, I have yet to discover the sansai of California. However, another classic Japanese spring vegetable, flowering brassicas, grouped under the name na no hana, "vegetable flowers," are abundant in the farmers' markets here in California. There, I can find yellow and white flowering Chinese broccoli and mustard greens, flowering bok choy shoots, and rapini. With tender florets and slight bitterness, rapini is an ideal vegetable for this simple nibitashi.

Unlike ohitashi, where the vegetables are soaked for an hour or two in the chilled seasoned dashi (see page 84), in this version, the rapini is quickly soaked in hot dashi, then spiked with spicy mustard powder. It is served warm and topped with finely shaved katsuobushi that dances in the steam.

Trim the bottoms from each rapini floret. Bring a medium pot of salted water to a boil and prepare an ice water bath. Add the rapini to the boiling water and blanch for 45 seconds. With tongs, transfer to the ice water bath to cool, then drain in a colander.

Bring the dashi, shoyu, mirin, and salt to a boil in a saucepan. Skim any foam. Add the powdered mustard and the drained rapini. Heat for less than a minute, until the rapini is warmed through. Remove from the liquid and arrange in a shallow bowl or rimmed plate (if you want to make it look fancy, arrange the rapini so all the stems are facing the same direction). Spoon a few tablespoons of the cooking liquid over the vegetables and garnish with a loose pile of the finely shaved katsuobushi.

VARIATIONS

Substitute flowering Chinese broccoli, flowering mustard greens, or turnip greens for the rapini. If you can find it, flowering rapeseed is the most classic version of this dish.

SHUNGIKU TO KAMO NO SARADA

CHRYSANTHEMUM AND GRILLED DUCK SALAD

春菊と鴨のサラダ

DRESSING

½ cup / 118ml rice wine vinegar

¼ cup / 35 g grated onion, grated with a rasp-style grater or on the finest holes of a box grater

¼ cup / 60ml shoyu

2 tablespoons sugar

1 tablespoon mirin

About 6 cups / 75 g loosely packed picked chrysanthemum greens

About 2 cups / 25 g loosely packed picked frilly mustard greens

2 tablespoons grated and lightly drained daikon (see page 54)

1 (10 to 12-oz / 283 to 340 g) boneless duck breast, grilled (see page 142)

2 kumquats, thinly sliced, seeds removed

MAKES 4 SERVINGS

Usually, the development of a new dish is a process of trial and error, sometimes ending in nothing but a bad mood. The Rintaro duck salad, however, was an honest-to-God epiphany. We had just started receiving a weekly delivery of impeccable Japanese vegetables from Hikari Farms, a family-run organic operation south of San Francisco. They were bringing us boxes of shungiku (chrysanthemum greens), which were as tender and delicate as any I'd ever seen. I'd been reluctantly blanching them (too nice to cook!) or adding them to udon or using them to garnish gyoza. But on a beautiful fall day, with fall tastes in mind, I thought, duck! Slices of smoky grilled duck breast from the yakitori grill, sweet and sour slices of ruby red pluots, and a bit of frilly mustard mixed in for heft. Eureka!

Admittedly, you're not likely to find shungiku in your produce section, although you may have more luck at farmers' markets, especially from Asian farmers (chrysanthemum greens are also known as Tong Hao in Chinese). And while I think the salad is best with the distinctive flavor of the shungiku, we have successfully served this salad with a mix of baby mustard greens, young mizuna, and wild arugula. During the summer, we use pluots and plums; in the fall and early winter, we use persimmons; and in the late winter and spring, we use thin slices of kumquat.

You'll find the method for grilling duck on page 142. It's basted with tare as it cooks, adding another layer of flavor, but if you don't have access to a grill, the duck breast can be cooked on the stove top, skin-side down, until the fat has rendered, then transferred to the oven to finish cooking. Don't brush with the tare until just before the duck goes into the oven; otherwise, it will burn.

To make the dressing: In a small bowl, stir together the vinegar, onion, shoyu, sugar, and mirin. The dressing will keep covered in the refrigerator for up to 2 weeks.

To prepare the greens: Remove the thick, tougher stems and rough outer leaves of the chrysanthemum and frilly mustard greens. Soak together in a bowl of cold water for a couple of minutes. Using your hands, lift the greens out of the water and place in a strainer. (Don't pour them into a strainer, because you'll end up pouring any sand and grit that's come off in the water back onto your greens.) Repeat if necessary. Spin dry and chill in the refrigerator until ready to use.

When ready to serve, in a large bowl, add the daikon and a few tablespoons of the dressing and mix together. Add the greens and toss carefully. Taste for seasoning, adding more dressing if necessary. Mound the greens in a tower on a large serving plate. Slice the grilled duck breast crosswise into thin slices and lean the slices against the bottom of your towering salad. Garnish with the kumquats.

TOFU
TO
TAMAGO
豆腐と卵

TOFU AND EGGS

TOFU AND EGGS ARE THE quiet stars in the kitchen; not flashy, but each playing a foundational role in Japanese cooking. The recipes in this chapter show the versatility of these ingredients, from very pared down (like the hot spring egg, page 96) and yosedofu (page 111), to the more complex (like the chawanmushi on page 107).

For good reason, tofu has long been maligned in the West. Much of what you can buy at the supermarket is chalky, slightly sour, and not fresh. In fact, those sealed plastic tubs have a shelf life of a couple of months. Freshly made soy milk is rich, naturally sweet, and slightly nutty. And the silken tofu we make every morning at Rintaro has a lovely texture, light and custardy. We'll sometimes add it along with pork to the mabodofu (see page 218), but mostly it's served chilled and unadorned, with ginger, scallion, and shoyu on the side. Fresh tofu is certainly not easy to find in the US, but in California there are a number of Japanese American tofu companies. You might also investigate the tofu made by Korean and Chinese shops, as both cuisines rely heavily on it.

Although some of the recipes in this chapter are proper tofu dishes—that is to say, made with soybeans, I've also included recipes for tofu-like dishes. There is the gomadofu which is a sesame "tofu" with a silken tofu-like texture that is achieved with arrowroot starch. And then we have tamago dofu, which is made with eggs and dashi and not a drop of soy milk.

Also included are our main egg dishes. Eggs are small wonders, more versatile than maybe any other ingredient, and we go through them by the case. They play a supporting role as the elegant hot spring egg that we serve with udon, or with the paper ribbon egg that we use with chirashizushi and cold sesame udon. And, for me, they are at their best when they play a starring role in the dashimaki tamago, a folded omelet that I contend is the most delicious (and technically challenging) in the history of omelets. I've always thought of pastured eggs—that is, eggs from chickens who live on grass, pecking for insects—as the world's most affordable luxury. They may be four times the cost of a standard supermarket dozen, but even the most expensive egg will cost you less than a dollar each.

ONSEN TAMAGO

HOT SPRING EGGS

温泉卵

---

9 large eggs, at room temperature

4 qt / 3.8L water

MAKES 8 EGGS (PLUS A TESTER)

For me, no trip to Japan is complete without a visit to one of the thousands of hot springs that can be found in almost every prefecture in Japan. In olden times, Japanese cooks used the even heat of the springs for cooking, and eggs, in particular, are well suited to this low-temperature cooking method. Hot spring eggs are essentially eggs poached in their shells. The water cooks them gently, resulting in whites that are barely set and creamy yolks. With no hot springs nearby, at the restaurant we mimic the method by using a sous vide circulator to keep a water bath at a consistent temperature, but with a bit of babysitting, you can also make them in a pot on the stove. The eggs are a wonderful addition to a bowl of udon, or they can be eaten on their own with a couple of drops of shoyu and a bit of grated wasabi or ginger. Note that you can cook fewer or more eggs using this same method.

Prepare an ice water bath. In a large saucepan over medium-low heat, heat the water until it registers 150°F / 66°C on an instant-read thermometer. (If you have an immersion circulator, you can also use that to maintain a water bath that's 150°F.) Add the eggs and bring the water back to 150°F. If you're working with a pot on a stove, you'll need to monitor the water temperature carefully to keep the water at a constant temperature, adding cold water as necessary. After 35 minutes, test an egg by cracking it into a bowl; the majority of the egg white should surround the yolk and be fully set; some white will gather in the bowl. Cut into the egg with a spoon; the yolk should resemble that of an over-easy egg. If the test egg looks underdone, cook the remaining eggs for another 5 minutes. Using a slotted spoon, remove the eggs from the water and transfer them to the ice water bath; let stand until cold.

When ready to serve, crack an egg into a bowl. Using a slotted spoon, transfer the eggs to a serving dish, leaving behind the watery egg white residue.

KINSHI TAMAGO

RIBBON EGG  錦糸卵

3 large eggs

1 teaspoon sugar

1 teaspoon cornstarch, dissolved in 2 teaspoons water

¼ teaspoon fine sea salt

1 tablespoon vegetable oil or other neutral oil

MAKES 4 SHEETS

This paper-thin omelet is useful in all sorts of dishes. At the restaurant, I slice the sheets thinly and use them as a garnish for the Hiyashi Udon (page 250). You can also use sheets of ribbon egg like nori to wrap an onigiri (rice ball). If you have one, use a square dashimaki tamago pan to make the omelets; if not, a round nonstick pan works well, too. Use the best eggs you can find. We use eggs from the pasture-raised chickens at Riverdog Farm in the Capay Valley, north of San Francisco. Unlike "free-range" chickens, Riverdog chickens spend their days pecking at grubs and grass outdoors in the fields in mobile enclosures. The yolks are a beautiful deep yellow, almost orange, color. They are expensive—for eggs— but remember there are twelve eggs in a dozen, and at 50 cents an egg, they are an affordable luxury.

Whisk the eggs, sugar, cornstarch slurry, and salt in a small bowl until well combined. Strain through a fine-mesh strainer into a clean bowl, rinse the first bowl, then strain the eggs a second time into the original bowl.

Pour the oil into a small bowl. Tear a paper towel in half and fold into quarters.

Heat an 8-inch / 20 cm nonstick skillet over medium-low heat. When the pan is hot, dip the folded paper towel in the oil and lightly coat the pan (if you have too much oil, the egg will not form a pancake).

Holding the pan off the heat, pour 3 tablespoons of the egg mixture into the pan, quickly tilting and swirling the pan so the egg coats the bottom in an even layer. Cook for 30 seconds, until the surface of the omelet is dry, then run a silicon spatula around the edge of the pan to loosen it. Using your fingers and chopsticks, carefully flip the omelet and cook for a few seconds on the second side, then turn out onto a plate, trying to avoid folds and wrinkles. Repeat with the rest of the egg mixture, wiping the pan with oil between each batch and layering each one onto the one below on the plate, until you've made four omelets.

Roll the stack of omelets into a cylinder and cut the roll crosswise into ⅛-inch / 3 mm-thick ribbons.

DASHIMAKI TAMAGO

FOLDED OMELET

だし巻き卵

6 large eggs, at room temperature

¾ cup / 180ml Dashimaki Base (recipe follows)

½ cup / 120ml vegetable or other neutral oil

2 tablespoons grated daikon, for serving

Shoyu, for serving

MAKES 1 OMELET: 2 TO 4 SERVINGS

The dashimaki tamago I make is a version of the one that was served at Soba Ro in Saitama, Japan. The first time I had it, I was amazed. This was a dish I had eaten my entire life, but I had never encountered one that was so juicy and, more crucially, served hot. Usually, when I was served dashimaki tamago or its cousin, tamago yaki (which is similar but seasoned with sugar and soy and no dashi), it was served cold or at room temperature. Tasting it hot from the pan, topped with a small Mt. Fuji–shaped mound of grated daikon and a drop of soy sauce, was a revelation.

I later learned that the juicier your dashimaki tamago is, the harder it is to cook; more dashi makes it more fragile and delicate. I'm always pushing the limits of juiciness. I recommend starting with 1 oz / 30ml of dashimaki seasoning base for each egg; as you get better at making the dashimaki, try increasing the amount of dashi slightly.

Don't be discouraged if it takes you a few (dozen) tries to get your dashimaki right. It requires a lot of skill and practice. When cooks are coming up in the kitchen, it's considered a rite of passage when I ask them to make the night's dashimaki. My biggest tip for home cooks is to ensure that your pan is in really good condition. It has to be *extremely* nonstick, so I season mine every night we have dashimaki on the menu. We use a square copper tamago pan, but you can also use a more affordable Teflon steel pan. It is also important to ensure that both your eggs and the dashimaki base are at room temperature or warmer. (Colder eggs and base get sticky and don't cook evenly.)

My last hint for beginners: When you're first learning, you can use a bamboo sushi roller to take your cooked, terrible-looking dashimaki and squish it into a shape that looks reasonably good. Roll the dashimaki in the sushi roller and secure it with a rubber band. Let it sit for five minutes; that will help the dashimaki coalesce, so that when you serve it, you won't be totally embarrassed.

Note: To season your pan, fill it a third of the way with vegetable oil. Heat the pan over high heat, until the oil starts to smoke, then turn off the heat and pour the oil into a small bowl to reuse later. When the pan has cooled, it's ready to use.

Crack the eggs into a large, spouted measuring cup and beat them with chopsticks. Once the whites and yolks are completely incorporated, add the dashimaki base and beat again until combined.

Set a small bowl of the oil on a plate near the stove (if you've just seasoned your pan, you can use that oil). Carefully fold half a paper towel into a 2-inch / 5 cm square. Dip the paper towel into the oil to saturate it and place it on the plate next to the bowl. (You want to use plenty of oil but don't leave the towel *soaking* in the oil or you'll end up with oily dashimaki.)

Using chopsticks, wipe the bottom and sides of a seasoned 7-inch / 17 cm

tamago pan with the oil-soaked paper towel. Heat the pan over medium heat. Test the pan temperature by flicking a bit of the egg into the pan from the tip of the chopsticks. The egg should sizzle with a slight crackle, not a searing hiss. If the pan is too hot, remove it from the heat, remove the test egg with your oiled towel, and wait for a few moments before testing again; the goal is to cook the egg without browning it, so you want to carefully monitor the pan temperature.

When the temperature is right, add one-quarter of the egg mixture. After a few seconds, using chopsticks, pop the bubbles that form on the surface. When the egg is almost fully cooked, carefully fold the sheet from the far edge of the pan toward you in three motions. The motion for folding the omelet is "in the wrist" (and similar to flipping a pancake), and the chopsticks guide the egg as you flip rather than actually lifting the egg from the pan. Wipe the far side of the pan with the oiled towel (resubmerge the towel in oil and set it back on the plate as needed), push the folded egg to the back of the pan, and wipe the near side of the pan with the oiled towel. Test the pan temperature again with egg flicked from the chopsticks. If it's not hot enough, wait a few seconds and test again.

Add another quarter of the egg mixture, lifting the front edge of the folded omelet with the chopsticks to allow the mixture to run underneath. Pop the bubbles as they form and fold the omelet toward you again, this time in two motions. Use chopsticks to guide, not lift, the omelet as you fold it and, simultaneously, use your non-dominant hand to lift, tilt, and jerk the pan, almost as if you were trying to flip a pancake without using a spatula (again, it's all in the wrist). If you have a

sticky spot, wipe the spot with another layer of oil.

Wipe the far side of the pan with the oiled towel and push the omelet to the back of the pan. Wipe the near side. Test the pan temperature.

Add another quarter of the egg mixture, lifting the front edge of the folded omelet to allow the mixture to run underneath. Pop the bubbles as they form and fold the omelet toward you again, this time in one motion. Wipe the exposed side of the pan with the oiled towel, push the folded omelet to the back of the pan, and oil the pan again. Add the last of the egg mixture to the pan, lifting the front edge of the folded omelet to allow the mixture to run underneath. Pop the bubbles as they form and fold the omelet toward you again in one final motion.

Turn off the heat. To help shape the dashimaki and to ensure that any raw egg is gently cooked with the residual heat of the pan, use the wooden lid that comes with the dashimaki pan (called the tamagoyaki yo kibuta) or a 7-inch / 17 cm-wide cutting board to gently press the dashimaki against the side of the pan closest to you. Hold for 10 seconds, then use the lid to push the egg to the far side of the pan and press gently for another 10 seconds. Invert the omelet onto the lid and return it, upside down, back into the pan, pressing gently for 10 seconds. Invert the omelet again and press the opposite side for 10 seconds more. Invert the dashimaki back onto your lid or board and cut immediately into ten even slices.

Serve hot with a small mound of freshly grated daikon topped with a few drops of shoyu.

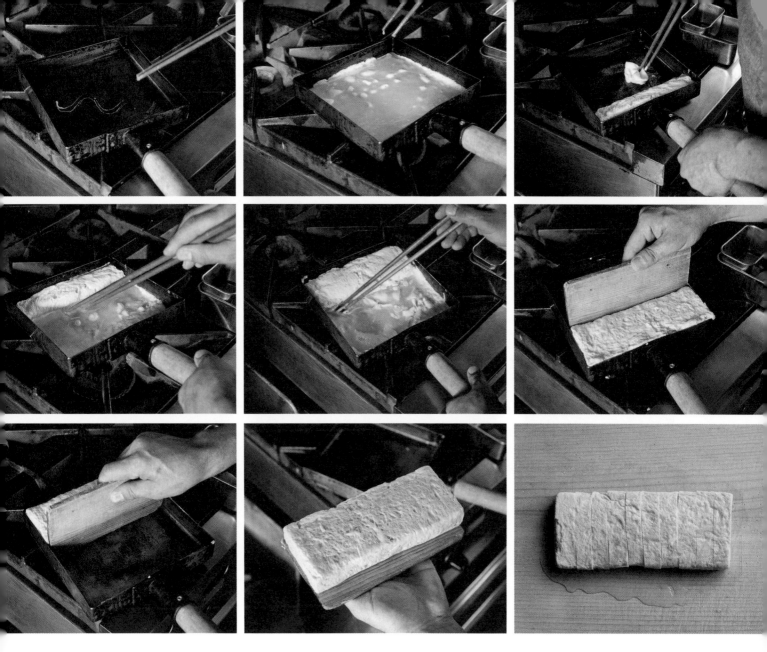

DASHIMAKI BASE

1½ cups / 375ml Katsuobushi Dashi (page 19)

1½ tablespoons plus ½ teaspoon white shoyu or usukuchi (light-colored) shoyu

1½ tablespoons plus ½ teaspoon mirin

2 teaspoons sugar

½ teaspoon fine sea salt

½ cup / 8 g freshly shaved katsuobushi

In a small pot, bring the dashi, shoyu, mirin, sugar, and salt to a boil. Using a slotted spoon, skim the foam from the top and discard, then add the katsuobushi and turn off the heat. Let it sit for 5 minutes.

Line a strainer with a damp paper towel, then strain the dashimaki through the towel into a small bowl, squeezing the towel gently to get the last bit of the katsuobushi essence. Discard the katsuobushi and paper towel. Use immediately or for longer storage, allow it to cool, uncovered, in the refrigerator, then cover and store in an airtight container for up to 3 days.

MAKES ABOUT 1¾ CUPS (ENOUGH FOR 2 DASHIMAKI)

GOMA DOFU
ごま豆腐

SESAME "TOFU"

---

2 teaspoons white or golden sesame seeds

2 cups / 472 ml Katsuobushi Dashi (page 18)

½ cup plus 4 teaspoons/ 63 g arrowroot starch

3 tablespoons / 50 g sesame paste (nerigoma)

⅓ teaspoon sea salt

FOR SERVING:

Wasabi

Shoyu

Sliced scallions

MAKES 4 SERVINGS

I remember my surprise when I first tried goma dofu as a teenager at a tofu restaurant in Kyoto. It had the texture of tofu, smooth and creamy, but was incredibly rich. For years, I didn't know that there weren't actually any soybeans in goma dofu—it is made with dashi and sesame paste and thickened with kuzu (arrowroot starch). Traditionally, it is a mainstay of Shojin Ryori or "temple cuisine," and as such is made with konbu-shiitake dashi to make it vegan. We use katsuobushi dashi, because I always have it available, and I prefer the flavor. It is also traditionally made with freshly toasted and ground sesame seeds, rather than the *nerigoma*, sesame paste, that we include in this recipe.

When I worked at Soba Ro, Chef Kanji-san would buy little baggies of sesame seeds at a roadside farmers' co-op. They were grown by his neighbors, were a bit smaller and darker than the ones I'd seen before, and were incredibly flavorful. When I returned to California, I searched high and low for sesame that was as flavorful, but it was a series of disappointments, and I refused to serve sesame seeds until we were able to source good ones. Now, all of the sesame we buy is from Wadaman, a fifth-generation sesame roaster in Osaka. In the last few years, their products have become available online in the United States. The difference between their sesame and what you might find at your local grocery is not subtle. They are significantly more expensive, but it's worth the small splurge.

In addition to sesame seeds, this recipe also calls for nerigoma (sesame paste). You might think that tahini would be a reasonable substitute, but there is one significant difference between the two: for nerigoma, the seeds are toasted before they're ground, so it's much nuttier in flavor than tahini, which, unfortunately, is not a great substitute.

Toast the sesame seeds in a dry skillet over medium heat, shaking constantly for several minutes, until they're fragrant and can be crushed easily between your fingertips. Sesame seeds burn easily, so pay close attention and taste them often. When done, pour them immediately into a suribachi grinding bowl or a mortar and pestle and grind until completely smooth. They should start to release oil. Transfer to a measuring cup, add the dashi, and stir to combine.

Line a strainer with heavy-duty paper towels, then strain the dashi through the towels into a small bowl, squeezing as much dashi as you can from the towel. Discard the residual seed husks and the paper towels.

Pour the sesame-dashi mixture into a medium saucepan. Add the arrowroot starch, sesame paste, and salt. Whisk until the starch has completely dissolved and then place the pan on the stove over medium heat. Bring to a

GOMA DOFU, CONTINUED

boil, whisking continuously with a stiff whisk. Once the mixture has boiled, turn down the heat to low and continue whisking for 10 minutes.

Fill a 5 by 5 by 1½-inch / 12 by 12 by 4 cm pan with water, then dump it out. This could be a Tupperware container, it just needs to have an area of 25 square inches / 144 square cm. Scrape the sesame mixture into the pan, then gently tap on the counter to remove bubbles. Smooth with a rubber or offset spatula into an even layer, cover with a damp paper towel, and then cover it with a sheet of plastic wrap into which you've poked some vent holes. Refrigerate for at least 4 hours or overnight, then slice into small squares and serve with a dab of wasabi, a few drops of shoyu, and scallions.

Note: The goma dofu will keep its lovely smooth texture for a couple of days, gradually getting firmer. At the restaurant, if we have two-day-old goma dofu, we coat it in potato starch and fry it in 330°F / 166°C oil, as registered on an instant-read thermometer, until it puffs slightly (about 3 minutes), then we serve it hot with a few drops of shoyu, grated ginger, and sliced scallions.

HARU NO CHAWANMUSHI

STEAMED EGG CUSTARD WITH SPRING VEGETABLES

春の茶碗蒸し

4 large eggs

1⅓ cups / 312ml Katsuobushi Dashi (page 19)

2½ tablespoons usukuchi (light-colored) shoyu

2 tablespoons mirin

8 asparagus spears

8 sugar snap peas

12 whole fava beans

4 oz / 115 g raw medium shrimp, peeled, deveined, and cut into ½-inch / 12 mm pieces, lightly salted

MAKES 4

Chawanmushi, like dashimaki tamago and tamago dofu, is another excellent combination of dashi and eggs. Delicate in texture, served straight from the steamer, the custard barely holds together on the spoon and melts in your mouth. As a *chawan* is a teacup and *mushi* means "steamed," this dish is usually served in a narrow lidded cup. It's often made with bits of chicken thigh, shrimp, shiitake mushrooms, and mitsuba greens. But the version I love most is made with first-of-the-season peas, asparagus, and fava beans.

This spring version is a bit more finicky than the standard, since it requires steaming in two steps. This allows you to cook the shrimp and the bulk of the egg mixture without overcooking the vegetables and prevents the vegetables from sinking to the bottom. For the spring chawanmushi, I prefer to use wide, shallow ceramic bowls, rather than the standard teacup, for a more glamorous presentation. I use a lid made of aluminum foil to keep the condensation that collects on the lid from dripping onto the dishes and spoiling their perfect surface.

To prepare the steamer: Fill the bottom of a steamer with 3 inches / 7.5 cm of water. Wrap the lid of the steamer with a large dish towel and tie at the handle. The towel will catch the condensed steam that will otherwise rain down, marring the surface of the chawanmushi. If you don't have a metal steamer pan, use a bamboo basket fit snugly over a pot filled with 3 inches / 7.5 cm of water and bring to a boil. Wrap the bamboo steamer lid with a dish towel.

In a medium bowl, whisk together the eggs, dashi, shoyu, and mirin. Pass the mixture twice through a fine-mesh strainer into a clean bowl and then back a third time into the original bowl. Set aside.

Trim the ends of the asparagus, then slice on the bias, about ⅓ inch / 8 mm thick. Remove the string from the sugar snap peas then cut along the string line, about ¼-inch / 6 mm deep, to open the pod and reveal the peas but keeping the pod and peas intact. Shuck the fava beans.

Bring a medium pot of heavily salted water to a boil and prepare an ice water bath.

Add the asparagus and peas and cook for 15 seconds. Remove from the water with a slotted spoon, plunge into the ice bath, then use a slotted spoon to transfer to a paper towel–lined plate.

Add the fava beans to the boiling water and cook for 30 seconds, then remove from the water and plunge them into the ice bath. Once cold, drain and peel each fava bean to reveal the brilliant green bean within.

Pour all but ¼ cup / 60 ml of the egg mixture into four shallow bowls, each about 5 inches / 13 cm wide and 1½ inches / 4 cm deep. Divide the shrimp amongst the four bowls, then cover each bowl tightly with foil. Set two bowls on each level of the steamer, then steam over medium-high heat for 10 minutes or until the chawanmushi is set in the center. The temperature in the steamer should be 195–200°F / 90–93°C. If the heat is too low it will not cook through, and if it's too high, it will bubble and puff up like a souffle. If you are using a two-layer bamboo basket, rotate the top and bottom baskets halfway through to allow the chawanmushi to cook evenly.

Remove the steamer from the heat, uncover, remove the aluminum foil from each bowl, and quickly arrange the asparagus, fava beans, and peas on top of the cooked chawanmushi, dividing evenly. Pour 1 tablespoon of the remaining egg mixture over the vegetables in each bowl, replace the foil cover—this time leaving it loosely covered so steam can reach the vegetables—return to the steamer and steam for another 8 minutes, or until the second layer of egg is completely set.

Serve immediately.

VARIATION

To make a chicken, shrimp, and mushroom chawanmushi, after adding the shrimp to your egg mixture add 4 oz / 115 g of boneless, skinless chicken thighs, cut into ½-inch / 12 mm pieces and 2 fresh shiitake mushrooms, cut into ¼-inch / 6 mm slices. Cover with foil and steam over medium heat for 10 to 12 minutes, or until the custard is set. Top with a mitsuba leaf and steam for another minute until the leaf is bright green. Serve immediately.

YOSEDOFU

SILKEN TOFU 寄せ豆腐

---

4 cups / 950ml fresh soy milk

2 teaspoons nigari

FOR SERVING:

Grated ginger

Sliced scallions

Freshly shaved katsuobushi

Shoyu

Ground sesame seeds (optional)

Wasabi (optional)

SERVES 4

When I was a small child, my mother attempted to make her own tofu. She soaked and then steamed the soybeans. Then things started to fall apart. Grinding and straining the hot beans to make the soy milk was a hot mess. After a couple of hours of hard work, she had made one block of tofu. Now, I'm not one to shy away from doing things the hard way, but her experience did not inspire me to make my own tofu.

Some years ago, I was introduced to Meiji Tofu, in Gardena near Los Angeles. It's a small tofu company run by the Sato family. They make absolutely delicious tofu—silky, rich, and nutty. I tried to have them ship it to me overnight, but the boxes were always delivered upside down, dripping. It then occurred to me that I could buy their soy milk, which comes in rugged plastic jugs, that would ship more easily. Now, we get a delivery from Meiji once a week and use their rich soy milk to make tofu each morning.

We serve the silken version of tofu at the restaurant. Since it isn't drained, it's quite soft, with a very light custardy texture. The process is straightforward: the soy milk is mixed with 1 percent nigari, a coagulant made from sea water, placed in a dish, and steamed until set. Of course, the success of your tofu will be completely dependent upon the quality of your soy milk. If you happen to be in Los Angeles, you're in luck—Meiji sells their products at a number of stores around town. Otherwise, see if you can source soy milk from a local tofu maker.

VARIATION

If you have access to good yuzu, try adding 1 tablespoon of finely grated zest to the soy milk before you add the nigari.

Fill the bottom of a steamer with 3 inches / 7.5 cm of water. Wrap the lid of the steamer with a large dish towel and tie at the handle. The towel will catch the condensed steam that will otherwise rain down, marring the surface of the tofu. If you don't have a metal steamer pan, use a bamboo basket fit snugly over a pot filled with 3 inches / 7.5 cm of water and bring to a boil. Wrap the bamboo steamer lid with a dish towel.

Reserve ¼ cup / 60ml of the soy milk and pour the rest slowly down the side of a medium bowl, taking care not to create any bubbles. Add the nigari and stir the mixture thoroughly with a rubber spatula, once again moving slowly so as not to create bubbles. With the addition of the nigari, the soy milk should thicken slightly.

Once set, the tofu is very fragile, and

you will be serving it directly from the bowl in which it's steamed, so keep that in mind when choosing the bowl. Carefully pour the mixture into four bowls. Cover tightly with aluminum foil, place in the steamer, and steam over medium-high heat until the center is set, 15-20 minutes. If using a two-layer bamboo steamer, rotate the steamer baskets after 7 minutes. Remove from the heat. For a perfectly smooth surface, distribute 1 tablespoon of the soy milk on top of each bowl of hot tofu. Smooth with the back of a spoon to create an even layer. The residual heat, along with the nigari, should set this top layer, leaving a perfect surface.

Serve chilled or at room temperature with the ginger, scallions, katsuobushi, and shoyu. Ground sesame seeds and wasabi are also delicious condiments.

KON TAMAGO DOFU

STEAMED EGG AND CORN "TOFU"

コーンたまご豆腐

3 ears white or yellow corn

7 tablespoons / 105ml Katsuobushi Dashi (page 19)

½ teaspoon sea salt

3 large eggs

MAKES 4 SERVINGS

During the summer, I serve this corn and egg "tofu." It makes a lovely side dish or a light first course. The success of the tamago dofu is really dependent on the sweetness and freshness of your corn. Look for corn with a bright green husk that's slightly damp. Or if you're like me, dig your fingernail into the kernels and have a surreptitious taste. Take care when steaming this custard; if the heat is too high, the edges will cook first and then begin to soufflé; this will ruin its delicate texture. Low and slow is the way to go.

With a sharp knife, cut the corn kernels off each cob into a bowl. Using the back of your knife, scrape the cobs to extract the juices into the same bowl. Transfer the kernels to a blender and blend at high speed until liquefied. Pass through a fine-mesh strainer, pressing on the solids to extract the liquid; discard the solids. You should have a bit more than 7 oz / 205ml corn juice. Add the dashi and salt to the corn juice.

Crack the eggs into a medium bowl and whisk until the whites and yolks are fully incorporated. Add the corn mixture, then pass twice though a fine-mesh strainer.

To prepare the steamer: Fill the bottom of a steamer with 3 inches / 7.5 cm of water. Wrap the lid of the steamer with a large dish towel and tie at the handle. The towel will catch the condensed steam that will otherwise rain down, marring the surface of the tamago dofu. If you don't have a metal steamer pan, use a bamboo basket fit snugly over a pot filled with 3 inches / 7.5 cm of water and bring to a boil. Wrap the bamboo steamer lid with a dish towel.

Pour the corn mixture into a shallow pan; the custard should be no more than an inch deep. When the water is boiling, set the pan in the steamer basket and turn down the heat to medium. Cover, leaving the lid slightly ajar, and steam for 20 to 25 minutes, checking occasionally to ensure the water isn't steaming too vigorously; the temperature in the steamer should be between 195–200°F / 90–93°C. Check to see if the custard is fully set by inserting an instant-read thermometer in the center of the pan; it should register at least 165°F / 75°C, and the custard should jiggle only slightly in the center. When it's cooked through, carefully remove the pan from the steamer, and cover with a sheet of plastic wrap into which you've poked some vent holes. Chill until cold or for up to 1 day.

To serve, cut the custard into square or rectangular portions and use a small offset spatula to remove them from the pan. Trim the edges so you have perfect pieces. Serve the pieces inverted, with the smooth surface facing up.

YAKITORI
やきとり

WHEN YOU SIT DOWN AT the counter at the famous Sukiyabashi Jiro in Tokyo, the chef will present you with a perfect piece of nigirizushi, along with the command, "Please, eat this immediately." You must enjoy this sushi at the height of its deliciousness, he insists, when the rice is still warm, the wasabi is still pungent, and the fish is still cool. Five minutes after it has been made, it will already have lost its essence.

The same principle applies to good yakitori.

There is a short window when yakitori is at its best. It's partly a product of the wisps of smoke from the grill, where the chicken juices and tare (a sweet, thick dipping sauce and marinade typically made from soy sauce and mirin) vaporize over the super-hot binchotan charcoal as they drip from the skewer. At Rintaro, I take the matter of yakitori immediacy very seriously. Delivering yakitori to a table is the highest priority, and our servers know that yakitori always has the right of way.

Of all the stations at my restaurant, the yakitori station is the most elemental. Once the skewers are made, it's just the cook and the fire. Specifically, a good yakitori cook must learn to control the heat: too hot and everything burns on the outside before it's cooked through; too cool and the yakitori is anemic, without the delicious smoky char that makes yakitori worth the trouble. The key to controlling the heat is controlling the oxygen.

We do this by adjusting the air vents on the front of the grill and with a paddle-shaped hand fan we always keep by our side. Once the heat is right, it's then a matter of focus: moving the skewers from a flare-up caused by rendering fat, dipping them in the tare to caramelize, turning and waiting until that optimal moment of deliciousness to pull them from the grill to serve. Our main yakitori cook, Coco Lim, is a master of this balancing act, always cool amidst the constant flux of orders, carefully tending to each skewer—all while chatting with the customers lucky enough to sit at the counter in front of him.

Although we buy whole bone-in legs for many of the basic skewers, we also butcher whole chickens so we have a wide variety of parts we couldn't get any other way. These are the odd bits: shoulder blade, neck meat, tail, rib, sternum cartilage, and so on. Each cut has a distinct flavor and texture, and they are all cooked in subtly different ways—some over a hotter or cooler part of the grill, glazed in tare or with just sake and salt.

By butchering whole chickens, we're able to have a steady supply of these odd bits. At home, of course, it's trickier, since you're not going to butcher a dozen chickens at once. But even if you're starting with whole bone-in chicken legs instead of a whole bird, you'll still be able to make a very nice variety of delicious yakitori. With a whole leg, you can make basic thigh skewers, as well as skewers of chicken oyster, achilles, inner thigh, and kneecap. In the pages that follow, I've included recipes and techniques for all of them. But if you're feeling ambitious (and cooking for a crowd), consider buying two or three whole birds to break into their parts, so you have the full array of bits to work with (see page 120 for detailed instructions on how to break down a whole chicken).

If you've been considering buying those very expensive pasture-raised chickens at the farmers' market, this is the time to do it. Pasture-raised birds live outside, usually in movable pens that are shifted every week or two to new grass. There, they live their lives running, scratching, and pecking and otherwise living as you would imagine a chicken should. Not only are pasture-raised chickens the most environmentally sustainable (they improve the soil with activity), but with all this outdoor exercise, their meat is denser and more flavorful. And as nearly every part of the chicken can be served as yakitori, it takes some of the sting out of paying that much more for pastured birds.

THE GRILL

For the best yakitori at home, you'll need to consider your grilling setup. A standard gas or charcoal grill will not provide the controlled, intense heat you will need to cook yakitori successfully. A yakitori grill is narrow, with two parallel iron bars upon which the skewers rest. The width of the opening directs heat onto just the part of the skewer that holds the meat, so the exposed ends of your skewers don't catch fire. Relatively inexpensive yakitori grills are available online, but you can make your own makeshift setup using materials that are easily found at your local hardware store: bricks and concrete pavers.

   I recommend setting up the makeshift grill on top of your existing gas or charcoal grill. Your existing grill will serve as the work surface—you will not actually be using it for heat. You will need eight bricks and two 16 by 2-inch / 40 by 5 cm-thick square cement pavers. Lay the pavers on the metal grill grate of your existing grill to form the base. Use the bricks to create the walls, positioning them three to a side, laid end to end with the remaining bricks capping the left and right sides. The grill opening should be about 4 inches / 10 cm wide. With this setup, you don't need the iron bars, since the bricks themselves will hold the skewers. For peace of mind and to burn off any chemicals used to treat the bricks and stone and resulting unpleasant odors, I'd recommend you fire up this makeshift grill once before cooking on it.

THE CHARCOAL

When we first started Rintaro, we imported binchotan charcoal directly from Japan. Binchotan is an incredibly dense charcoal that clinks like porcelain when knocked together. It burns extremely hot, produces little ash, and is the preferred charcoal at the best yakitori-ya. It's also extremely expensive and is becoming rare even in Japan, since there are fewer and fewer artisans left who make it. The charcoal that we use now is called ogatan. It's a compressed Japanese charcoal, not as dense as binchotan but far denser than standard mesquite charcoal and briquettes, and it burns very hot and lasts for hours. It's widely available online. At the end of the night, we pull the hot charcoal from the grill and put it in a metal ash bucket with a lid. Once covered, the oxygen is quickly depleted, and the charcoal extinguishes. We save it for the next night, where, toward the end of the night, we add it to fill in the gaps between the charcoal in the grill. You can do the same. I've found that inexpensive Chinese clay pots work well for storing hot charcoal at home.

THE TOOLS

The tools you will need are simple: a paddle-shaped fan, a small spray bottle of water, and a pair of long-handled tongs. The fan is used to raise the temperature of the grill in two ways: it adds oxygen to the fire, and it also blows away the insulating layer of ash that forms as the charcoal burns. The fan is also useful for blowing out small flare-ups that are inevitable as the fat renders from the chicken and drips onto the coals. Essentially tiny grease fires, the flare-ups produce black smoke that will discolor the yakitori and give it an unpleasant flavor. If the fan is not enough to blow out a flare-up, use a quick spritz of water from the spray bottle. Use the tongs to adjust the charcoal as you are cooking.

PREPARING THE FIRE

To prepare the grill for cooking, start your charcoal early using ogatan charcoal and a standard charcoal chimney. Once the charcoal is hot, plan to load it in your grill at least a half hour before you're ready to cook. Both a makeshift brick grill and real yakitori grill need time to absorb the heat to create the intense, even heat you will need for grilling. You will need enough charcoal to lay a single layer at the base of the grill, end to end and side to side, without gaps. The first time you set up the grill, I'd recommend preloading your grill with cold charcoal to determine the right quantity. Use a hammer to break the ogatan into manageable lengths before adding it to the chimney.

Once the charcoal is red hot in the chimney, use tongs to organize your charcoal: place the first row of charcoal against the far side of the grill, end to end. Place a second row against the near side of the grill, end to end. If there isn't space to insert the final middle row of charcoal, place them sitting atop the first two rows. Once the charcoal has burned down, it will fall down into place.

The key to controlling the fire is controlling the oxygen. Gaps between the burning ogatan charcoal introduce more oxygen, so paradoxically your grill can start to get too hot after an hour or two when the charcoal has burned down and gaps have started to form.

JUDGING THE HEAT

To test the temperature of the charcoal, I test it with my hand. Generally speaking, I want to be able to hold my hand where the skewers will sit for 5 seconds before needing to pull it away. Any longer and the fire needs to be hotter; any shorter and you will likely be burning your yakitori before it cooks through. There are exceptions to this rule. For some thicker cuts, such as the chicken oyster (page 139), you will want a fire that is a bit cooler (6-7 seconds with the hand test) to allow the meat to cook through without burning the outer layer of skin. Other skewers, like the inner thigh (page 138), which are quite small and in order to develop good color without overcooking, need to be cooked quickly over a blisteringly hot fire (4 seconds with the hand test). In any case, it's advisable to use the tongs to shift the charcoal to increase the heat on one side of your grill and reduce the heat on the other, creating a multizonal fire.

HOW TO BREAK DOWN A WHOLE CHICKEN

Early in my cooking career, I was very proud of myself when I learned how to butcher a chicken. I'd start with a whole chicken and I'd end up with the legs, thighs, breast, and wings. I felt like a real professional. Alas, I had to start from square one when learning how to break down a chicken for yakitori. Although some of the Western techniques apply, for yakitori there are many, many more specific steps to yield the enormous variety of cuts that a chicken can offer.

When we cut chicken for yakitori at the restaurant, we usually cut no fewer than a dozen birds. The issue is one of scale. Each chicken has only two shoulder blades, for instance, and it takes three of them to make a single skewer. If you are in no mood to break down three chickens (the minimum for many of the skewers pictured below), you can skip ahead and start with whole bone-in legs. Three whole legs will yield plenty for an assortment of skewers, including Negima (page 133), Achilles (page 137), and Oyster (page 139), and at least one skewer each of Aka Momo (page 138) and Hiza Nankotsu (page 140). If you buy six whole legs, you will have enough for all the above, plus the meat you'll need for the Tsukune (page 134). However, the whole chicken does yield a wide and wonderful diversity of cuts. If you're looking to serve the super-fatty and crispy tail, the distinctively chewy neck meat, or the excellent shoulder blades, for instance, there is no way to get them except by butchering the whole chicken yourself.

For chicken butchery, I use a small Japanese single-bevel knife called a honesuki, which has a distinctive triangular shape. Its thin tip is good for separating joints, and its relatively thick blade is sturdy enough to cut through bone. A medium paring knife works well, too. In either case, just make sure your blade is razor sharp. The skin on a chicken is tough, and a sharp knife will allow you to make clean, precise cuts without a struggle.

Begin with a whole chicken.

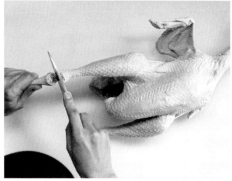

To remove the feet, flex them and then cut through the joint on each leg.

To remove the tail, cut horizontally from the back of the chicken.

Cut a shallow horizontal line across the center of the back of the chicken, then a vertical line, creating a cross.

To remove the legs and thighs, cut the skin between the leg and breast, repeat on other side.

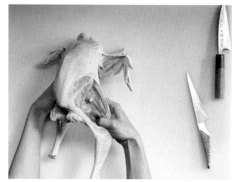

Push the legs downwards and pop the leg joints on both legs.

Return to the cross on the back of the chicken to cut through the skin connecting the leg and back.

Cut the oyster from the scalloped divot on the back of the chicken, where the thigh meets the back.

Turn the chicken over and cut through the joint and flesh to remove the leg, repeat on the other leg.

To remove the wing, flex it and cut through the joint. Repeat with the other wing.

To remove the shoulder blade, insert your knife under the shoulder blade.

Cut to the top of the shoulder blade, then rotate the knife to snap the shoulder blade off at the joint.

CONTINUED →

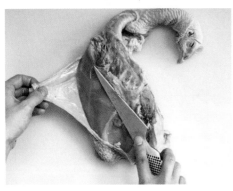
To remove the skin, sever the connection at the breast.

Pull the skin away from the breast and cut at the tail and the neck to remove.

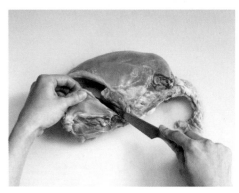
To remove the rib meat, cut along the bottom of the breast.

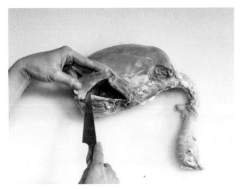
Continue cutting the rib meat away along the backbone.

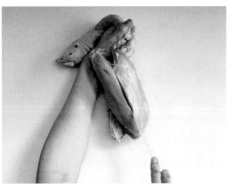
To remove the breast meat, cut between the breasts.

Pull the breast meat away from the carcass and with shallow knife strokes, remove the breast.

To remove the tender, slide your blade along between the tender and the breast bone.

To remove the cartilage along the breast-bone, cut under the breast bone to separate it from the carcass.

Snap off and remove the cartilage tip of the breastbone.

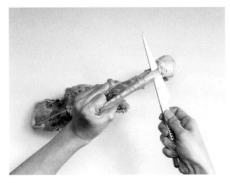
To remove the neck meat, hold the chicken carcass to put the neck under tension, insert your blade under the neck meat and use a sawing motion.

See page 128 for how to break down the chicken leg and thigh.

All the parts of a single chicken.

TAIL

WING

SHOULDER

GIZZARD

LIVER

INNER THIGH

OYSTER

KANZURI

KNEECAP

THIGH SANSHO

HEART

THIGH ONION

TENDER

BREAST

SKIN

RIB

CARTILAGE

NECK

SHOULDER

TENDER

GIZZARD

CARTILAGE

BREAST

RIB

HEART

SKIN

NECK

WING

TAIL

KANZURI

THIGH
SANSHO

HOW TO BREAK DOWN A WHOLE LEG

Although you'll end up with the widest and most interesting variety of yakitori skewers by breaking down a whole chicken, it is something of a time commitment that might be best reserved for an elaborate weekend dinner. However, if three whole bone-in legs will yield a surprisingly interesting assortment of skewers, including Negima (page 133), Achilles (page 137) and Sori (page 139) and at least one skewer each of Aka Momo (page 138) and Hiza Nankotsu (page 140). If you buy six whole legs, you will have enough for all the above, plus the meat you'll need for the Tsukune (page 134).

For chicken butchery, I use a small Japanese single-bevel knife called a honesuki, which has a distinctive triangular shape. Its thin tip is good for separating joints, and its relatively thick blade is sturdy enough to cut through bone. A medium paring knife works well, too. In either case, just make sure your blade is razor sharp. The skin on a chicken is tough, and a sharp knife will allow you to make clean, precise cuts without a struggle.

If you've been considering buying those very expensive pasture-raised chickens at the farmers' market, this is the time to do it. Pasture-raised birds live outside, usually in movable pens that are shifted every week or two to new grass. There, they live their lives running, scratching, and pecking and otherwise living as you would imagine a chicken should. Not only are pasture-raised chickens the most environmentally sustainable (they improve the soil with activity), but with all this outdoor exercise, their meat is denser and more flavorful. And as nearly every part of the chicken can be served as yakitori, it takes some of the sting out of paying that much more for pastured birds.

Begin with a whole chicken leg.

Separate the leg and thigh by cutting through the joint.

To remove the leg bone, begin by cutting along the top of the leg bone.

Cut along the bottom edge of the leg bone.

Sever the connection between the bone and meat at the thigh joint.

Sever the connection between the bone and meat at the foot joint.

To remove the thigh bone, begin by cutting along the top of the thigh bone.

Cut along the bottom edge of the thigh bone.

Sever the connection between the bone and meat at the hip joint.

Sever the connection between the bone and meat at the thigh joint.

Separate the thigh into two parts: top is thigh meat, bottom is oyster and kneecap.

Separate the kneecap from the oyster meat.

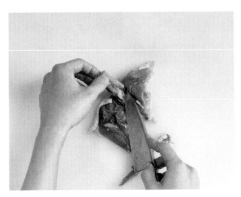

Separate the flap of inner thigh meat.

The parts of a whole leg and thigh. Clockwise: leg meat, thigh meat, kneecap, oyster, and inner thigh.

YAKITORI

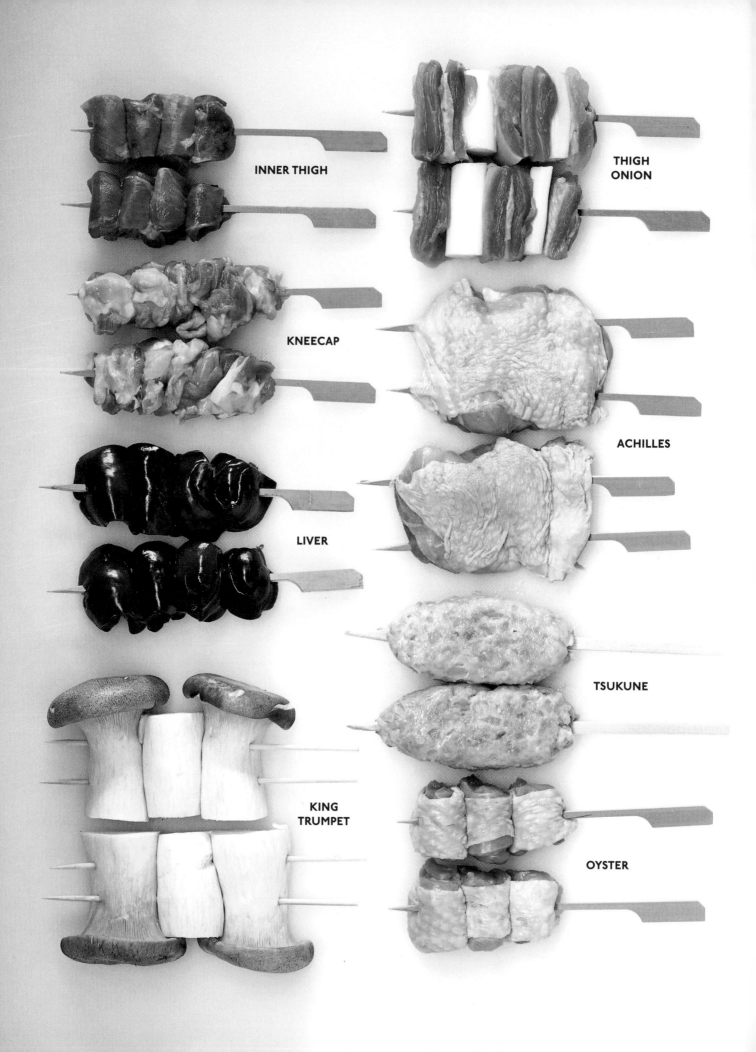

INNER THIGH

THIGH ONION

KNEECAP

ACHILLES

LIVER

TSUKUNE

KING TRUMPET

OYSTER

TSUKUNE

KING
TRUMPET

THIGH
ONION

ACHILLES

OYSTER

LIVER

KNEE

INNER THIGH

YAKITORI TARE

YAKITORI GRILLING SAUCE

やきとり たれ

---

1 cup / 236ml cooking sake

1 cup / 236ml shoyu

½ cup / 118ml mirin

½ cup / 106 g unrefined Japanese sugar (zarame) or raw sugar

MAKES 2½ CUPS / 600ML

This tare is used in nearly every recipe in this chapter. There are many far more complicated tare recipes in the world; by contrast, mine is extremely simple. But it becomes more flavorful as you use it; each skewer that gets dunked into the sticky sauce enhances the sauce's flavor, adding depth and deliciousness (and, in turn, the tare then enhances the flavor of anything it touches).

At the restaurant, our tare has become something of a master sauce. Each night we dip hundreds of skewers into it, and by the end of the night, it's full of flecks of char and onion bits from the Tsukune (page 134) and deeply flavored from the meaty juices that have dripped off the skewers. When service is over, we strain the tare and boil it; the next day, we use it as the base for a fresh batch of tare. It just gets better with time; elements of our tare are more than ten years old. I recommend taking the same approach at home and saving any tare that's left over after a night of grilling. It will keep, refrigerated, for a month, or can be frozen indefinitely.

In a heavy-bottomed saucepan, combine all the ingredients. Bring to a boil over high heat, then reduce to a low boil. Let cook, stirring frequently and checking to ensure it's not charring on the sides of the pan, until the sauce is reduced by 20 percent, about 30 minutes.

YAKITORI NEGIMA

CHICKEN THIGH AND SPRING ONION

---

16 (6-inch / 15 cm) round bamboo skewers

6 skin-on, boneless chicken thighs (about 2 lb / 900 g (see page 128)

11 spring onions, with at least 6 inches / 15 cm from root end to start of the green tops

1 batch Yakitori Tare (page 132)

Sea salt

Shichimi, for serving

Lemon wedges, for serving

MAKES 16 SKEWERS

VARIATION

When we can't get our hands on large negi (green onions), we substitute with pieces of yellow onions. Cut a small onion in half from root end to stem end and then trim the root and stem ends to leave a 2-inch / 5 cm-wide piece of onion. Slice into ½-inch / 12 mm-thick pieces. Skewer as above, making sure to run the skewer through each of the layers of the onion.

If you would like to skip the onion altogether, you can make thigh-only skewers. And, as with most yakitori, you can choose to grill with tare or with only a dip in sake and salt and dust with sansho powder before serving.

Negima is one of a handful of the most basic yakitori skewers, and the one I order every time I go out for yakitori. *Negi* is a general word for "green onions," but the ones used in this skewer are the enormous variety called Naganegi, or Tokyo negi. They grow up to 2½ / 76 cm feet tall, with long white stems that are 1inch / 2.5 cm thick, with hollow green tops. Their thick stems hold up well on the grill and become sweet and tender as they cook. You see them growing in backyard gardens and in fields all over Japan, but they are harder to find in the United States. You can substitute with spring onions or gigantic scallions if you spot them at the market. When we can find neither, we substitute with yellow onions (see Variation below).

Place the chicken on a plate and transfer to the freezer for 15 minutes. (When the meat is cold, it is firmer and easier to cut and skewer.)

Place the chicken thighs, skin-side down, on a cutting board and cut each chicken thigh in half, against the grain, into two strips, each approximately 1¾ by 3 inches / 4½ by 7½cm. Cut each strip crosswise into four ¾-inch / 2 cm pieces, each about ½ oz / 15 g.

Trim the root ends off the spring onions and remove any dried or discolored leaves. Cut the white section of the onions into 1¾-inch / 4 cm lengths; this should yield three per onion.

Each skewer is comprised of three pieces of thigh and two pieces of onion. Organize your portions for skewering with the largest pieces of thigh at the top, with the skin facing away from you, a thicker piece of onion next, another piece of thigh, another piece of onion, and, finally, a smaller piece of thigh. As with all yakitori, you want the largest and thickest pieces of meat at the top of the skewers, since they will sit at the hottest part of the grill. Thread the alternating pieces of chicken and onion

on the skewer, starting from the bottom; only ¼-inch / 6 mm of the tip of the skewer should be visible. Adjust the ingredients on the skewers as needed, so the weight is balanced, then trim the sides of each skewer to make them even.

Pour the tare into a narrow, tall vessel, such as a jam jar or a drinking glass. Prepare a grill for medium-heat grilling, as directed on page 118.

Lightly salt the chicken and onion pieces, place the skewers on the grill, and grill until the meat starts to brown, about 2 minutes. Flip the skewers and cook on the other side until the meat begins to brown, about 2 minutes more. When both sides have developed a little color, dip the skewers into the tare one at a time, gently knocking off the excess back into the tare container before returning the skewer to the grill. Repeat the dipping and grilling process twice more, until the skewers are richly glazed with tare and the chicken and onions have cooked for a total of 10 minutes. The chicken should be opaque without a trace of pink.

Serve immediately, with the shichimi and lemon wedges alongside.

TSUKUNE

CHICKEN MEATBALL

16 (6-inch / 40 cm) flat
bamboo skewers

About 2 lb / 900 g skin-
on whole chicken
legs, or ground
chicken

1 small yellow onion,
finely diced

1 tablespoon minced
yuzu or lemon peel

1 tablespoon plus 1½
teaspoons mirin

2 teaspoons fine sea
salt

3 cups / 480 g mochiko
(glutinous rice flour)

1 batch Yakitori Tare
(page 132) for dipping

Shichimi, for serving

Lemon wedges, for
serving

MAKES 16 SKEWERS

Most yakitori-ya (grilled chicken shops) have their own version of tsukune, for the simple reason that they use up chicken scraps that might otherwise go to waste. And of all the dozens of grilled chicken preparations on a yakitori-ya's menu, tsukune might be the most telling of the restaurant's quality and point of view. Some chefs cook tsukune from a raw state, while others first poach them in oil or steam them before grilling.

For years, we formed the tsukune into balls, poached them in oil until just cooked through, then skewered and grilled them over charcoal. They were very good, but our new method is even better: We shape the raw chicken mixture into oblong logs, coat them with mochiko flour (glutinous rice flour), and then steam the meatballs until barely cooked. The rice flour forms a very thin outer layer as it steams; when they're grilled, this layer soaks up the tare and gives the tsukune a subtle snap. We also add lemon peel to our ground chicken mixture because I love the brightness it adds, but you could mix in sliced shiso or scallions instead.

It's important to incorporate enough fat into the ground meat mixture (what in French cuisine we would call a farce). Chicken breast meat is far too lean, yielding tsukune that are dry and dense. But skin-on chicken legs have the perfect ratio of meat to fat to produce a tender, juicy bite. Ask your butcher to bone out and grind the thighs and drumsticks with the skin on. You could also do it yourself and chop the chicken legs with a heavy chef's knife or cleaver. If you must start with preground dark meat chicken, add a bit of finely chopped chicken skin to the mixture to keep the tsukune juicy. Some finely diced onion adds more texture to the farce, providing a tiny crunch with each bite. For the tsukune, I recommend using flat (rather than round) bamboo skewers that will hold the meatball steady as it's grilled. If you can't get flat skewers, you can substitute round ones, but use two skewers for each tsukune instead of one to prevent them from spinning.

If using whole chicken legs, debone the thighs and drumsticks (see page 128). Save the bones for chicken stock, then cut the chicken into smaller pieces.

Using a meat grinder with a ¼-inch / 7 mm die or a heavy knife, grind or finely chop the chicken meat and skin. Divide the ground/chopped chicken into two equal portions. Place one half into a bowl, then pass the remaining meat through the meat grinder a second time (or finely chop it again by hand) and add it to the bowl. Add the onion, yuzu, mirin, and salt. Mix vigorously by hand to ensure the ingredients are thoroughly combined.

Make a small test patty and cook in a skillet (or microwave) just until done; taste and adjust the seasoning. It should be slightly less salty than you might like, since you'll be grilling the tsukune with salty shoyu-based tare.

Line a sheet pan with parchment paper. Divide the meat into ¼-cup / 64 g balls and then form the balls into 34-inch by 1½-inch/ 10 by 3.8 cm-wide oval logs, laying them neatly side by side on the prepared sheet pan. Refrigerate for 30 minutes (this will make the next step of forming the tsukune on the skewers a bit easier).

To prepare the steamer: Fill the bottom of a steamer with 3 inches / 7.5 cm of water. Wrap the lid of the steamer with a large dish towel and tie at the handle. If you don't have a metal steamer pan, use a bamboo basket fit snugly over a pot filled with 3 inches / 7.5 cm of water and bring to a boil. Line the steamer basket with parchment paper. Put the mochiko in a shallow dish. Working one at a time, gently transfer the chilled tsukune to the flour and dredge to coat on all sides. Brush off any excess flour and skewer the dredged tsukune, one per skewer; only the tip of the skewer should be visible. Take time to smooth the tsukune into an appealing oval shape, then place them in the prepared steamer basket. Set the steamer basket over a pan of simmering water, then steam the tsukune in batches over high heat for 6 to 8 minutes, or until the meat is just cooked through.

Prepare a yakitori grill for medium-heat grilling, as described on page 118. Place the tare in a tall, narrow vessel such as a jam jar or a drinking glass.

Place the skewers on the grill and grill until the tsukune start to brown, about 2 minutes. Flip and grill the skewers on the second side for 2 more minutes. Dip the tsukune into the tare, one at a time, knocking the excess back into the tare container before returning them to the grill. Grill for 1 minute on each side, then dip the skewers into the tare a second time. Repeat this process of grilling and dipping twice more, until the tsukune are richly glazed with tare and deeply caramelized—a little bit of char is okay—about 7 to 9 minutes total.

Serve immediately, with shichimi and lemon wedges alongside.

YAKITORI LEBA

GRILLED CHICKEN LIVER

---

12 (6-inch / 15 cm) round bamboo skewers

GARLIC PASTE

1 head garlic

Vegetable or other neutral oil for frying

1 teaspoon toasted sesame oil

¼ teaspoon sea salt

¼ teaspoon konbucha (kelp tea powder), optional

1 lb / 450 g chicken livers

1 batch Yakitori Tare (page 132)

Shichimi, for serving

Lemon wedges, for serving

MAKES 12 SKEWERS

Early in my teenage years, a family friend turned me off to chicken livers, when he referred to them as "little oil filters." Of course, I've since changed my mind. Well-prepared chicken livers have a rich, creamy texture. I often order chicken liver pâté, as a first course, and I love them sautéed with capers and sherry and even coated with potato starch and deep fried. But these richly glazed grilled chicken livers, take the cake. They are particularly good with oil-poached garlic paste.

To make the garlic paste: Place the garlic head in a very small saucepan and add enough vegetable oil to cover. Heat the oil until it registers 220° to 230°F / 105° to 110°C, then turn down the heat and poach over low heat for 45 minutes, until the garlic has caramelized a bit and a skewer pierces the cloves with little resistance. Remove the pan from the heat and let cool to room temperature. Cut the garlic head in half crosswise and squeeze the cloves out into a bowl. Reserve the oil for another use (garlic oil is excellent for sautéing just about anything). Press the garlic through a fine-mesh strainer. Season with the sesame oil, salt, and the konbucha (if using). Set aside.

Soak the livers in a bowl of ice water for 5 minutes to remove the blood. Drain them through a colander, gently shake off the excess water, and dry them on a double layer of paper towels.

To clean the livers, remove the membrane that connects the large and small lobes. Leave the smaller lobe intact and cut the larger one in half. If you see any green-tinged spots, cut them out and discard. That green is bile from the gallbladder, and no amount of washing will remove its bitter taste.

Depending on the size of the livers, you will need three to five pieces per skewer. Beginning with a smaller piece, fold the liver onto itself and thread onto a skewer, keeping the meat under a bit of tension as you go. Repeat with a second piece, then thread a third (and fourth or fifth piece, if using); only a quarter inch of the tip of the skewer should be visible. Adjust the liver pieces on the skewers so the weight is balanced.

Pour the tare into a tall, narrow vessel, such as a jam jar or a drinking glass. Prepare a yakitori grill for medium-heat grilling, as directed on page 118.

Salt the skewers lightly and grill on one side over medium heat for 4 minutes. Flip and cook the other side for 4 minutes.

When the livers have started to firm up, dip the skewers into the tare, one at a time, gently knocking off the excess back into the tare container before returning them to the grill. Repeat this process of grilling and dipping twice more, until the livers are richly glazed with tare and deeply caramelized—a little bit of char is okay—about 10 minutes total. To test for doneness, remove a skewer from the heat and peek between the lobes. It should still be pink and opaque, not bloody and transparent.

Serve immediately, with the garlic paste, shichimi, and lemon wedges alongside.

YAKITORI ACHILLES

CHICKEN LOWER LEG

アキレス

24 (6-inch / 15 cm) round bamboo skewers.

6 skin-on chicken drumsticks (about 1¾ lbs / 780 g, boned (see page 128)

2 cups / 472ml cooking sake

Sea salt

Shichimi, for serving

Lemon wedges, for serving

MAKES 12 SKEWERS

As much as I've always enjoyed eating drumsticks, there is a very high concentration of sinew and gristle where the calf muscles connect to the bone end. We often reserve the meat from the drumstick for the tsukune: When ground into small bits, the tendon adds collagen and a silky richness to the mix. Inspired by our friends at Yardbird, a fabulous yakitori restaurant in Hong Kong, we've recently been skewering and cooking the leg meat on its own. The whole leg is significantly thicker than what you might skewer for a negima (thigh), and grilling over low, slow heat renders the skin and melts the tendon in the meat, yielding an especially juicy skewer. We skewer the whole leg using two skewers. Once it's grilled, we let the meat rest, so the juices reabsorb into the meat, then cut it in half, turning the one leg into two portions and revealing a surprising swirl of meat and melted tendon within.

Place the chicken on a plate, transfer to the freezer, and freeze for 15 minutes. (When the meat is cold, it is firmer and easier to cut and skewer.)

Arrange the boned chicken legs on a cutting board, skin-side down. Trim off and discard ½ inch / 12 mm, where the sinews connect to the bone end of the drumstick, removing the section where the tendon is thickest. Trim the leg meat so that it's more or less an even thickness, about 2½ to 4 inches / 6.5 to 10 cm; each piece should weigh about 4 oz / 115 g. Flip the chicken pieces skin-side up and orient them so the narrower side is facing you. Insert two skewers through the leg, from bottom to top; only ¼-inch / 6 mm of the tip of the skewer should be visible.

Pour the sake into a narrow, tall vessel, such as a jam jar or a drinking glass.

Prepare a yakitori grill for medium-low heat grilling, as directed on page 118.

Dip each skewer into the sake, then season both sides generously with salt. Place the skewers on the grill and cook, skin-side down, for 4 minutes, until the skin starts to render and brown. Beware of flare-ups; move the chicken immediately out of any flames. Flip the skewers and cook on the other side for 8 to 10 minutes, until the meat is well browned. Flip again and cook for 2 more minutes. To test for doneness, remove a skewer from the grill and insert an instant-read thermometer into the thickest part of the chicken; it should register 160°F / 71°C. Let the skewers rest for 5 minutes before slicing the double skewer into two single portions.

Serve immediately, with the shichimi and lemon wedges alongside.

YAKITORI AKA MOMO

CHICKEN INNER THIGH

あかもも

2 (6-inch / 15 cm) round
    bamboo skewers

6 inner thigh pieces
    from 6 whole chicken
    thighs (see page 128)

Yakitori Tare (page 132)

Sea salt

Shichimi, for serving

Lemon wedges, for
    serving

MAKES 2 SKEWERS

When I was learning about butchering whole chickens for yakitori (see page 120), discovering the inner thigh cut was one of the greatest revelations. The inner thigh is a small muscle that sits, barely attached, on the inside of the thigh. It is similar to the chicken oyster, incredibly tender and flavorful. And like chicken oysters, there is only one per thigh, so you will only be able to make a couple of skewers from six whole legs. But what skewers they will be! Their distinct texture adds a lovely diversity to a yakitori platter.

Arrange the inner thigh pieces in two rows on a cutting board, orienting the largest pieces farthest from you. As with all yakitori, you want the largest and thickest pieces of meat to be at the top of the skewers, since they will sit at the hottest part of the grill.

Beginning with a smaller piece, fold the meat onto itself and thread onto a skewer, keeping the meat under a bit of tension as you go. Repeat with a second piece, then thread the third, largest piece on the end of the skewer; only 1/4-inch / 6 mm of the tip of the skewer should be visible. Repeat with the second skewers. Adjust the ingredients on the skewer as needed, so the weight is balanced.

Pour the tare into a tall, narrow vessel, such as a jam jar or a drinking glass. Prepare a yakitori grill for high-heat grilling, as directed on page 118.

Salt the skewers lightly and grill until the meat colors slightly, 1 to 2 minutes. Flip the skewers and cook on the other side for 1 to 2 minutes. When both sides have developed a little color, dip each skewer into the tare one at a time, gently knocking off the excess back into the tare container before returning the skewer to the grill. Repeat the dipping and grilling process twice more, until the skewers are richly glazed and the chicken has cooked for 6 to 8 minutes. To test for doneness, remove a skewer from the grill and pull the meat down the stick to peek between the pieces of meat. The chicken should be opaque without a trace of pink.

Serve immediately with the shichimi and lemon wedges alongside.

YAKITORI SORI

CHICKEN OYSTER ソリ

---

6 (6-inch / 15 cm) round bamboo skewers

6 skin-on chicken oysters from 6 whole chicken thighs (see page 128)

2 cups / 472ml cooking sake

Sea salt

Shichimi, for serving

Lemon wedges, for serving

MAKES 6 SKEWERS

Like a pearl in an oyster, the chicken oyster is a treasure, and there is no skewer more hotly sought after at Rintaro. The oyster is a roundish, small piece of dark meat on the top of the chicken thigh, in the hollow of the hip bone. It's the most tender dark meat on the chicken and is covered with a thick layer of back fat. When grilled, the skin covering the oyster renders and becomes incredibly crisp, and the meat is rich and succulent.

A final note: The oyster skewer at my restaurant has three segments. Don't tell anyone, but only the top piece is the actual chicken oyster. The other two are the tender pieces of thigh meat adjoining it.

Place the chicken on a plate and transfer to the freezer for 15 minutes. (When the meat is cold, it is firmer and easier to skewer.)

The oyster section is rectangular, about 2 by 4 inches / 5 by 10 cm, with the oyster itself at the thickest part and the adjacent thigh meat attached. Using a sharp knife, cut the meat into three sections: the largest, with the oyster, then two other pieces, comprising pieces of thigh meat. Arrange the pieces in a row, skin-side up and oriented with the short side facing you, with the largest piece the farthest from you. As with all yakitori, you want the largest and thickest pieces to be at the top of the skewers, as it will sit at the hottest part of the grill.

When you skewer the pieces, you want to make sure to preserve the skin covering each piece. However, the skin is tough, and to ensure you can push your skewer through, use the tip of a sharp paring knife to poke an incision into the skin before inserting the skewer. Thread the meat on the skewer, starting with the smallest thigh piece, folding the meat onto itself and keeping the meat under a bit of tension as you thread. Carefully thread your skewer through the layers of muscle before piercing through the skin on the other side. Repeat with the second piece of thigh, and finally the oyster; only ¼-inch / 6 mm of the tip of the skewer should be visible. Adjust the ingredients on the skewer so it's balanced.

Pour the sake into a narrow, tall vessel, such as a jam jar or a drinking glass.

Prepare a yakitori grill for medium-low heat grilling, as directed on page 118.

Dip the skewered chicken into the sake and season both sides generously with salt. Grill, skin-side down, until the skin starts to render and brown, about 3 minutes. Beware of flare-ups; move the chicken immediately out of any flames. Flip the skewers and cook on the other side until well browned and the fat in the meat starts to crackle, 5 to 7 minutes. Flip back to the first side and cook for 2 more minutes. To test for doneness, remove a skewer from the grill and pull the meat down the stick to peek between the pieces. The chicken should be opaque without a trace of pink.

Serve immediately, with the shichimi and lemon wedges alongside.

YAKITORI HIZA NANKOTSU

CHICKEN LEG AND KNEE

ひざなんこつ

2 (6-inch / 15 cm) round bamboo skewers

6 knee sections from 6 whole chicken legs (see page 128)

1½ to 2 cups / 360 to 472ml cooking sake

Sea salt

Shichimi, for serving

Lemon wedges, for serving

MAKES 2 SKEWERS

When butchered carefully, the whole of the chicken can be enjoyed in all its textural glory. The cartilage in the knee has an especially satisfying crunch. Encased in bits of the leg and thigh, it is meaty as well. The chicken knee is an "odd bit" that doesn't require you to break down a whole chicken. However, you will need at least six whole legs to yield two skewers. Plan to make these when you are breaking down legs for Tsukune (page 134) or the other whole leg skewers, such as the Negima (page 133), the Sori (page 139), the Aka Momo (page 138), and the Achilles (page 137).

Check to make sure the knee cartilage doesn't have any bone still attached to it. You can tell the difference by feel (the bone is sharp and hard) and by sight (the bone is opaque while the cartilage is slightly translucent).

Arrange two rows of three kneecap pieces on a cutting board, orienting the largest pieces farthest from you. As with all yakitori, you want the largest and thickest pieces of meat to be at the top of the skewers, since they will sit at the hottest part of the grill.

Start with the smallest piece by threading the skewer through the loose flap of meat, then pierce the meat under the cartilage and thread onto the skewer, keeping the meat under a bit of tension as you go. Repeat with the second kneecap and third kneecap pieces; only ¼-inch / 6 mm of the tip of the skewer should be visible. Adjust the ingredients on each skewer so they are balanced.

Pour the sake into a narrow, tall vessel, such as a jam jar or a drinking glass. Prepare a yakitori grill for medium-hot grilling, as directed on page 118.

Dip each skewer into the sake and season both sides generously with salt. Place on the grill and cook on one side until it starts to brown, about 3 minutes. Flip and cook on the second side for 3 to 4 minutes, until well browned and the fat in the meat starts to crackle. Flip again and cook for another 3 minutes. To test for doneness, remove a skewer from the heat and pull the meat down the stick to look between the pieces. The chicken should be opaque without a trace of pink.

Serve immediately, with the shichimi and lemon wedges alongside.

YAKITORI ERINGI

GRILLED KING TRUMPET MUSHROOMS

---

16 (6-inch / 15 cm)
round bamboo
skewers

1 lb / 450 g trumpet
mushrooms

1 cup / 236ml cooking
sake

1 batch Yakitori Tare
(page 132)

Sea salt

3 scallions, thinly
sliced, for serving

Shichimi, for serving

MAKES 8 SKEWERS

King trumpet mushrooms have wonderfully meaty, dense flesh; basting with yakitori tare gives them a lovely caramelized glaze. If you can't find trumpet mushrooms, you can substitute with shiitake mushroom caps.

Since king trumpets are grown on sawdust blocks, there is usually some sawdust impregnated in the base of the stems when they are harvested. Trim off the sawdusty bits and cut the mushrooms in half crosswise into 2 to 2½-inch / 5 to 6 cm lengths (depending on the size of the mushrooms). Cut the halves in half again lengthwise.

The cap and stem pieces will fit together like a puzzle. Arrange them on a cutting board in approximately 2-oz / 60 g portions, ideally with a mushroom cap piece at the top. Keeping the mushrooms on the surface of the board, skewer them with two bamboo skewers. They shrink a lot as they cook, and the double skewers will keep them from rotating on the grill; only ¼-inch / 6 mm of the tip of the skewers should be visible.

Prepare a yakitori grill for medium-hot grilling, as directed on page 118. Pour

the sake and the tare into two separate tall, narrow vessels, such as jam jars or drinking glasses.

To cook, dip each mushroom skewer into the sake, then season both sides lightly with salt. Place on the grill and cook for 2 to 3 minutes, until the mushrooms start to brown. Flip and grill on the second side for another 2 to 3 minutes, until they begin to brown. Dip the skewers in the yakitori tare one at a time, gently knocking the excess back into the tare container before returning it to the grill, and grill on one side for 3 minutes. Dip in tare again and grill on the second side for 3 minutes more. Repeat the dipping and grilling twice more, until the mushrooms are richly glazed with tare and have cooked for 15 to 20 minutes total. Transfer to a plate, sprinkle with the scallions, and serve immediately, with shichimi alongside.

KAMO YAKI

GRILLED DUCK BREAST

2 duck breasts (about
10 oz / 280 g each)

Sea salt

1 batch Yakitori Tare
(page 132)

MAKES 4 SERVINGS

I've been buying duck from Sonoma's Liberty Ducks for more than a decade. Before I opened the restaurant, when I was cooking out of my garage, the owner of Liberty Ducks, Jim Reichardt, used to deliver my (very small) orders of duck directly to my house. I'll always remember it as a kindness, since most other companies couldn't be bothered to deal with such small orders. And his duck is delicious. It's a strain of Pekin duck with a mild flavor and lots of delicious fat.

I find it easiest to grill the breasts after the fat has been partially rendered in a pan. Without proper rendering, it's extremely challenging to grill them because the fat drips onto the charcoal, and seconds later, your duck is engulfed in a fireball. I also find that grilling the duck soon after rendering, while it's still warm from the pan, helps it cook more evenly.

Grilled duck breast plays a key role in the duck and chrysanthemum greens salad (page 90), but it is also wonderful served on its own.

To prepare the duck: Remove the tender, which is loosely attached to the inside of the breast, and reserve for another use. Trim the quarter-sized piece of silver-skin membrane and discard. Score the skin in a crosshatch pattern and salt heavily on both sides, using about 1 teaspoon of salt per breast.

Prepare a yakitori grill for medium-heat grilling, as directed on page 118.

Place the duck, skin-side down, in a cold pan and set the pan over medium heat. Cook until the fat has rendered

from beneath the skin and the skin has turned golden brown, about 5 minutes.

Set a wire grill rack over the grill, then set the duck breast skin-side up on the screen. Grill, turning and basting four or five times with the tare; be careful to move the duck away from any flare-ups on the grill (they'll make your duck taste like a tire fire). Grill for 10 to 12 minutes until medium rare, or until an instant-read thermometer inserted into the thickest part of the breast registers 130°F / 55°C. Let rest for at least 10 minutes before slicing.

AGEMONO あげもの

FRIED DISHES

DEEP-FRIED FOODS ARE AS POPULAR and as ubiquitous in Japan as they are here in the United States. And many of my favorite foods, both here and there, are fried. The biggest difference, though, is a matter of cultural attitude. With maybe the exception of fried chicken, fried foods don't get a lot of respect in the US. They are rarely made at home and are mostly featured on the menus at "family restaurants." Think jalapeño poppers, fish sticks, and French fries. While there is still plenty of mass-produced fried food in Japan, the country has also developed a rich diversity of more refined fried dishes—both ones that are commonly made at home and at higher-end restaurants—and frying is considered a skill worthy of refining.

The three main styles of fried food in Japan are panko dishes like katsu and korokke that are coated in breadcrumbs, karaage dishes like teba karaage that are dusted with potato starch, and tenpura dishes in which fish or vegetables are coated in a flour and water batter. Each method requires a different oil temperature and comes with its own set of subtleties and techniques. And in Japan, you will find restaurants dedicated to a single fried dish. Tonkatsu restaurants are a genre unto themselves, as are high-end tenpura restaurants and, to a lesser extent, joints specializing in chicken karaage. With such specialization comes a kind of refinement that you don't often see elsewhere. At my favorite tonkatsu restaurant, for example, you can order a specific cut of pork, and it's fried in a blend of vegetable oil and beef tallow for an especially deep flavor. And the restaurants specializing in tenpura can be incredible; foods are plucked from the hot oil and placed in front of you one at a time, an experience similar to eating an omakase sushi meal.

The frying setup we use at the restaurant can be replicated at home. We use canola (rapeseed) oil for nearly all of our frying. It has a light, neutral flavor and is durable enough for a heavy night of frying. Instead of a standard deep fryer with baskets, we use a shallow Comstock Castle Doughnut Fryer and an extremely wide and heavy cast-iron pot (that I carried on my lap flying back from Japan). The doughnut fryer is set between 305° to 310°F / 152° to 154°C for the panko-breaded foods. It's a relatively gentle heat that cooks the katsu and korokke through at just about the same time it takes to beautifully brown the panko. The second pot is kept at around 330°F / 166°C. It's a much more aggressive heat that's suited to crisping the potato starch for truly crunchy fried karaage. We also use the higher heat for the quick-fry tenpura, which fries for a shorter period of time. Both are fairly shallow (about 6 inches / 15 cm) and wide. This allows us to clean the oil constantly with a fine wire spider strainer. At home, a heavy 3 to 4-qt / 2.8 to 3.8L Dutch oven is a good substitute for them both.

Whereas Japanese home cooks seem to be tolerant of the oily smells of deep frying penetrating the house, most Americans don't relish the idea of frying at home. Even the strongest hood fan in a home kitchen is a poor match for the pungent aerosols of a whole fried fish. But there is a simple solution: fry outside. Back in my catering days, I had a makeshift kitchen in my garage. My main burner was a phenomenally strong propane-powered wok burner. I bought it in Chinatown for less than $80, and when I was frying something, I'd move the burner and its tank outside to a picnic table to do my cooking. If you can grill outside, why not fry outside?

And a final note about the oil. If the oil is still relatively light colored after you're done with your frying, you can save it for another use. Let it cool to 250°F / 120°C and strain it through a coffee filter into a 2-qt / 1.9L canning jar. Seal the jar once the oil has cooled to room temperature and store it in the refrigerator for future use.

CHIIZU TORIKATSU

CHICKEN AND CHEESE KATSU

チーズとりかつ

8 cups / 1.9L canola or other neutral oil for frying

4 oz / 115 g Cowgirl Creamery Wagon Wheel cheese or other soft, flavorful cow's milk cheese

2 boneless, skinless chicken breasts (about 9 oz / 255 g each)

Sea salt

½ cup / 60 g all-purpose flour

2 large eggs, lightly beaten

2 cups /80 g Nama Panko (page 150)

FOR SERVING:

Snowy cabbage (see page 176)

Lemon wedges

Tonkatsu sauce

MAKES 4 KATSU

In the early years of the restaurant, I always had a glut of chicken breasts. We bought whole chickens from Riverdog Farm in the Capay Valley, then butchered them into a dozen parts for yakitori. These chickens spent their lives running around in the fields, eating farm scraps and scratching for bugs. They had dense, flavorful meat, and we used every bit, from the neck to the feet. The grilled chicken oyster, shoulder blade, liver, heart, and thighs were delicious when grilled. But the breast meat? It wasn't really suited to grilling—adequate but kind of dull. It wasn't until we thought to stuff the breasts with cheese, coat them in panko, and fry them until crispy and golden brown, that I started to get really excited about those chicken breasts. The reign of the chicken cheese katsu began.

As with many cheese-stuffed Japanese foods (chiizu typically refers to processed cheese), it's a bit of a junky dish: basically, it's fried chicken but with cheese in the center that oozes immodestly when you cut it. And it's addictive. When we started serving it, I ate one a day for six days straight. We don't use processed cheese; instead, we use a cheese called Wagon Wheel from Cowgirl Creamery, a local cheesemaker. It's a washed-rind cow's milk cheese that is aged for a few months, with a deep, pungent flavor. It also melts beautifully. When Wagon Wheel isn't available, we substitute raclette, which is similarly pungent with excellent meltability. But any tasty, meltable cow's milk cheese such as fontina, provolone, or Gruyère would be suitable.

Chicken breasts come in a range of weights. I look for breasts that are 9 to 10 oz / 255 to 283 g each, but if yours are larger (or smaller), you can still use them for this recipe. The key is to make sure they are not too thick after you've butterflied them; if necessary, pound the breasts with a meat mallet. When the cutlets are the correct thickness, about ½ inch / 12 mm, they cook evenly, the cheese melts satisfyingly, and the panko fries to a lovely golden brown in the time it takes for the meat to cook through.

In a large Dutch oven or heavy-bottomed pot over medium-high heat, heat the oil until it registers 310°F / 154°C on an instant-read thermometer.

Cut the cheese into four batons, each about 4 by 1 by ¼-inch / 10 by 2.5 cm by 6 mm.

To portion each breast, remove the tender and reserve for another use. Then,

cutting on the diagonal, with the knife nearly parallel to the cutting board, cut each breast crosswise into two portions about 4 oz / 115 g each.

To make a space for the cheese, make a slit on the long side of each piece of chicken, then continue cutting until you're about ½ inch / 12 mm from the opposing side, taking care not to cut all the way through. Open the chicken

CHIIZU TORIKATSU, CONTINUED

breast like a book; you should have a piece of chicken that's about ¼-inch / 6 mm thick. If yours is thicker, place it between two sheets of parchment paper and gently pound it with a rolling pin to the correct thickness but not so hard that you tear the meat. Place one piece of the cheese on one half of the piece of chicken and close the "book" to enclose the cheese. Lightly salt both sides of each breast. Repeat with the remaining chicken and cheese.

Set a wire rack over a rimmed sheet pan.

Place the flour, egg, and panko in three separate shallow dishes or pie pans. Working with one cutlet at a time, dredge the chicken in the flour. Make sure the entire surface is covered and shake off any excess. Next, dip it in the egg mixture, turning to coat completely. Then drop the egg-dipped chicken into the panko. Cover the cutlet with panko and press firmly on the top and sides so the panko adheres. Lightly shake off any excess and arrange on the prepared sheet pan. Repeat with the remaining pieces of chicken. It's best to fry the katsu immediately when the panko is

at its fluffiest. If you're not planning to fry right away, cover loosely with plastic wrap and refrigerate for up to 3 hours.

When the oil is hot, slide two of the breaded chicken katsu into the oil. With a fine-mesh strainer, immediately scoop up and discard the loose panko bits that float to the surface of the oil. Adjust the heat to maintain the oil temperature at approximately 310°F / 154°C and fry for 2 minutes. Using tongs or chopsticks, turn the katsu over and fry for another 2 minutes on the other side. Continue cooking, flipping every 2 minutes, until the chicken has cooked for 7 minutes. When the katsu is nearly cooked, it will start to sit higher in the oil, the bubbles surrounding it will become smaller, and the panko will be golden brown. Using the tongs, remove the katsu from the oil and set it on the wire rack to drain. Allow the oil to return to 310°F / 154°C and repeat with the remaining katsu.

To serve, cut the katsu into six to eight slices and serve with the snowy cabbage, lemon wedges, and tonkatsu sauce alongside.

NAMA PANKO
FRESH PANKO 生パン粉

1 lb / 450 g loaf soft white bread, such as pain de mie or sandwich bread

MAKES APPROXIMATELY 10 CUPS

To make nama panko, use a sharp knife to trim the crusts as closely as possible. Cut the denuded loaf into cubes, roughly 1-inch / 2.5 cm square. In a food processor, pulse a handful of cubes at a time into shaggy breadcrumbs. Don't overprocess: the larger pieces fry into delightful crunchy bits. Store your processed panko in an airtight container for up to 3 days in the refrigerator or up to a month in the freezer.

TONKATSU

PORK LOIN KATSU

とんかつ

---

2 qt / 1.9L canola or
    other neutral oil, for
    frying
1 boneless pork loin
    (about 1½ lb / 680 g)
Sea salt
1 garlic clove

¼ cup / 30 g all-purpose
    flour
1 large egg, beaten
2½ cups / 100 g Nama
    Panko (page 150)

FOR SERVING:
Snowy cabbage (see
    page 176)
Tonkatsu sauce
Japanese mustard

MAKES 4 KATSU

Tonkatsu can be so good. When the pork is sweet and juicy and the panko is
perfectly fluffy and crisp, it's a real treat. Done poorly (as, sadly, is often the case),
it's a minor tragedy. Restaurants specializing in tonkatsu are a genre of their own
in Japan, and at a good one, you can order *hire-katsu*, which is made with pork
tenderloin, or *rosu-katsu*, which is made with pork loin. You can also often choose
between different breeds of pork. Unlike the other panko-fried dishes in this
chapter, with tonkatsu there is relatively little room for error. Like a pork chop, the
meat must be cooked through but just barely so, or all the vital juices will escape
into your frying oil, and the tonkatsu will become dry.

At Rintaro, we use pork from Becker Lane Organic in Iowa. Jude Becker, the
farmer and owner, is a low-key pork evangelist and champion of the old ways. He
raises heritage breed Berkshire pigs that have plenty of fat marbling as opposed
to the "other white meat" pork that became popular during the 1980s. And rather
than the indoor confinement horror show (and antibiotics it requires), he raises his
pigs outdoors, with plenty of straw and room to be their piggy selves. And apart
from his humane practices and lovely demeanor, his pork is absolutely delicious.
You may not be able to source Becker Lane where you live, but look for something
similar, since good meat will give you the best-tasting tonkatsu.

In a large Dutch oven or heavy-bottomed pot over medium-high heat,
heat the oil until it registers 310°F /
154°C on an instant-read thermometer.
Set a wire rack over a rimmed sheet pan.

Place the loin on a cutting board and
trim the layer of fat covering the loin to
no more than a ½-inch / 12 mm thickness; discard the fat or save for another
use. Using a sharp knife, slice the loin
into ½-inch / 12 mm thick cutlets,
approximately 5 inches / 13 cm long and
3 inches / 7.5 cm wide at the thickest
point. Lightly salt each cutlet on both
sides. Cut the clove of garlic in half and
rub each cutlet on both sides with the
cut side of the garlic.

Place the flour, egg, and panko in three
separate shallow dishes. Working with
one piece of pork at a time, dredge the
pork in the flour. Make sure the entire
surface is covered and shake off any
excess. Next, dip it in the egg mixture,
turning to coat completely. Then drop
the egg-dipped pork into the panko.
Cover the pork with the panko and
press firmly on the top and sides so the
panko adheres. Lightly shake off any
excess and arrange on the sheet pan.
Repeat with the remaining pieces of
pork. It's best to fry the katsu immediately when the panko is at its fluffiest.
Otherwise, cover loosely with plastic
wrap and refrigerate for up to 3 hours.

When the oil is hot, slide two of the katsu into the oil. With a fine-mesh strainer, immediately scoop up the loose panko bits that float to the surface of the oil. Adjust the heat to maintain the oil temperature at approximately 310°F / 154°C and fry for 2 minutes. Using tongs or chopsticks, turn the katsu over and fry for another 2 minutes on the other side. Continue cooking, flipping every 2 minutes, until the katsu has cooked for 7 to 8 minutes. When the katsu is nearly cooked, it will start to sit higher in the oil, the bubbles surrounding it will become smaller, and the panko will turn golden brown. Using the tongs, remove the tonkatsu from the oil and set it on the wire rack to drain. Allow the oil to return to temperature and repeat with the remaining katsu.

To serve, cut the tonkatsu in six to eight slices and serve with the snowy cabbage, tonkatsu sauce, and hot Japanese mustard alongside.

KARE KABOCHA KOROKKE

カレーかぼちゃ
コロッケ

KABOCHA CROQUETTES

**1 small kabocha squash
(about 13 oz / 375 g)**

**1 small russet potato
(about ½ lb / 225 g)**

**1 lb / 450 g German
Butterball, Yukon
Gold, or Bintje
potatoes**

2 teaspoons sea salt

**2 tablespoons plus 6
cups / 1.4 L canola
or other neutral oil,
divided**

**1 large yellow onion,
diced**

**1½ teaspoons S&B
brand curry powder**

½ teaspoon sugar

**½ cup / 60 g all-purpose
flour**

3 large eggs, beaten

**2 ½ cups / 100 g Nama
Panko (page 150)**

FOR SERVING:

**Snowy cabbage (see
page 176)**

Lemon wedges

Tonkatsu sauce

**MAKES ABOUT 16
KOROKKE**

I spent many summers visiting my grandmother at her house in a small town between Osaka and Kyoto. While we were there, my mother and I frequently visited the grocery store, which was always exciting. There were the assorted summertime fireworks, the perfectly packaged Super Sentai chocolates that came with a tiny plastic toy, Doraemon fruit jellies, and red tins of Milky candies with Peko-Chan's tongue-smacking grin. And I was always drawn to the smell of the prepared foods section. There was a deli shelf with a variety of panko-fried foods, but the smell of the kabocha korokke was always the strongest. They were almost always available, still warm, five packed in a flimsy plastic box with a little packet of tonkatsu sauce. I ate dozens of them. When I first thought of opening an izakaya, I immediately thought of including the kabocha korokke on the menu. I wasn't sure how much my future customers would know about Japanese food, but I knew that if I loved them as a seven-year-old, they'd appeal to everyone…and they do.

Aside from using fresh panko, the key to this recipe is to make sure that the korokke base is not too wet. When choosing a kabocha squash, you want a dry one. So rather than choosing the most beautiful, bright green, fresh one, look for an older kabocha whose color has faded to olive drab. As it cures, the kabocha will have lost some of its moisture and should feel light for its size. After roasting the kabocha, I also leave it to dry out further in the oven, with the door cracked. As for the potatoes, I like the fluffy (and dry) texture of the russet potato but the flavor of a yellow potato, so I use a combination. My favorite yellow potato is the German Butterball, but Yukon Gold works well, too. As with the kabocha, once the potatoes are cooked, I like to give them some time to dry, spreading them out on a rimmed sheet pan in a single layer.

Korokke store well and can be kept frozen, ready to fry when you'd like to serve them. The patties are thin enough you can fry when frozen.

Preheat the oven to 450°F / 230°C. Line a sheet pan with aluminum foil.

Using the back of a heavy chef's knife, knock the stem off the kabocha. Cut the kabocha in half. Use a large spoon to scoop out the seeds and stringy bits and scrape the kabocha clean. Place the kabocha, cut side down, on the prepared sheet pan and roast for 45 minutes, or

until the squash collapses and is tender enough to be easily pierced by a knife. Turn the oven off, but leave the kabocha in the oven to dry with the door propped open, 10 to 30 minutes (or until the potatoes are done).

While the squash is cooking, scrub the potatoes and place them, whole and unpeeled, in a large pot. Cover them with 2 inches / 5 cm of cold water and generously salt the water. Bring the water to a boil and then turn down the heat to a simmer. Cook until the potatoes are cooked through, about 25 minutes. Test one with a skewer: it should pass through easily. Strain well and spread out on a rimmed sheet pan in an even layer to cool and dry. Once cool enough to handle, remove the skins and discard. Place in a large bowl and mash coarsely, leaving some small chunks.

When the kabocha is cool enough to handle, scoop out the flesh and discard the skin. Add the kabocha to the mashed potatoes.

In a large frying pan over medium heat, heat 2 tablespoons of the oil. Add the onion and salt and cook, stirring, until tender and translucent but not caramelized, about 7 minutes; they should maintain a bit of a crunch. Add the onion to the potato-kabocha mixture. Add the curry powder and sugar and mix until thoroughly combined. Taste and add more salt, if needed, and more curry powder, if desired.

Line a rimmed sheet pan with parchment paper. Divide the potato-kabocha mixture into 2-oz / 60 g balls. Using your hands, shape the balls into oval patties about 3 by 2½ by ½ inch / 7.5 by 6 cm by 12 mm. Arrange the patties on the prepared sheet pan. Once one layer is complete, cover with parchment paper, and add another layer. Freeze until the patties are rock hard, at least 1 hour.

Place the flour, egg, and panko in three separate shallow pans. Working with one piece at a time, dredge the korokke in the flour. Make sure the entire surface is covered and shake off any excess. Next, dip it in the egg mixture, turning to coat completely. Then drop the egg-dipped korokke into the panko. Cover the korokke with panko and press firmly on the top and sides so the panko adheres. Lightly shake off any excess and arrange on the prepared sheet pan. Repeat with the remaining korokke. Fry immediately or if you're not planning to fry right away, cover loosely with plastic wrap and refrigerate for up to 6 hours.

The korokke can be frozen in a single layer on a parchment-lined sheet pan. Leave a bit of space around each korokke; if they are too tightly packed, when you pull them out to fry, you'll have bald spots where the sides have frozen together. Once frozen solid, transfer to a freezer storage bag; they'll keep, frozen, for up to 1 month.

To cook, heat the remaining 6 cups / 1.4L oil in a large Dutch over or heavy-bottomed pot until it registers 310°F / 154°C on an instant-read thermometer. Working in batches, add a few korokke to the oil and fry, turning occasionally, until golden brown, about 6 to 8 minutes. Remove from the oil with a spider or slotted spoon and transfer to a paper towel–lined plate to drain. Allow the oil to return to temperature and repeat with the remaining korokke. Serve hot with snowy cabbage, lemon wedges, and tonkatsu sauce alongside.

KON KURIMU KOROKKE

CORN AND BECHAMEL CROQUETTES

コーンクリームコロッケ

BÉCHAMEL

3 ears corn, shucked

2¼ cups / 530ml whole milk

4 oz / 113 g unsalted butter

¾ cup plus 2 tablespoons / 105 g all-purpose flour

1½ teaspoons sea salt

½ cup / 60 g all-purpose flour

2 large eggs, beaten

3 cups / 120 g Nama Panko (page 150)

6 cups / 1.4L vegetable oil or other neutral oil

FOR SERVING:

Snowy cabbage (see page 176)

Lemon wedges

Tonkatsu sauce

MAKES ABOUT 16 KOROKKE

Korokke—fried croquettes—are most often made with a base of potatoes and, according to the Japan Croquette Association, were introduced to Japan by the French in 1872. There are the kabocha and potato korokke; the ubiquitous beef and potato korokke; the green pea, carrot, and potato korokke; the tuna fish and potato korokke—you get the picture. But a subset of korokke, called "cream" korokke, are made with béchamel. Once the béchamel is chilled, it firms up and can be formed into patties, which are then deep-fried until crunchy. They are tremendously delicious (and also, it bears mentioning, insanely burn-your-mouth hot—so eat them with caution!).

For these corn croquettes, some of the corn is pureed and added to the milk used to make the béchamel. Then whole kernels are folded in, making the korokke extra corn-y.

Although it goes without saying, these korokke are best when made with fresh corn on the cob; if corn is not in season, thawed frozen corn can be used, or you can try the shrimp version described on page 158.

To make the béchamel: Use a dish towel to wipe off any stray corn silk from the cob. Holding the corn vertically by its stem on a large cutting board, cut the corn kernels off the cob, being careful not to cut into the cob itself. Reserve the kernels in a measuring cup; you should have a scant 2½ cups / 425 g of kernels. Once you've removed all the kernels from the cobs, using the back of a knife, scrape the length of the cob to extract any leftover corn bits. Set aside 1 cup / 170 g of the kernels and transfer the remaining 1½ cups / 255 g of kernels along with the juice to a blender or a food processor and blend or process until smooth.

In a medium saucepan, combine the milk and corn puree and heat over medium heat until warm. Meanwhile, in a large saucepan, melt the butter over medium heat. Add ¾ cup plus 2 tablespoons / 105 g flour and, using a rubber spatula, mix constantly until the mixture begins to barely color and smells toasty, about 5 minutes. Mixing vigorously, add ladlefuls of the warm corn-milk mixture to the roux, mixing between each addition.

Turn down the heat to low and cook the béchamel for 5 minutes, constantly scraping the bottom of the pan to keep it from sticking, until it thickens visibly. Add 1¼ teaspoons of the salt, then remove the pan from the heat and fold in the remaining whole corn kernels. Taste again and add the remaining ¼ teaspoon of salt if necessary.

Scrape the corn béchamel into a baking dish (any size is fine, since you'll be forming the mixture into patties after it cools), smooth into an even layer with a rubber spatula, and cover with plastic wrap, pressing the wrap directly onto the surface to prevent a skin from forming. Chill for at least 1 hour in the refrigerator or until the mixture is completely cold and has congealed.

Line a rimmed sheet pan with parchment paper. Divide the mixture into 2-oz / 60 g balls. An ice cream scoop can be useful, as the mixture is sticky. Using wet hands, shape the balls into oval patties about 3 by 2½ by ½ inch / 7.5 by 6 cm by 12 mm. Arrange the patties on a sheet pan lined with parchment paper. Transfer to the freezer and freeze until the patties are rock hard; if you'd like to store them longer, once frozen solid, transfer to a freezer storage bag; they'll keep, frozen, for up to 1 month.

Place the flour, egg, and panko in three separate shallow dishes. Working with one piece at a time, dredge the frozen korokke in the flour. Make sure the entire surface is covered and shake off any excess. Next, dip it in the egg mixture, turning to coat completely. Then drop the egg-dipped korokke into the panko. Cover the korokke with panko and press firmly on the top and sides so the panko adheres. Lightly shake off any excess and return to the sheet pan. Repeat with the remaining korokke. Fry immediately or if you're not planning to fry right away, cover loosely with plastic wrap and refrigerate for up to 6 hours.

In a large Dutch oven or other heavy-bottomed pot, heat the oil until it registers 310°F / 154°C on an instant-read thermometer. Working in batches, add a few korokke to the oil and fry, turning occasionally, until golden brown, about 6 minutes. Using a spider or a slotted spoon, remove the korokke from the oil and transfer to a paper towel–lined plate to drain. Allow the oil to return to temperature and repeat with the remaining korokke.

Serve hot, with the snowy cabbage, lemon wedges, and tonkatsu sauce.

VARIATIONS

Another favorite korokke is Ebi Kuriimu Korokke, shrimp cream croquettes. The basic recipe is the same, but instead of the corn, you substitute 1½ lb / 680 g medium shrimp, deveined and cut into ½-inch / 12 mm pieces. Sauté the shrimp in 2 tablespoons unsalted butter, until they begin to turn pink, then deglaze the pan with a splash of white wine and continue cooking until the shrimp are cooked through. Add the chopped shrimp to the béchamel and stir to combine, then proceed with the recipe directions above.

TEBA NO KARAAGE

CHICKEN WINGS

手羽の唐揚げ

---

2 lb / 900 g whole
    chicken wings

1½ teaspoons sea salt

1 teaspoon sugar

MARINADE

2 tablespoons grated
    ginger

1 tablespoon grated
    garlic

1 tablespoon cooking
    sake

1 tablespoon mirin

2 teaspoons sesame oil

6 cups / 1.4L vegetable
    oil or other neutral oil

2 cups / 380 g potato
    starch

3 tablespoons Yakitori
    Tare (page 132)

FOR SERVING:

Ground sansho pepper

Lemon wedges

Arugula (optional)

I never intended to serve chicken wings at my restaurant, but each week at Rintaro, we butcher dozens of chickens for yakitori, leaving us with a lot of wings. More recently, there has been an American renaissance of chicken wing cookery. Now there are all sorts of restaurants serving wings, from buffalo sauced to Taiwanese-style to, of course, KFC (that's Korean Fried Chicken). Even though it's a crowded field, Rintaro's teba no karaage hold their own. Unlike most recipes for chicken karaage, my marinade doesn't include shoyu (which burns easily). Instead, after they're cooked, we dress the wings lightly with a shoyu-based yakitori tare that has been reduced to the consistency of warm maple syrup. But use a light hand with the tare; if you drown the fried wings with it, they'll lose their crispiness, and the tare will overwhelm the flavor of the chicken itself. The sprinkle of sansho pepper at the end adds a pleasant citrusy flavor, along with some tongue-tingling spice.

To prepare the wings: Cut off the wing tips and reserve for stock. Cut the wings into two pieces: upper wing (or flat) and drumette. Cut a slit in each wing down to the bone, transfer to a large bowl, and toss with the salt and sugar. Let stand at room temperature for at least 10 minutes or up to 1 hour.

To make the marinade: In a small bowl, combine the ginger, garlic, sake, mirin, and sesame oil. Pour the marinade over the chicken, toss to coat, then cover the bowl and marinate, refrigerated, for at least 2 hours and up to 2 days.

In a large Dutch oven or heavy-bottomed pan over medium-high heat, heat the canola oil until it registers 330°F / 166°C on an instant-read thermometer. Set a wire rack over a rimmed sheet pan.

Put the potato starch in a large bowl. Toss the marinated wings with the potato starch, knocking the wings against the side of the bowl to shake off excess potato starch.

When the oil is hot, drop half of the chicken wings into the oil and increase the heat to high. Fry until the wings float, approximately 4 minutes. Using a spider or tongs, remove the wings from the oil and transfer to the wire rack. Allow the oil to return to temperature and repeat with the remaining wings. When all the wings have been fried, transfer them to a clean bowl and toss with the tare.

Place the wings on a serving platter, dust with the ground sansho, and serve hot with lemon wedges and arugula (if using) alongside.

IWASHI NO NANBANZUKE

SOUTHERN BARBARIAN MARINATED ANCHOVIES

3 dried Thai red chiles

2 medium carrots

1 medium yellow onion

1 sweet red bell
   or gypsy pepper
   (optional)

¾ cup plus 2
   tablespoons / 205ml
   Katsuobushi Dashi
   (page 19)

6 tablespoons / 90 ml
   shoyu

2 tablespoons mirin

2 tablespoons sugar

¼ cup / 60ml rice
   vinegar

2 tablespoons lemon
   juice

8 oz / 225 g whole
   anchovies, about 20
   pieces

6 cups / 1.4L vegetable
   oil or other neutral oil

1 cup / 190 g potato
   starch

Sea salt

FOR SERVING:

4 kumquats, thinly
   sliced (optional)

1 scallion, finely sliced
   (optional)

½ carrot, peeled and
   finely diced

MAKES 4 SERVINGS

I'm often asked which dish on the menu is my favorite. I love them all, of course—they wouldn't be on the menu if I didn't—but the nanbanzuke does have a special place in my heart. The nanban part of the name refers to "barbarians," specifically the Portuguese, who were the first Westerners to trade with Japan. They came from the south in the mid-16th century, and during the seventy years that they were allowed to trade, they had an enormous influence on Japanese cuisine. They introduced what would become tenpura, the Castella cake, chile peppers, corn, and sugar candies. They also brought Christianity to Japan, for which they were eventually banned (and boiled alive in hot springs).

Nanbanzuke is a Japanese version of Portuguese escabeche, small fried fish marinated in a sweet and spicy vinegar sauce. Like the European version, the one I grew up eating was served at room temperature. The long soak in the seasoned vinegar helped to soften the fine bones of the fried smelts or anchovies. That version is delicious but is not particularly *dynamic*, if that's something food can be. It wasn't until I visited an izakaya in Meguro, in Tokyo, that I realized how thunderously delicious the same dish could become if served HOT. Rather than soaking the fish in the marinade, the fish were fried, tossed quickly in spicy vinegar, served with vegetables pickled in the same sauce, and eaten while still crisp. Really, it's an extremely lovable dish.

You can make nanbanzuke with all sorts of small fish. In addition to anchovies, I've used sardines, large day smelts, tiny night smelts, herring, and even the sunfish that I caught on Minnesota's Lake Minnetonka while visiting relatives. If using smelts, be sure to wash in several changes of water to remove the sand and grit. If using the larger sardines or herring, use a sharp knife on the back of the fish to make an incision the length of the fish along the spine. This will allow the oil to reach the inner bones and crisp them, so they become edible. Larger herring and sunfish will take longer to fry than smaller fish; fry them until they float and the bubbles subside, then taste for crispiness; you want to fry them long enough for the bones to become edible.

Soak the chile peppers in 1 cup / 236ml of boiling water for 10 minutes, then stem, seed, and thinly slice. Peel, then cut the carrots into batons. Cut the onion into thin slices. Repeat with the sweet red pepper (if using).

In a medium saucepan, combine the dashi, shoyu, mirin, and sugar and bring to a boil over medium-high heat, then remove from the heat and chill to warm bath temperature. Add the vinegar, lemon juice, and chile peppers (I never like to heat lemon juice, since it dulls its

flavor). Add the sliced carrots and onion and soak while you prepare the anchovies. The vegetables can be prepared up to a day ahead; refrigerate until ready to serve.

Using a paring knife, gently scrape the fine scales off the anchovies. Pinch the gills with your fingers and remove. Cut open the bellies of the anchovies and scrape out the guts. Rinse in cold water, rubbing the blood and guts carefully from the cavity of the fish. Set a sheet pan on the countertop with one end elevated and line the anchovies on it to drain. Then transfer them to a paper towel–lined sheet pan to dry.

In preparation for plating the anchovies, scoop the pickled vegetables from the marinade and arrange them on a serving platter. Reserve the marinade.

Arrange a wire rack over a rimmed baking sheet.

Heat the oil in a large Dutch oven or heavy-bottomed pot over medium-high heat until it registers 330°F/ 166°C on an instant-read thermometer. Arrange a wire rack over a rimmed baking sheet

and set nearby. Put the potato starch in a medium bowl. Lightly salt the anchovies, then dredge in the potato starch. Knock the anchovies gently on the side of the bowl to shake off excess potato starch.

When the oil is hot, drop half of the anchovies into the oil. increase the heat to high and continue to fry for about 5 minutes. When they are ready, the anchovies will float, with notably smaller bubbles surrounding them. Using a spider, scoop the anchovies from the oil and drain on the wire rack. Allow the oil to return to temperature and repeat with the remaining anchovies. You can keep the first batch warm (placed on a wire rack over a baking sheet) in a low oven while frying the second.

When all the anchovies have been fried, quickly transfer them to a large bowl and toss with ½ cup / 120ml of the reserved marinade. Arrange the anchovies on the serving platter over the pickled vegetables. Garnish with the kumquats, scallions, and diced carrot (if using). Serve hot.

HANETSUKI GYOZA

GYOZA WITH "WINGS"

羽根つきぎょうざ

WRAPPERS

4 ¼ cups plus 3 tablespoons / 525 g all-purpose flour

1 cup / 236ml warm water, plus more as needed

1 tablespoon toasted sesame oil

1 teaspoon sea salt

Potato starch, for rolling out

FILLING

¾ pound / 340 g green cabbage, cored

5 tablespoons / 80ml chicken stock

1 teaspoon powdered gelatin

1¾ pound / 795 g fatty ground pork

2 tablespoons plus ¾ teaspoon shoyu

1 tablespoon plus 1½ teaspoons cooking sake

1 tablespoon plus 1½ teaspoons toasted sesame oil

1 tablespoon plus 1½ teaspoons sugar

1½ teaspoons sea salt

6 tablespoons / 56 g finely chopped scallion

1 tablespoon plus 1½ teaspoons minced ginger

1 tablespoon plus 1½ teaspoons minced garlic

Generous ¼ teaspoon black pepper

Between the ages of four and twenty, I could, without hesitation, say that my three all-time favorite foods were, in order of preference, my mother's gyoza, her Japanese curry (page 221), and her lasagna. My mother's gyoza were locally famous. The recipe even made it into a tiny cookbook put together by my (only) neighbor and set the standard for these dumplings in my (admittedly very white) county.

Making gyoza was always something of a production. When I was very young, my job was to spoon the pork mixture onto the gyoza wrappers and, with a moistened finger, wet the edges for sealing. As I got older, I graduated to pleating them closed. When my mother was feeling ambitious, she and I would even make the wrappers ourselves from scratch. The version that we serve at the restaurant are a version of my mother's original recipe. They're larger than most Japanese gyoza, with handmade wrappers and the addition of "chicken foot jelly." This is simply a very gelatin-rich chicken stock that, when chilled, turns to a solid aspic that we fold into the meat mixture. As with Chinese soup dumplings, this gelled stock melts as you cook the gyoza, and bursts out when you bite into the gyoza.

During the early Peko Peko catering years, we made gyoza feverishly. We froze them (they store best frozen) and sold them, packaged, by the dozen. Then, as part of a huge Japanese food event at the Culinary Institute of America, we were asked to serve 1,500 of them as part of a tasting event with chefs from all over Japan. Some of the most well-known chefs in Japan were in attendance, dressed in their pristine chef's whites, making sushi with fish, rice, and water (to cook the rice!) flown in from Japan. We were, by comparison, a ragtag bunch of home cooks. A then-famous Japanese TV personality stopped by our gyoza-making operation with his entourage behind him, gave us one look, and sniffed that "gyoza aren't even Japanese food." Of course, he was right—kind of. Gyoza were adopted from the Chinese. But just as ramen (which are also considered "not Japanese" in Japan) were adopted from the Chinese, they have both been so thoroughly Japanified, there is no doubt they qualify as part of the cuisine. Incidentally, we managed to shape (by hand!) and cook those 1,500 gyoza for that CIA event. They were extremely popular, and I even spotted that sniffy TV personality in our line, waiting to try them.

While completely optional, I've also included directions for making the "wings" when you steam the gyoza. By adding some potato starch and flour to the steaming water, you can create a very crispy crepe-like layer in the pan. When you invert the gyoza onto a plate, the wings hold the gyoza together and add a little drama to the presentation. Only attempt the wings if you have a truly nonstick pan.

While I can take credit for the general recipe, my gyoza "section chief," Tomoko Tokumaru, has refined it and the production of gyoza far beyond what I could have imagined. Tomoko-san was one of the old guard of cooks who worked

FOR COOKING
1 DOZEN:

1½ teaspoons potato starch

1 cup / 236ml cold water

½ teaspoon all-purpose flour

1 tablespoon canola or other neutral oil

Gyoza tare (2 parts rice vinegar, 1 part shoyu), for serving

Chile oil, for serving

MAKES 60 GYOZA

with me out of my kitchen garage and then helped open Rintaro. She was (and is) a highly trained chef from Fukuoka, one of my favorite food cities in Japan, who worked there developing recipes before moving to the States. But alas, restaurant life is not for everyone, and after she left, I turned to her for help producing our gyoza, which in addition to being ever more popular, are time-consuming to make. Over the years, she's assembled a gyoza team—all Japanese women—who, each with their particular role in the production, make gyoza by hand for us with machine-like consistency. By my calculation, she and her team have made nearly a quarter million gyoza. It's a good recipe.

To prepare the dough for the wrappers: Combine the flour, water, sesame oil, and salt in the bowl of a stand mixer fitted with the dough hook or in a large bowl. Mix with the machine or your hands until a dough forms, then knead on low speed (or by hand) until the dough is smooth and elastic, 5 to 10 minutes in the stand mixer or 10 to 15 minutes by hand. If the dough isn't coming together, you can add additional water by the tablespoon, though don't add too much; the dough should be hydrated but this is a dry dough. Cover the bowl with plastic wrap and let rest at room temperature for 1 hour to allow the gluten to relax.

To prepare the filling: While the dough is resting, bring a large pot of water to a boil, add the cabbage, and cook for 4 minutes. Drain and rinse with cold water until cool enough to handle, then finely chop the cabbage, wrap it in a kitchen towel, and squeeze it well over the sink to remove as much water as possible.

Pour the chicken stock into a small bowl and sprinkle the gelatin over it; let stand until the gelatin has dissolved and the mixture is firm and jiggly like Jell-O.

Combine the pork, shoyu, sake, sesame oil, sugar, salt, and jellied chicken stock in a large bowl and, using your hands, mix well. Add the chopped cabbage,

scallions, garlic, ginger, and black pepper and mix well to combine. Place the bowl in the refrigerator for 30 minutes while you finish the wrappers.

To make the wrappers: Divide the dough into four equal pieces. With your hands, form the dough into four logs, approximately 1-inch / 2.5 cm thick. Cut the logs into 15 coin-sized pieces, about ⅓ oz / 10 g each. Use both thumbs to press each coin into a disk on the cutting board. Dust them lightly with potato starch and using a small rolling pin, roll them into 3-inch / 7.5 cm rounds. As you're working, cover the dough and finished wrappers with a sheet of plastic wrap to keep them from drying out. Alternately, if you have a hand-crank pasta machine, it will speed up the process: Pass each disk of dough through the rollers twice until you have a circle that is 3 inches / 7.5 cm in diameter.

To form the gyoza: Working with one wrapper at a time, place about 1 tablespoon plus 1 teaspoon of filling in the center of each wrapper and spread it into a disk, leaving a ¼-inch / 6 mm border. Use a finger dipped in water to moisten the outer edge of the wrapper. Fold the dumpling in half like a taco (but don't press together to seal) and hold in your dominant hand. Using the thumb and index fingers of your dominant hand, pinch the edge closest

AGEMONO

to you to seal. Then use the thumb and forefinger of your non-dominant hand to pleat one edge of the dough, enclosing the filling (while taking care that no filling is squeezed out). Continue crimping the seam until you reach the end, making about five pleats, squeezing out any excess air as you go.

Unless you plan to cook all sixty gyoza immediately, they are best stored frozen. When left refrigerated, the moisture from the filling turns the wrappers into a sticky mess. To freeze them, line them up on a rimmed sheet pan lightly dusted with potato starch, taking care not to let them touch. Cover with plastic wrap and freeze overnight. Once frozen solid, transfer them to sealed containers or freezer storage bags. They will keep, frozen, for up to 1 month.

To cook each 1 dozen gyoza, in a small bowl, mix the water with the potato starch and flour. Coat the bottom of a 10-inch / 25 cm nonstick frying pan with the canola oil. Place 12 gyoza in the pan in a pinwheel formation. Whisk the water and flour mixture and pour it over the gyoza. Cover the pan with a tight-fitting lid and cook on high heat for 8 to 10 minutes, until most of the water has evaporated. When you start to hear the oil sizzling and the edges have browned, turn down the heat to low, remove the lid, and continue cooking for another minute or two until the water has completely evaporated. Bang the pan firmly on your stovetop to release the gyoza and the thin crepelike "wings." Cover the pan with a serving plate and invert to serve them crispy side up. Repeat for any additional batches of gyoza, being sure to mix more of the flour-water mixture.

Serve with the tare and chile oil alongside.

KAISEN KAKIAGE TENPURA

MIXED SEAFOOD TENPURA

海鮮かき揚げてんぷら

BATTER

2 cups / 425ml ice water

1 large egg

2 cups / 212 g pastry
    flour

6 cups / 1.4L vegetable
    oil or other neutral oil

4 oz / 115 g medium
    shrimp, peeled,
    deveined and cut into
    ¼-inch / 6 mm pieces

4 oz / 115 g scallops,
    side muscles
    removed, rinsed well,
    and cut into ¼-inch /
    6 mm pieces

½ small yellow onion,
    sliced on a mandoline
    ⅛ inch / 3 mm thick
    from top to bottom

20 mizuna leaves and
    stems, washed and
    cut into 1-inch /
    2.5 cm lengths

½ cup / 95 g potato
    starch

Sea salt, for serving

Lemon wedges, for
    serving

MAKES 4 SERVINGS

In my twenties, I helped on a magazine photo shoot about restaurants in Tokyo. We visited many great ones, but the one I'll always remember is Kondo, a tenpura restaurant in Ginza. It was morning, before the restaurant opened, and the chef, Fumio Kondo, worked alone at his polished copper pots of oil. I was completely unaware of his fame, but his enthusiasm for his work and his skill were mesmerizing. He is a wizard with the oil, judging the temperature by sight and working with a fluidity of four decades of practice. His produce and fish were laid out in bamboo baskets. The asparagus had the blush of ones just picked that morning, and the spot prawns were still trying to snap their way back into the water. As he explains in his cookbook, his work is to highlight the flavor and color of the ingredients themselves. Rather than coat the ingredients in a thick batter, he makes his tenpura batter as thin as possible. He says that his tenpura can be thought of as both a fried food and a *steamed* food. That is, while the outer layer of batter is fried, under this thin "jacket," the moisture within the ingredient steams it, concentrating the flavor. Everything he fried that morning was light, crisp, and beautiful. I was particularly impressed with his *hanabi ninjin*, "firework carrots." He dropped a handful of extremely finely cut carrots, dressed in an especially thin batter, into the oil. They spread across the top of the oil in a mat, and with a few sweeps of his chopsticks, he gathered them together into a haystack. The rapidity of the motion was like magic, and the final dish, a tangle of crispy, carrot-y floss, is one of the finest fried foods I've ever eaten.

We don't serve much tenpura at Rintaro. Logistically, it's difficult to manage during a busy service, and I'd hate to see it cool off and lose its luster before it reaches the table. One thing we do make with regularity is kakiage, a mixed tenpura of finely cut fish and vegetables. Its volume makes it a little more durable, and there are endless variations. The recipe below is one possibility, but feel free to experiment with other ingredients. To prevent the creation of gluten, which makes the batter tough rather than crispy, we use pastry flour and mix the batter until barely combined; overstirring contributes to gluten development. Warm water also kickstarts gluten activity, so make the batter with cold water; it's a good idea to put a few ice cubes in with your water and egg mixture as well to keep it chilled. You should use the batter within 30 minutes of mixing it.

To make the batter: In a small bowl, beat the egg. In a medium bowl, combine the water and half of the beaten egg (discard what remains). Sift the flour into the water-egg mixture and whisk it together quickly. Don't worry if there are a few lumps; it should be the consistency of thin pancake batter.

Set a wire rack over a rimmed sheet pan and have ready a fine-mesh strainer or spider and a small bowl.

Heat the oil in a large Dutch oven or heavy-bottomed pot, until it registers 330°F / 166°C on an instant-read thermometer. (For kakiage, it's best for the oil to be no more than 2½ inches / 6 cm deep; any deeper and it becomes hard to control the shape of the kakiage.)

Divide the shrimp, scallop, onion, and mizuna into four batches, using equal quantities of each item in each batch; each batch should weigh about 3 oz / 90 g. Place one batch in a bowl and add 2 tablespoons of the potato starch. Toss to coat well, then transfer to a wire strainer and shake off any excess. Wipe the bowl clean and return the starch-coated ingredients to the bowl. Add ⅓ cup / 80ml batter and mix with

a slotted spoon until everything is well coated.

When your oil is hot, using your slotted spoon, spoon up half of the mixture, letting it drain for a few seconds. Gently slide the mixture into the oil along the edge of the pot. Use the edge of the pot and the spoon to hold the mixture together; it will want to spread and break apart. After a few seconds, once the kakiage has set, spoon the remaining mixture into the hot oil, right on top of the first. Use the fine-mesh strainer or spider to scoop any loose tenpura or ingredients from the oil, depositing them in the small bowl. Check to make sure the oil is still at 330°F / 166°C and adjust the heat as necessary.

Allow the kakiage to cook for 2 minutes undisturbed. Flip it over and cook for another 2 minutes. When it's finished, the bubbles will be smaller, and it should be floating and lightly browned. Scoop the kakiage from the oil, gently shake off the excess oil over the pot, and drain on the wire rack. Repeat with the remaining batches.

Serve simply with a sprinkle of sea salt and a lemon wedge.

KAREI NO KARAAGE

WHOLE CRISPY FRIED PETRALE SOLE

カレイの唐揚げ

½ bunch komatsuna
(about 4 oz / 113 g)

1 whole Petrale sole, 8
to 12 oz /226 to 340 g

Sea salt

1 cup / 190 g potato
starch

2 qt / 2 L vegetable oil
or other neutral oil

FOR SERVING:

⅓ cup / 79 ml Mori
Tsuyu (see page 248),
warmed

2 tablespoons grated
daikon

Lemon wedges

**MAKES 2 TO 4
SERVINGS**

Plates of fried fish are a dime a dozen, but this preparation renders the entire sole—bones and all—edible, and is a very special way to prepare whole fish. But, as with all good things, it requires care. You must choose the right-size fish; I prefer sole that are between 8 oz / 225 g and 12 oz / 340 g; any larger than 1 pound / 455 g and the bones are too thick to eat. If you can't find Petrale sole, you can substitute another flat fish, such as Dover sole or flounder; just make sure they're the right size.

The fish must be carefully butchered so the vertebrae and rib bones are exposed to the hot oil, otherwise they won't become crisp. And, lastly, you must be vigilant when frying: if the oil is too hot or the fish fries too long, the flesh will become very dry. On the other hand, if the oil isn't hot enough, or doesn't fry for long enough, the bones won't become crisp and edible.

Mori tsuyu (see page 248) is typically served as a dipping sauce for soba, but this flavorful sauce has many uses. Here, hot mori tsuyu is poured over the fried fish just before serving—if you've gotten the timing right, when you pour the tsuyu over the ragingly hot, freshly-fried sole, it should sizzle.

It takes a lot to balance the heaviness of a large deep-fried fish, but blanched greens, grated daikon, and lemon wedges alongside do a fine job. The greens are unseasoned and offer a bit of freshness, and the grated daikon and lemon help cut the oil.

If you have an outdoor propane burner, this recipe will give you a good reason to use it. If not, crank up your hood fan, open the doors and windows, and get to it. Nothing (except, perhaps the fried anchovies on page 162), will do such an excellent job of making every room in the house smell like a Maine fry shack. But what a small price to pay for such magnificent eating!

Rinse and trim the komatsuna and bundle the greens with a rubber band. Bring a large pot of salted water to a boil and prepare an ice water bath. Hold the greens by the tops with the stems in the water for 45 seconds before dropping the entire bunch in. Cook for 2 minutes. Remove with a spider strainer and transfer to the ice bath. Once cool, squeeze firmly with your hands to remove the excess liquid, then cut into 1½-inch /3.8 cm lengths. Set aside.

You can ask the person at the fish counter to clean the fish for you. If you're

cleaning it yourself: Using the back of your knife, remove any scales from both sides of the fish. Remove the gills with a sharp knife, cutting them from the inside of the collar. With your fingers, reach in to remove the guts. Use the tip of a fine spoon to scrape out the bloodline at the base of the spine. Wash and dry well with paper towels, inside and out.

In order for the entire fish to be edible and for the bones to become crispy, the ribs and vertebrae will need to be exposed to the oil. You will be cutting the fillet from the skeleton, as though you were cutting the fillets off the fish, while leaving the skin intact and fillet attached at the top and bottom fins (dorsal and anal fins).

Using the lateral line that runs down the middle of the fish on the top as a guide, slice the fish from head to tail along the backbone. Starting with the side closest to you, run the tip of your knife ½ inch / 12 mm deep along the length of the incision along the rib bones, cutting the meat from the bones. Continue with long shallow cuts, using the ribs as a guide, until the tip of your knife has nearly cut through the skin at the fins. Turn the fish over and repeat on the bottom and top fillets on both sides. Make sure to cut the meat from the bones at the top of the spine near the head and in the pocket under the pelvic fin.

Sprinkle the fish lightly with salt, inside and out. Pour the potato starch into a rimmed baking dish and dredge the fish with the starch, coating the bones, as well.

In a large Dutch oven or other heavy-bottomed pot over medium-high heat,

heat the oil until it registers 350°F / 180°C on an instant-read thermometer and set a wire rack over a rimmed baking sheet. Shake off any excess potato starch from the fish, and, when the oil is at temperature, carefully slide the fish into the oil. Increase the heat to maintain the oil temperature at 350°F / 180°C.

Fry the fish for 7 to 10 minutes, turning once or twice with tongs. The flesh around the slits will pucker, exposing the backbone. Cook until the tail bones are brittle and crackly. Using tongs to hold it by the head, remove the fish from the oil, shake it several times over the pot to drain the oil, and set it on a wire rack.

Place the fish on a large platter. Bring to the table immediately and pour the mori tsuyu over the fish—it should sizzle. Serve with the blanched komatsuna, grated daikon, and lemon wedges alongside. With the exception of the saber-like collar bone, the entire fish should be edible, from head to tail.

SNOWY
CABBAGE
AND OTHER FRIENDS
OF KATSU

While sitting at a counter at a small tonkatsu restaurant in Yokohama, I noted how, despite working in a kitchen barely large enough for two people to stand side by side, cooks in Japan are still able to make extremely delicious food. I also caught a glance inside the closet next to their cramped kitchen—the entire space was reserved for their industrial-sized electric cabbage slicing machine. At the time, it seemed to me like an incredible waste of precious space, like putting a trampoline in a two-person tent. But finely sliced cabbage is served by the softball-sized mound with every katsu, and by volume, it makes up almost half the food on the plate. If you're selling a lot of katsu, this could easily mean slicing a dozen cabbages a day. Now, having sliced several tons of cabbage by hand myself since I opened my restaurant (I never bought an electric cabbage slicer), I understand their decision to dedicate the entire closet to the cabbage machine.

At some point, I started calling this snowy cabbage, since the usual "shredded cabbage" didn't convey its lightness. For me (and the entire nation of Japan), there is no better accompaniment for katsu. It is refreshing and unobtrusive, and it perfectly cuts the oiliness and heaviness of panko-fried foods. We serve it with all our katsu and korokke.

Apart from the electric slicer, I've only ever seen snowy cabbage made using a very sharp mandoline called the Benriner. This is an essential kitchen tool. It's simple, sharp, and inexpensive. And as its name suggests—*benri* means "handy" in Japanese—it's useful for all sorts of cutting tasks.

To make snowy cabbage, peel away any brown and bruised leaves. Cut it in half lengthwise, from stem to tip, and trim the end of the stem, but keep the core intact to hold the leaves together as you cut. Adjust the mandoline with a few turns of the screw open and begin by slicing the cut edge the length of the cabbage. The slices should be very fine, and when they emerge from the blade, they should curl like thin ribbons of paper onto your hand. If the slices are rigid and too thick, adjust the mandoline a couple of turns thinner. This is not like making coleslaw (although the Benriner is handy for that, too). Once you've sliced to the core on one side, rotate the cabbage and slice from the other side. At the end, you should have only the core and a small wedge of cabbage left. Put the sliced cabbage in a bowl, cover it with cold water, and let it sit for ten minutes. Although the soak in cold water does wash away some of the sweetness, it also crisps it up and removes much of the sulfurous odor. Drain well and store the snowy cabbage, covered, in an airtight container in the refrigerator for up to a day.

Apart from the snowy cabbage, the other essential for panko-fried foods is tonkatsu sauce, a condiment so important in Japan that it's simply called "sauce." This is the only food that we regularly serve at Rintaro that comes in a bottle. For me, it's kind of like ketchup: I like the *idea* of homemade ketchup, but somehow it never hits the mark. And the ketchup analogy is an apt one, because as a kid growing up far from any Asian markets, we almost never had proper bottled *sausu* in the refrigerator. We would "make" it by combining two parts Heinz ketchup with one part Lea & Perrins Worcestershire sauce. It makes a pretty good substitute for the most famous brands (Otafuku, Bulldog, and Kagome) and for good reason. *Sausu* was adapted from English Worcestershire shortly after World War II, and although anchovies are no longer an ingredient in most Japanese tonkatsu sauces, they do share that clove-y piquant sweetness of ketchup and Lea & Perrins.

NIMONO TO ODEN

煮物とおでん

...ED DISH

NO MATTER THE CUISINE, I'VE always been drawn to simmered dishes. Poule au pot, bollito misto, lamb tagines: They all fill the house with lovely smells and make you feel as if you've cooked something proper for dinner. The same goes for Japanese nimono. This is a giant category, of which I've only included a tiny selection of some of my favorites. For the most part, the majority of nimono use the same simmering liquid: katsuobushi dashi and sake, with mirin and shoyu for seasoning.

But the bulk of this chapter is devoted to oden, a subcategory of nimono, but a whole genre unto itself. Generally speaking, it consists of a rich broth, with (very) long-simmered satsumaage fish cakes, vegetables, and tofu. Mostly unknown in the West, it never fails to bring waves of nostalgia and home-sickness to our Japanese expatriate customers.

A month before the world shut down because of COVID-19, I went to Japan on an oden research trip. I visited my favorite oden restaurants in Tokyo, including slightly upscale places, where the counters are built around shallow vats arranged with fish cakes of every shape and size, daikon, cabbage rolls, and tofu bathing in golden dashi. But my ideas of oden were upended when Hitoshi Okamura, an old friend and connoisseur of the nooks and crannies of Japanese restaurants, took me on a tour of the city of Shizuoka, just south of Tokyo. The day started with breakfast oden at a tiny spot by the train station. It was then oden for lunch, dinner, and a second dinner. In Shizuoka, the oden is sold on skewers, and the broth is heavier, darker, and murkier than I'd ever seen before. I learned that rather than being made with katsuobushi dashi, some Shizuoka shops make theirs with konbu (dried kelp) and beef tendon broth, and in the old days, it used to include whale meat broth. Powdered katsuobushi, dried anchovies, and hot mustard are served alongside as condiments. The fourteen-hour tasting tour ended at Shizuoka Aoba Koen Oden Alley, a collection of more than thirty oden restaurants, each seating no more than a dozen customers, jammed side by side on a covered street in the middle of town.

Satsumaage fish cakes are the heart of oden, so the great oden tour also included a visit with a small mom and pop fish cake shop in the town of Ichikikushikino in Kagoshima. Kagoshima is the birthplace of satsumaage (the word Satsuma is the ancient name of the prefecture), and there, in a bare-bones workshop, a husband and wife duo showed me how to gut and clean mackerel; press it through a fine-mesh sieve to remove the bones, scales, and skin; process it with salt; and mix it with soft tofu and the local black sugar.

Back in Odawara, just south of Tokyo, my friend Yuri Nomura took me to visit the Suzuhiro Kamaboko fish cake factory that's been in business since 1865. After we donned hairnets, face masks, white jumpsuits, and sterile white boots, the president of the company showed me their giant fish grinders, extruders, mixers, and conveyor ovens and fryers. He told me about the importance of water in washing away excess enzymes, of proper grinding and pressing, and the science of transforming fish protein with the use of salt. As mechanized as the factory was, it was dependent most of all on its highly skilled workers, hand shaping the fish cakes and carefully managing each step in the process. Suzuhiro sells upward of three hundred distinct kinds of fish cakes. I tried a couple dozen varieties, including a few new items developed over the last decade, and they were all delicious.

When I returned from my trip, I was full of ideas and enthusiasm. And then, like the rest of the world, we went into lockdown. It wasn't until the spring of 2021, when we were able to open again for limited service outdoors, that I could put all my oden research to work. We refurbished a seventy-year-old yatai food cart that I'd acquired a few years earlier, hung a red lantern, and set it up in the courtyard in the front of the restaurant. We offered a menu that was called the Oden Set. Excited to leave their houses and hungry for something new, it was a hit with our customers, who ate the steaming oden outdoors, distanced but together. We still use the outdoor cart as our oden station. It's a charming scene, with a large pot of golden dashi and our assortment of satsumaage, vegetables, and tofu steaming in the cool night air. A small selection of our oden recipes begins on page 183.

KINKI NO NITSUKE

SHOYU AND SAKE-SIMMERED ROCK COD

きんきの煮付け

SIMMERING LIQUID

½ cup plus 2 tablespoons /150ml Katsuobushi Dashi (page 18)

7 tablespoons / 100ml cooking sake

7 tablespoons / 100ml water

¼ cup / 60ml shoyu

3 tablespoons mirin

1 tablespoon sugar

2 whole rock cod (about ¾ lb / 340 g each), scaled, gilled, and gutted

1 piece ginger (about 1 ounce / 28 g)

1¾ ounce / 50 g gobo (burdock root)

3 scallions, thinly sliced, green tops reserved

MAKES 4 SERVINGS

This very common Japanese method for cooking a whole fish is one of my favorites. As it braises, you baste the fish with the simmering liquid that dissolves the collagen in the fish skin and head, adding richness and gloss to the sauce. Japanese kinki is a deliciously oily rockfish, but this recipe works well with many types of whole fish. The only requirement is that the fish be small, ideally three-quarters of a pound and no more than one pound. Sea bass, mackerel, snapper, or flounder are all good choices. If you can't find a small fish or would prefer something boneless, you can substitute skin-on fish fillets. In either case, blanching the fish will remove any unpleasant fishiness.

To prepare the simmering liquid: Mix the dashi, sake, water, shoyu, mirin, and sugar in a small bowl. Stir to dissolve the sugar. Set aside.

To prepare the fish: Rub the sharp side of a paring knife along the skin of the fish to remove any errant scales; pay particular attention to the areas near the fins and on the belly, where the scales are often missed. Rinse and dry with a paper towel.

The bones on a rock cod are especially thick and sharp. To make the fish easier to eat, remove the dorsal (top) fins and bones: starting at the base of the head, cut along one side of the dorsal fins to the tail, about ½ inch / 12 mm deep. Repeat on the other side. Starting at the tail, and using a paper towel for better grip, pull back toward the head; you should be able to pull out the strip of bones and fins in a single motion. Cut two or three slashes on both sides of the fish, almost to the bone, to allow the simmering liquid to penetrate the flesh as it cooks.

Peel the ginger and reserve the peel. Using a mandoline or a knife, cut it into eight to ten paper-thin slices.

To prepare the gobo, bring a large saucepan of water to a boil over high heat. Cut the gobo into lengths that are short enough to fit in the pot, then scrape the skin off each piece with the back of a knife. Once skinned, gobo oxidizes extremely quickly. To keep the pieces from turning brown, put the skinned gobo into the pot as you go. Boil for 3 to 4 minutes, then use a slotted spoon to transfer to a bowl of cold water. Once cool enough to handle, cut into 3-inch / 7.5 cm lengths. Cut each segment lengthwise into ¼-inch / 6 mm-thick segments; reserve the water.

Return the water to a boil over high heat and add the reserved ginger peel, scallion tops, and fish. Return the water to a boil, 2 to 3 minutes, then use a spider to transfer the fish to a rimmed sheet pan. Discard the blanching water and solids.

Line the bottom of a 10-inch / 25 cm frying pan with the ginger slices. Lay the fish on the ginger, their heads facing in the same direction. Scatter the pieces of gobo alongside. Pour the dashi mixture over the fish. Cut a 10-inch / 25 cm circle of parchment, then cut a ½-inch / 12 mm circle in the center. Cover the fish with the parchment, then bring the liquid to a boil over high heat. Once at a boil, immediately turn down the heat to keep the liquid from boiling over. Adjust the heat so the simmering liquid boils up onto the parchment paper, basting the top of the fish but doesn't boil over the side of the pan. Cover the pan with a lid, slightly ajar to allow the steam to escape, and cook for 12 minutes. Remove the lid and discard the parchment. Return the heat to low, then baste the top of the fish with the simmering liquid for another minute or two, until the flavor of the simmering liquid becomes concentrated; it should be rich, sweet, and salty but not syrupy.

Transfer the fish to a warmed rimmed platter. Arrange the ginger under and around the fish and the gobo into a tidy bundle, leaning it against the side of the fish. Pour the simmering liquid through a fine-mesh strainer over the fish. Garnish with the scallions. Serve immediately.

TEBAMOTO NO SHOYU MAMAREDO

SHOYU AND MARMALADE CHICKEN DRUMETTES 手羽元のしょうゆ
マーマレード

2 tablespoons
    vegetable oil or other
    neutral oil

16 chicken drumettes
    (about 1 lb / 450 g)

1 cup / 236ml cooking
    sake

½ cup / 120ml usukuchi
    (light-colored) shoyu

4 garlic cloves, grated

1 cup / 320 g orange
    marmalade

MAKES 4 SERVINGS

My mother used to make this marmalade chicken as part of the New Year's Day osechi meal. Although the osechi menu is fairly codified with elements that are considered crucial, there is still room for improvisation and add-ons. In Japan, most people buy their osechi foods from restaurants or department stores, and it's not uncommon to see roast beef and French cheeses included. The osechi meal is made a day or two in advance and served from lacquered boxes. These chicken wings work well in this context, since they taste just as good at room temperature.

Unlike the other recipes in this book, I don't actually serve these wings at the restaurant, but I do serve them at home for New Year's Day, and because they are so simple, quick, and beloved by everyone who tries them, they deserve a spot in your regular weeknight meal rotation. You'll note that in this recipe, the simmering liquid is just a relatively small amount of sake and shoyu, with no added dashi. Together with the marmalade, they cook down into a thick, sticky glaze that coats the wings.

Heat the oil in a large heavy skillet over medium-high heat. When the oil is hot, add the drumettes and fry, turning, until browned on both sides, about 7 minutes. Pour in the sake and shoyu, then add the garlic and marmalade and stir to coat the chicken wings. Turn down the heat to medium-low and cook, stirring occasionally at the start, then more frequently as the glaze thickens to prevent scorching, until the sauce thickens to a glaze and the chicken is cooked through, about 30 minutes.

Serve warm or at room temperature.

BUTA NO KAKUNI

SHOYU AND BLACK SUGAR–SIMMERED PORK BELLY

---

4 lb / 1.8kg pork belly

2 tablespoons vegetable oil or other neutral oil

1 medium onion, coarsely chopped

1 large carrot, coarsely chopped

3 whole scallions, root ends trimmed

1 whole garlic head, halved across its center

1½ oz / 45 g coarsely chopped ginger (unpeeled is fine)

3 cups / 710ml cooking sake

1½ cups / 355ml Katsuobushi Dashi (page 19)

1 cup / 236ml mirin

2 tablespoons kurozato black sugar or dark brown sugar

1 (4 by 4-inch / 10 by 10 cm) piece konbu

1 whole star anise (optional)

1 cup / 236ml shoyu

3 dried Japanese chiles, seeded

FOR SERVING:

Furofuki daikon (page 197; optional)

Blanched mustard greens (optional)

Japanese hot mustard

Hot rice

MAKES 8 SERVINGS

When shopping for the pork belly, ask for a piece with the rib meat still attached and with the skin and some of the belly fat removed. This is the same cut used for making bacon. Parboiling the meat first removes blood and gaminess. As with many Japanese simmered dishes, the meat is long-cooked with the sweet elements to allow the sugars to penetrate, before adding salt in the form of shoyu. In Japan, when I asked why this was done, my chef told me with a shrug, "It's osmosis. Science!" I nodded. I still don't really understand, but the sweet before salt rule has stuck with me ever since.

Given that it's so rich, I like to balance the pork belly with simmered daikon (see page 197) or with blanched mustard greens (see Note below) and Japanese hot mustard. Served with a bowl of rice, it makes a meal.

If you'd like, you can press the pork belly flat under a weight during the blanching and simmering process, then refrigerate it in its liquid overnight. Doing these steps doesn't really change the flavor but does help to make a beautiful, shapely final dish. Perfectly shaped or not, this dish is a crowd pleaser.

Bring 2 qt / 1.9L of water to a boil in a large, heavy-bottomed pot over high heat. Add the pork belly, reduce the heat to medium and to a simmer. Cook until an instant-read thermometer inserted in the thickest part of the belly registers 150°F / 66°C. Drain and rinse the pork. Wash the pot for the next step.

Return the pot to the stove over high heat and add the oil. When the oil is shimmering but not yet smoking, add the onion, carrot, scallions, garlic, and ginger and cook, stirring constantly, for 1 minute. Add the sake, dashi, mirin, and black sugar. Add the pork belly, skin-side up, then add the konbu and star anise (if using). Cover the pot with a small heatproof plate or pot lid to keep the meat submerged in the simmering liquid. Turn down the heat until the liquid is simmering gently, then simmer for 3 hours, until the pork is easily pierced with a metal skewer. Add the shoyu and chiles and simmer for 1 more

hour. Remove the pot from the heat and let cool to room temperature.

Place the pork belly in an 8 by 12-inch / 20 by 30 cm baking dish, fatty side up. Strain the simmering liquid into a bowl and discard the vegetables. Use a fat separator to strain the seasoning liquid from the impressive quantity of fat that is rendered from the belly. If you don't have a fat separator, use a large resealable storage bag: pour the stock into the bag, hold it upright to allow the oil to float to the top, snip a small hole in the bottom corner of the bag, and drain the sauce into a saucepan. Discard the fat.

Cut the pork belly into 2½-inch / 6 cm squares. Place the baking dish under the broiler and broil until the top of each piece of pork has caramelized to a dark lustrous brown. To serve, return the pork cubes to the saucepan with the liquid, along with the furofuki daikon, if using, and bring to a simmer to heat through. Serve with blanched mustard greens, if using, with hot Japanese mustard and rice alongside.

Note: To blanch the mustard greens: While the pork is simmering, in a large pot of salted water, boil the greens until tender, about 3 minutes, then plunge them into cold water to stop the cooking. Using your hands, gather the greens by the stems so the leaves all face in the same direction. Squeeze gently to remove most of the water, forming a log, then cut into 2-inch / 5 cm pieces.

GYUSUJI NIKOMI

SIMMERED VEAL SHANK AND TENDON

---

8 lb / 3.6kg veal shanks

8 oz / 225 grams unpeeled ginger, cut into ½-inch / 12 mm-thick slices

4 bunches scallion tops

7 dried Japanese chile peppers

½ cup / 106 g demerara or dark brown sugar

8 ½ cups / 2L Katsuobushi Dashi (page 19)

1 cup / 236ml cooking sake

1 cup / 236ml mirin

1 cup / 236ml dark shoyu

½ cup / 115 g red miso

6 tablespoons / 75 g hatcho miso (if not available, substitute red miso)

FOR SERVING:

Shichimi

Sliced scallions

Finely sliced yuzu or lemon peel, pith removed

MAKES 8 TO 10 SERVINGS

I love a giant pot of gyusuji nikomi gurgling away on the back burner. There is nothing light about this dish. It's nearly black because of the dark shoyu and hatcho miso, and the veal shanks cook long past where the meat has fallen from the bones. The connective tissues in the shank, after hours of simmering, begin to melt, enriching the sauce and giving it a deep luster. In Japan, gyusuji nikomi is made from beef tendon, which is sold with a bit of meat attached and is widely available in grocery stores. It's hard to find it here (tendons are often turned into dog chews), so this recipe uses mostly the hardworking leg muscle meat with the tendons that connect them to the bone. If you happen to find beef tendons sold on their own, substitute them for a third of the shanks in the recipe.

Put the veal shanks, half of the ginger, and half of the scallion tops in a large pot. Add cold water to cover by a few inches / 5 centimeters and bring to a boil over high heat. Turn down the heat so the water is simmering and simmer for about an hour, or until the shanks are totally cooked through (an instant-read thermometer inserted into the thickest part of the shank should register 145°F / 63°C). Drain, discard the vegetables, and rinse the beef in a bowl of fresh water. Wash the pot.

Once the shanks are cool enough to handle, cut the meat and tendons from the bones; discard the bones. Cut the meat and tendons into bite-sized pieces. Wrap the remaining scallion tops and chile peppers in a piece of cheesecloth and secure with kitchen twine. Place the cloth package at the bottom of the clean pot and cover with the cut meat and the remaining ginger slices. Add the sugar, dashi, sake, and mirin and bring to a boil over high heat. Using a spider or a slotted spoon, skim any foam that rises to the surface. Turn down the heat to low and simmer for 1 hour, periodically skimming any foam that rises to the surface, until the tendons become soft and gelatinous. Remove the cloth package and discard. Add the shoyu and red and hatcho miso, stirring to dissolve the miso. Cook for another 10 minutes, until the sauce is glossy.

Ladle into bowls and serve with shichimi, scallions, and yuzu alongside.

ODEN TSUYU

ODEN SIMMERING BROTH

---

8 ½ cups / 2L Katsuobushi Dashi (page 19)

2½ tablespoons white or usukuchi (light-colored) shoyu

¼ cup / 60ml cooking sake

¼ cup / 60ml mirin

1½ teaspoons sea salt

MAKES ABOUT 2 QT / 1.9L

The dashi you use for the oden broth—as with udon or miso soup—is the foundation of the dish. But the seasoned tsuyu is just the beginning. Each element you add to the simmering broth not only becomes seasoned by the broth but it also adds its own flavor to the whole. The satsumaage fish cakes and daikon are particularly important, and over the hours of simmering, they make the simmering broth rich and flavorful.

In a large pot, combine the dashi, shoyu, sake, and mirin and bring to a boil over high heat. Once boiling, add the salt. Like magic, the impurities in the dashi will rise immediately to the surface in the form of foam. Skim with a fine-mesh skimmer. The tsuyu is best used on the same day it's made. If you have any left over after serving the oden, it can be saved by bringing it to a boil, straining it through a fine-mesh strainer, and then cooling. It will keep in an airtight container in the freezer for up to a month.

ODEN SATSUMAAGE

FRIED FISH CAKES さつま揚げ

- 1 lingcod fillet (about 1 lb / 450 g), skin and pin bones removed; other whitefish can be substituted
- 1¼ teaspoons sea salt
- 1 tablespoon sugar
- ¼ cup / 60ml mirin
- 3 tablespoons potato starch
- 2 large eggs
- 3 tablespoons Katsuobushi Dashi (page 19)

MAKES 1½ LB / 680 G FISH CAKE BASE, ENOUGH FOR APPROXIMATELY 20 SATSUMAAGE

I first fell in love with satsumaage fish cakes when my friend Shin Nakahara brought an assorted pack to a photo shoot I was assisting at in Kagoshima, Japan's southernmost prefecture. They are ubiquitous there, eaten cold as a snack, or hot, just out of the fryer in all their chewy glory, with a bit of ginger and shoyu. At Rintaro, we serve them mostly in our oden.

The old way of making them, using a grooved ceramic suribachi mortar and wooden pestle, is a workout, but with a food processor, satsumaage are fairly easy to make. Most of our satsumaage are made with lingcod, but any lean white fish will work, including cod, haddock, flounder, or halibut. The satsumaage base is extremely versatile. It can be shaped into patties and fried as is, or you can experiment, folding in finely cut root vegetables, such as sweet potatoes, carrots, gobo roots, or lotus roots or seafood, such as shrimp, crab, or squid. You can form them in all sorts of shapes and sizes. We've served ones the size of ping-pong balls, the size of tennis balls, and as thin, flat disks or as oblong patties. An assortment of shapes and flavors, all using the same satsumaage base, makes for the most exciting oden.

This recipe makes about 1½ pounds / 680 g of satsumaage base, while the variations are scaled to use ½ pound / 225 g of base. This is by design so that you can make a few different types of satsumaage from a single batch of the base.

Cut the lingcod into roughly 1-inch / 2.5 cm chunks. Soak in a bowl of ice water for 10 minutes to remove any residual blood and strong fishy flavor. Dry in a colander and pat between sheets of paper towels to dry.

Add the lingcod and salt to a food processor and pulse until the fish is a uniform paste. It will be quite springy and dense. Add the sugar, mirin, potato starch, eggs, and dashi. Process for 1 full minute, scraping the sides down with a spatula halfway through.

Transfer the satsumaage base from the food processor to a medium bowl, cover with plastic wrap, and refrigerate for 30 minutes.

At this point, the satsumaage base can be seasoned and shaped in many ways; a few are listed on the next page.

GINGER AND SCALLION SATSUMAAGE

MAKES 4 PIECES

Slice two scallions as finely as you can, cutting up to the "shoulder" of the scallion. Fold the scallions and 2 tablespoons of minced ginger into 8 oz / 225 g of the satsumaage base. Lightly grease your hands with a bit of vegetable oil to keep the base from sticking to your hands, then shape into four balls, about 2 oz / 60 g each. Using your hands, shape the balls into oval patties about 3 by 2½ by ½ inch / 7.5 by 6 cm by 12 mm thick. Heat 6 cups / 1.5L vegetable oil or other neutral oil in a large Dutch oven or heavy-bottomed pot over high heat until it registers 300°F / 150°C on an instant-read thermometer. Add the satsumaage and fry, turning occasionally, until they are golden brown and slightly puffed, 8 to 10 minutes. Drain on a wire rack before serving.

CORN SATSUMAAGE

MAKES 9 PIECES

Cut the kernels off two ears of corn. Fold the corn kernels into 8 oz / 225 g of the satsumaage base. Lightly grease your hands with a bit of vegetable oil to keep the base from sticking to your hands, then shape into nine balls, about ¾ oz / 25 g each. Heat 6 cups / 1.5 L vegetable oil or other neutral oil in a large Dutch oven or heavy-bottomed pot over high heat until it registers 300°F / 150°C on an instant-read thermometer. Add the satsumaage and fry, turning occasionally, until they are golden brown and slightly puffed, 5 to 7 minutes. Drain on a wire rack before serving.

SHIITAKE SATSUMAAGE

MAKES 6 PIECES

Prepare eight small shiitake mushrooms: Remove and discard the stems, then cut an x pattern into the cap of the mushroom. Using a pastry brush, dust the inside of the mushrooms with a thin layer of potato starch. Using a spoon or small rubber spatula, fill each mushroom cap with about 1 oz / 30 g of the satsumaage base. Heat 6 cups / 1.5 L vegetable oil or other neutral oil in a large Dutch oven or heavy-bottomed pot over high heat until it registers 300°F / 150°C on an instant-read thermometer. Add the satsumaage and fry, turning occasionally, until they are golden brown and slightly puffed, about 8 to 10 minutes. Drain on a wire rack before serving.

ODEN KINCHAKU

MOCHI-FILLED TOFU "PURSES"

1 (1 oz / 30 g) bag
  kanpyo (dried gourd)

12 pieces aburaage
  (fried tofu)

6 pieces komochi (small
  mochi)

MAKES 12 PIECES

For most of my life, I've loved mochi with shoyu and nori, browned and puffed in the broiler. It was a common after-school snack for me, although my mother always warned me not to choke. Mochi is a silent killer in Japan. It's all at once crunchy, sticky, and chewy and is perfect for lodging in your throat. The Japanese government issues yearly warnings around New Year's, when mochi is most often consumed. These little "purses" are another great, if potentially lethal, way to eat mochi. The *aburaage*, thin fried tofu, soaks up the oden tsuyu (page 192), and the mochi becomes molten inside. Resist the urge to eat the entire kinchaku in one bite, and you'll likely be fine.

In a good Japanese market, look for aburaage (as opposed to *atsuage*, thick-fried tofu). Except for the weeks around New Year's, mochi usually isn't available fresh, but frozen ones work fine. Look for the *komochi*, small mochi, about twelve pieces to a pound. The purses are tied with *kanpyo*, long strips of edible dried gourd. All three ingredients are available at Japanese grocery stores.

Cut the kanpyo into twelve 6-inch / 15 cm lengths and soak the pieces in cold water for a few minutes, then squeeze them to remove the water and set aside.

Aburaage absorbs liquid, including the oil in which it was fried. To remove the oil, place the aburaage in a bowl of hot tap water and gently squeeze. Pour out the water and repeat a few more times, then lay the pieces on a cutting board and roll out the excess water with a rolling pin. Cut one of the edges open with a knife and gently open the aburaage into a little pouch. Cut the mochi in half and place half inside each pouch. Tie each bundle closed with a length of *kanpyo*, sealing with a double knot. The kinchaku can be made a day or two in advance. To cook, see instructions on page 189.

ODEN FUROFUKI DAIKON

ふろふき大根

"BATHING" DAIKON

---

2 lb / 900 g daikon

10 cups / 2.3L starchy water or plain water plus 2 tablespoons uncooked rice (see headnote)

MAKES 12 PIECES

Along with the satsumaage fish cakes, daikon is a key ingredient in oden and is always the first item that I order at an oden restaurant. Cooked properly, daikon become almost translucent, and the texture is tender and creamy, its peppery flavor having mellowed during the long cooking process. Unlike the satsumaage, which don't need much time in the oden tsuyu (page 192), daikon needs a few hours to absorb the flavor of the broth. Long white Japanese daikon are best suited for this recipe, although the green-topped Korean varieties work well, too.

We cut the whole daikon into 4-inch / 10 cm lengths and then roll-cut them to turn them into perfect cylinders before slicing them into rounds. You can also simply peel them with a vegetable peeler and cut them into uniform chunks. In either case, bevel the cut edges. Called mentori, this detail will make your finished daikon both more attractive and will keep the edges from disintegrating as they simmer for hours.

You can prepare the daikon a day in advance. The first step involves cooking it in starchy water; doing this helps draw out some of the pungency and spice. This water can be the water left over from washing rice or water to which you have added 2 tablespoons of uncooked rice.

Remove the skin of the daikon with a vegetable peeler. Remove and discard the top stem end and the thin tail root end. Cut the daikon in half and then cut the halves in half again lengthwise. Cut the lengths into half-moon pieces, each approximately 2 oz / 60 g. Using a knife or a vegetable peeler, create a fine ⅛ to ¼-inch / 3 to 6 mm bevel along all the cut edges. Discard the scraps.

In a large pot over high heat, add the daikon and starchy water. (If using plain water, add the uncooked rice.) Bring to a boil, uncovered. Once the water has reached a boil, immediately turn down the heat to low and add 1 cup / 236ml of cold water to lower the temperature. Simmer the daikon for 45 minutes to an hour, until they are translucent and easily pierced with a skewer. Remove from the heat, drain in a colander, and rinse thoroughly in a bowl of cold water to remove the starch.

Store for up to a day in the refrigerator, submerged in cold water.

ASSEMBLING THE ODEN

1 recipe Oden Satsumaage, about 20 pieces (page 193)

1 recipe Oden Tsuyu (page 192)

1 recipe Oden Furofuki Daikon (page 197)

6 hard-boiled eggs, peeled

1 recipe Oden Kinchaku (page 196)

Hot Japanese mustard, for serving

Yuzu kosho, for serving (optional)

MAKES 6 TO 8 SERVINGS

Oden is a bit like making a cassoulet, with many different components that are made separately and then assembled in the final dish. I find it's easiest to break down the work over a few days and then combine the ingredients a few hours before serving so they can simmer in the oden tsuyu (page 192), each ingredient absorbing the flavor of the broth. The satsumaage fish cakes (page 193) can be made three or four days in advance, and the par-cooked daikon (page 197), the mochi-filled tofu purses (page 196), and the eggs can be made the day before. I would also suggest making the dashi for the tsuyu simmering broth the day you'll be serving it.

Serve the oden at the table. It's an exciting presentation, and it's all the better if you can keep it warm with a tabletop butane burner. Use a high-walled stockpot to simmer the ingredients and then transfer the oden to a shallow enamel casserole for serving at the table.

To rinse off excess oil, submerge the satsumaage in a bowl of hot tap water. Rinse three times and drain in a colander.

Bring the oden tsuyu to a boil over high heat in a large, high-sided stock pot. Add the satsumaage, daikon, and eggs, submerging them in the tsuyu. Bring the tsuyu back up to 165° to 175°F / 75° to 79°C, adjusting the heat to maintain this temperature. To keep the broth clear, prevent the daikon from turning mushy and the satsumaage from losing their bounce, it's important to not let the oden tsuyu boil.

Simmer uncovered at 165° to 175°F / 75° to 79°C, for at least 2 hours (and up to 6 hours) to allow the flavors to blend nicely and the seasoning to penetrate

the daikon and eggs. Forty-five minutes before you plan to serve, add the oden kinchaku. The mochi is ready to serve when it becomes molten and hot inside (it will leak out if it cooks too long).

With a spider or a slotted spoon, transfer the satsumaage, daikon, eggs, and kinchaku to a shallow Dutch oven or similar pot. Ladle the tsuyu over the top, then bring the pot to the table, setting it over a tabletop burner set to low heat (if using). Serve with the hot Japanese mustard and yuzu kosho alongside.

GOHAN
ごはん

RICE

WHAT I REMEMBER FROM DIRECTOR Akira Kurosawa's Seven Samurai is not the gleaming katana and sword fights but the rice. In the film, the samurai were paid for their services in rice; bandits pillaged the village for rice, and the only currency the masterless samurai possessed was a small bag of rice, tucked into his tattered overcoat. Although the movie took place in the 16th century, when Japan was a feudal society, it's easy to forget that until recently, Japan was a very poor country. For most people, daily life revolved around planting, growing, and harvesting rice. With government support, Japan is still a country shaped by rice. Not only do you see miles of rice paddies on every long train ride, but even in the middle of ultramodern Shibuya, you'll see oddly shaped triangular or very narrow modern buildings, the shape of the old rice paddies on which they were built.

The word gohan is both the word for cooked rice and the word for meal. Although a Westernized diet is common in Japan, for many people a meal wouldn't be a meal without a bowl of rice. You start the day with it (rice cookers have a timer that can be set to start in time for breakfast), you end the day with it, and it's often the centerpiece of a midday meal. In the 1970s, when my father was working as a temple carpenter apprentice in Kyoto, he would come to work with a multilayered bento with egg, vegetables, and fish, prepared by my young mother. The other carpenters would look on enviously as they opened their lunch of white rice with a single red pickled umeboshi plum in the middle. This most basic bento, called hinomaru, or rising sun, looks like the Japanese flag, and for many years following the war, it was a symbolic, austere, and slightly nationalistic lunch.

Rice also plays an important role at Rintaro. It's usually served at the end of the meal as the shime, or final dish, to fill you up after a night of drinking and small dishes. Allowing myself a little melodrama, I tell my new cooks that rice is the real food and that if it's not cooked perfectly, we might as well close the restaurant. We use a blend of Koda Farms' Kokuho Rose rice and another California Koshihikari varietal and cook it in 4-cup batches in a Japanese donabe (clay pot) every 30 to 45 minutes, then transfer it to a rice warmer. Rice in the donabe is significantly better than rice made in an electric rice cooker—the cooked rice is shinier with better texture—although the modern electric rice cookers with their "fuzzy logic" do an excellent job.

Apart from the basic recipe for rice, the recipes in this chapter are for what are essentially elaborate condiments for a bowl of rice. The suffix -don (as in ikura don, yukke don) is shorthand for donburi, the word for an oversized rice dish. Donburi bowls are typically quite large and can hold around 4 cups of cooked rice. Typically, though, you'd fill a donburi halfway with rice and then top it with okazu, a general word that means "food meant to be eaten with rice." No matter the variety, donburi are a substantial meal and can be eaten alone or with a bowl of miso soup and a side of pickles.

NI KAPPU NO KOME

TWO CUPS OF RICE

ニカップの米

Although simple in theory, cooking perfect, aromatic rice is not easy. It's always the most daunting project for me when cooking for a large group. Al dente rice is terrible. Mushy rice is worse. At home, I never cook less than 2 cups / 420 g or more than 4 cups / 840 g at a time.

I grew up eating Koda Farms' Kokuho Rose rice. That's fitting, I suppose, since this rice varietal is, like me, half Japanese. The Koda family first migrated from Fukushima, Japan, in 1908, and hybridized Kokuho Rose after returning to the San Joaquin Valley from internment camps. Raised in California but of Japanese extraction, this variety has a slightly longer grain than most of what's eaten in Japan, but it shares the same toothiness and fragrance of the popular Koshihikari rice, a Japanese short-grain varietal, such as California's Luna Koshihikari .

To make rice: Carefully measure *exactly* 2 cups / 420 g of dry rice into a 2-qt / 1.9L capacity heavy-bottomed pot, Dutch oven, or donabe (Japanese claypot) with a tight fitting lid (or an electric rice cooker). Next, you must wash the rice; washing is important. Equally important is to wash it decisively: the longer the grains stand in the water, the more water they absorb. So, to wash it properly, add enough cold water to cover and vigorously swish the rice with your fingertips. Pour off the milky water, using a wire-mesh strainer to catch any stray grains. Quickly fill the pot three-quarters full of water, then swish and strain again. Repeat until the water runs clear (I wash it five to seven times). Pour the washed rice into the wire-mesh strainer and let drain for 30 minutes.

Pour the rice back into your pot and, if using a Koshihikari varietal (like Luna Koshihikari), add precisely the same amount of water as rice. If using a Kokuho Rose varietal (like Koda Farm) add 1 cup plus 2 tablespoons / 270ml water for every 1 cup / 210 g of rice. To complicate matters, if you buy new crop rice (which comes out in the fall and will be labeled as such on the bag) you'll find 5 to 10 percent less water is needed; the longer rice sits in storage, the more water evaporates from the grain and the more water you'll need to add.

If you're cooking the rice on the stove rather than in a rice cooker, place the pot of rice and water on the stove cover tightly with a lid. I usually place a single sheet of aluminum foil under the lid for a better seal. Bring the pot to a boil over medium-high heat; this should take about 10 minutes. If it boils in less time, you'll want to decrease the heat. You'll know when the rice has reached a boil by the steam spitting out from beneath the lid. Turn down the heat to the lowest possible setting and cook for 15 minutes. Turn off the heat and let the rice sit, undisturbed, for 10 minutes (don't open the lid!). Uncover and mix carefully with a wet bamboo rice paddle.

If you will not be serving immediately, cover the pot with a damp cloth to absorb condensation that may drip from the lid and store, covered, until ready to serve (no longer than 15 to 30 minutes).

To serve, scoop the rice into small rice bowls using a bamboo paddle dipped in water.

TAKENOKO OKOWA

BAMBOO SHOOT RICE

竹の子おこわ

1½ cups / 315 g Japanese rice

¾ cup / 175 g mochi (sweet glutinous) rice

2 or 3 dried shiitake mushrooms

¾ cup plus 2 tablespoons / 200ml warm water

1½ tablespoons mirin

4½ tablespoons / 90 ml usukuchi (light-colored) shoyu

1 tablespoon canola or other neutral oil

½ teaspoon toasted sesame oil

2 freshly picked bamboo shoots (about 1 lb / 450 g), processed (see page 85) or store-bought vacuum-sealed whole bamboo shoots

1¾ cups plus 2 tablespoons / 450ml Katsuobushi Dashi (page 19)

MAKES 6 SERVINGS

Bamboo shoots have a relatively short growing season in the spring. They emerge around the same time as asparagus and, like asparagus, pop out of the ground so quickly you can almost see them growing. Japan is literally covered in bamboo. I used to wander into the bamboo forest behind my grandmother's house, but would quickly leave after seeing the giant spiders. As my father says, everything is small in Japan except the insects, which are hideously oversized. It's common to see baskets of freshly picked shoots on the side of the road with a box to deposit a few hundred yen.

In California, fresh bamboo is a bit harder to find. Through a series of phone calls to the Bamboo Association of California (yes, that's a thing), I found a retired firefighter an hour's drive from San Francisco who maintains his own bamboo grove. For years, every spring I'd drive out to his place and stomp around, looking at the ground for the tips of new shoots. He has several bamboo varieties, all edible, although he doesn't grow the most prized one, called Moso. I now have less time to traverse the state looking for ingredients, but I have found a wonderful farm, Penryn Orchard, which now supplies the restaurant with Moso takenoko. As the bamboo is grown specifically for the shoots, the farmer tends to his grove attentively, watering and mulching as necessary. I look forward to bamboo shoots every year, and we use them on as many dishes as we can during the month-long season. If you can't find fresh bamboo shoots, the par-cooked vacuum-packed ones are a reasonable substitute. You can find them at a good Japanese market. Canned bamboo shoots should be avoided.

This recipe uses a mix of standard Japanese rice and mochi rice (aka sweet glutinous rice). The addition of the mochi rice gives the dish a denser, chewier texture and a lush glossy finish that I love. With the addition of the mochi rice, this becomes an okowa, a special occasion rice dish. There are many versions of okowa, the most famous of which is Sekihan, made with mochi rice and adzuki beans. For hundreds of years, it has been thought to bring good luck on New Year's Day and for weddings and other happy celebrations. I think the start of bamboo season is cause enough for celebration and reason enough to make this special dish.

Combine the two varieties of rice and wash with cold water until the water runs clear. Strain and let stand for 30 minutes.

Put the mushrooms in a small saucepan and add the water. Let stand until soft, about 30 minutes. Add the mirin and 1½ tablespoons of the shoyu to the saucepan, then bring to a simmer over medium-low heat and simmer for 15 minutes. Remove the pan from the heat and let the mushrooms cool in the liquid. Once cool, use your hands to remove the mushrooms from the liquid and gently squeeze them over the pot.

Slice into ⅛-inch / 3 mm strips.

Line a fine-mesh strainer with damp paper towels. Pour the simmering liquid through the prepared strainer into a medium bowl and reserve.

In a small frying pan over medium heat, combine the canola and sesame oils. When the oil is hot, add the sliced mushrooms and cook, stirring, for 3 minutes. Add 2 tablespoons of the reserved simmering liquid and continue to cook, stirring, until the mushrooms have absorbed the liquid, 1 to 2 minutes longer. Remove the pan from the heat and transfer the mushrooms to a small bowl.

Slice the bamboo shoots into thin wedges, about ¼-inch / 6 mm thick. Place the wedges in a medium saucepan and add the dashi and the remaining 3 tablespoons shoyu.

Cut out a circle of parchment paper the size of your saucepan, then press the parchment down into the water so the bamboo stays submerged. Bring the mixture to a boil over high heat, then turn down the heat and simmer for 15 minutes. Remove the pan from the heat and, using a slotted spoon, transfer the bamboo shoots to a small bowl. Strain the simmering liquid through a fine mesh

strainer lined with damp paper towels. Combine with the reserved shiitake simmering liquid; you should have 2⅓ cups / 545ml. Discard any extra.

Put the rice in a 2-qt / 1.9L heavy-bottomed pot, Dutch oven, or donabe (clay pot) with a tight-fitting lid (or an electric rice cooker) and add the reserved liquid. Layer the bamboo shoots and mushrooms on top. To cook rice on the stove: Place the pot on the stove, tightly cover with a lid, and bring to a boil over medium-high heat; this should take about 10 minutes. If it boils in less time, you'll want to reduce the heat on your stove. You'll know when the rice has reached a boil by the steam spitting out from beneath the lid. Reduce the heat to the lowest possible setting and cook for 20 minutes. Turn off the heat, and let the rice sit, undisturbed, for 10 minutes (don't open the lid!). Uncover and mix carefully with a wet bamboo rice paddle. Serve immediately or cover with a damp cloth to absorb condensation that may drip from the lid and store covered until ready to serve, not longer than 15 to 30 minutes.

To serve, scoop the rice into small rice bowls using a bamboo paddle dipped in water.

IKURA DON

CURED STEELHEAD ROE OVER RICE

いくら丼

2 tablespoons plus 1 teaspoon sea salt

4 cups / 950ml cold water

1 lb / 450 g uncured steelhead roe

7 oz / 207ml sake (any kind you like to drink will do)

1 recipe Mori Tsuyu (page 248), chilled

FOR SERVING:

Hot rice

4 to 6 shiso leaves

Toasted nori

Wasabi (see page 57)

MAKES 4 TO 6 SERVINGS

For the last ten years, beginning in the first week of December, I start pestering Shane, my contact at Quinault Pride Seafood, about the steelhead salmon run. Quinault Pride is the fishing arm of the Quinault Indian Nation in Washington's Olympic Peninsula, and they have exclusive rights to commercially fish on the Quinault River. Steelhead is a lovely fish, but it's the roe I get most excited about. During peak spawn, which lasts until February, the eggs are large, firm, and a gorgeous red-orange color.

While the roe are still in their membranes, they are called sujiko, but once the eggs have been separated out and cured with salt, they are called ikura. Although ikura can be stored, heavily salted or frozen, for months, they become gummy and strongly flavored. Fresh, they're like tiny jewels that pop delicately in your mouth with a gentle, briny flavor.

Although the steelhead roe is my favorite, coho and even King salmon roe can be cured as well. They don't have the same size and texture of the steelhead, but they can still be delicious. Once cured, ikura will last, refrigerated, for three or four days. Apart from a thimbleful on a mixed sashimi platter, my favorite way to eat ikura is over rice, with a bit of wasabi and some crisp nori to wrap them into little hand rolls.

Steelhead roe is available in the early winter; you should be able to special order it from any good fish market.

In a small bowl, dissolve the salt in the water and set aside.

To separate the roe if they are still enclosed in their membranes: Place a colander in the sink and set a large bowl of ice water on the counter.

Hold a membrane under a steady stream of very hot tap water (you can wear latex gloves to protect your hands from the heat) and massage the roe sacks with your fingers, freeing the eggs to fall into the colander below. Don't worry about any small pieces of membrane that fall with the eggs. Discard any larger pieces of membrane. When you've worked through about half of the roe, dump the freed eggs into the prepared ice water bath, then finish the

rest. You'll notice that the roe become slightly opaque in the ice water; this is normal.

The next step is to clean away the remaining bits of membrane. The eggs will sink to the bottom of the bowl while the bits of membrane will float. Swirl the eggs and gently pour off the ice water, being careful not to pour the roe down the drain. Fill the bowl again with cold tap water, swirl, and again pour off the water. Repeat several times, until the roe are nearly totally clean. By this point, the roe will be completely opaque and very delicate; drain any remaining water in the bowl and add the prepared salt water.

Almost immediately, as if by magic,

the roe will regain their former translucence and color. Allow them to sit in the salted water for 10 to 30 minutes. The best way to know if they're sufficiently cured is to taste them, beginning at the 10-minute mark and repeating every 5 minutes, until the roe pop in your mouth. If you don't cure them long enough, they'll be too soft and will break immediately; if you let them cure too long, they'll become rubbery balls. Pour the ikura into a colander and let drain for 10 minutes.

To finish the cure, transfer the drained ikura to a medium nonreactive bowl and pour the sake over them; it should just barely cover the eggs. Refrigerate for at least 30 minutes. The sake will wash away some of the salt, help with preservation, and, well, make them taste like sake. At this point, the ikura are stable.

You can continue with the final seasoning or allow them to rest a day or two in the refrigerator, stored in the sake.

For the final seasoning, pour the ikura into a colander and let them drain for 10 minutes. You'll notice that the ikura will be plumper, having absorbed much of the sake. Return them to the bowl and pour the tsuyu over them. As before, it should be enough to barely cover the eggs. Let stand for at least 30 minutes. The ikura can be served immediately or covered and kept refrigerated in the tsuyu for up to 2 days.

To serve, fill each bowl with hot rice. Arrange a shiso leaf on top of the rice and, using a slotted spoon, scoop out a few spoonfuls of ikura and spread them in a thin layer. Garnish with a dab of wasabi. Serve with the sheets of nori to make hand rolls.

MAGURO NO YUKKE DON

MARINATED TUNA OVER RICE

まぐろのユッケ丼

---

1 lb / 450 g sashimi-grade bigeye, yellowfin, or bluefin tuna

Sea salt

TARE

½ cup / 118ml Udon Kaeshi (page 239)

½ cup / 118ml shoyu

1 small garlic clove, finely grated

2 teaspoons ginger juice (from grated ginger)

Scant ⅛ teaspoon sesame oil (a few drops)

FOR SERVING:

Hot rice

4 shiso leaves

4 large egg yolks

2 scallions, thinly sliced

1 tablespoon toasted sesame seeds

Toasted nori

MAKES 4 SERVINGS

I'm always annoyed when people refer to our maguro no yukke as a "poke bowl." It's not that I haven't had delicious poke, but yukke has its own history: it's a Japanese adaptation of yukhoe, the steak tartare from Korea that comes accompanied by a raw egg yolk. The tare, or marinade, for the tuna is extremely simple, especially if you happen to have kaeshi on hand already. Use the garlic sparingly and be sure to put in only a few drops of sesame oil. These flavors are strong and can easily overwhelm the flavor of the fish. Because you'll be eating the fish raw, buy the best-quality sashimi-grade fish you can find.

Pat the tuna with a damp paper towel and cut into ½-inch / 12 mm cubes. Lightly salt and store between layers of paper towels in the refrigerator while you prepare the tare.

To make the tare, combine the kaeshi, shoyu, garlic, ginger juice, and sesame oil in a small bowl. Add the tuna and gently stir to combine. Let stand for 1 minute, then strain, discarding the liquid.

To serve, place a generous amount of rice in four bowls. Arrange a shiso leaf on top of the rice and cover with the tuna, dividing evenly. Form an indentation in the centers of the mounds of tuna and place an egg yolk in each of the indentations. Garnish with the scallions and sesame seeds. Serve with the sheets of nori, either torn and mixed into each dish, or use to make hand rolls.

KATSUDON

PORK KATSU AND EGG OVER RICE

KATSUDON TSUYU

1¼ cups / 300ml
Katsuobushi Dashi
(page 19)

¼ cup / 60ml mirin

¼ cup / 60ml white
shoyu or usukuchi
(light-colored) shoyu

1 tablespoon sugar

1¼ cups / 20 g shaved
katsuobushi

KATSUDON

½ recipe Tonkatsu
(page 151)

1 tablespoon vegetable
or other neutral oil

1½ yellow onions, thinly
sliced

2 large eggs

5 stems mitsuba, leaves
separated, stems cut
into 1-inch / 2.5 cm
lengths

Hot rice, for serving

Ground sansho powder,
for serving

MAKES 4 SERVINGS

One summer a few years ago, my friend Shin Nakahara took me to a tiny basement restaurant in Tokyo. It was barely visible from the street, just a few blocks from the famous Shibuya Crossing, a cramped space that could seat no more than ten people shoulder to shoulder. They had one item on the menu: katsudon. Two cooks worked together, one frying tonkatsu and slicing it, the other simmering the tonkatsu with seasoned dashi, onion, and a glossy coating of barely cooked egg. It came served over rice with a side of miso soup and pickles. Now I've written before about how Japan excels at the one-dish restaurant, and this was one of the best examples. Their katsudon always comes to mind when I make this dish. When made properly, the pork is perfectly cooked, and the crunch of the panko is mostly, but not totally, softened by the simmering. The egg and seasoned dashi combine to form a loose custard on the bottom, but the egg yolk on the top remains bright orange and jammy.

Katsudon, like oyakodon (page 217), are typically made in individual portions. I've scaled up the recipe to serve four and cook it in a larger pan. If mitsuba is not available, substitute one scallion, cut as described on page 74, adding it as a garnish at the end.

To make the tsuyu: Combine the dashi, mirin, shoyu, and sugar in a small saucepan. Bring to a boil, then remove from the heat and add the katsuobushi. Let the katsuobushi settle, then set aside to cool. Once cool, strain the liquid through a fine-mesh sieve lined with a damp paper towel.

To make the katsudon: Prepare the tonkatsu and slice it as directed for serving. The tonkatsu should be freshly fried when you begin, although they do not need to be piping hot; room temperature is fine.

Heat a 12-inch / 30 cm skillet over medium heat. Add the oil and when the oil is hot, add the onion. Cook, stirring, until the onion is soft, 3 to 4 minutes.

Add ¼ cup / 60ml of the tsuyu and bring to a low boil.

Crack the eggs into a small bowl and break the yolks but don't beat them. Turn down the heat to medium-low and lay your sliced katsu in the pan. Pour the egg mixture over the katsu. Add the mitsuba leaves and stems. Cover and let cook undisturbed for 5 to 6 minutes, until the egg whites are set but the yolks are still runny. Using a spatula, divide the katsudon into four pieces.

To serve, spoon hot rice into four bowls, then top each with a section of katsudon. Serve immediately with the sansho alongside.

OYAKODON

CHICKEN AND EGG OVER RICE

親子丼

OYAKODON TSUYU

1¼ cups / 300ml
Katsuobushi Dashi
(page 19)

¼ cup / 60ml mirin

¼ cup / 60ml white
shoyu or usukuchi
(light-colored) shoyu

1 tablespoon sugar

1¼ cups / 20 g shaved
katsuobushi

OYAKODON

1½ lb / 680 g skin-on
boneless chicken
thighs, cut into bite-
sized pieces

Sea salt

1 large yellow onion,
thinly sliced

8 large eggs

20 mitsuba stems,
leaves separated and
stems cut into 1-inch /
2.5 cm pieces

¼ cup /60ml vegetable
oil or other neutral oil

Hot rice for serving

Ground sansho powder,
for serving

MAKES 4 SERVINGS

This egg and chicken recipe is the most famous of the *oyako* ("mother and child') dishes in Japan—a concept that is both charming and a touch disturbing. The idea, if it's not obvious, is that you are serving the chicken, the mother, along with its child, the egg. I like to use the best-pastured eggs I can find for oyakodon, both because they're the most flavorful and because their yolks are an almost orange-yellow. Rather than beating the eggs into the mixture, I like to simply break the yolks. The egg cooks together with the seasoned dashi to make a half-set custard, with any unset dashi settling into the rice below. Be careful not to overcook the egg. The whites should be set, but some of the yolk should still be a little runny and bright. Oyakodon is typically garnished with mitsuba, a common herb in Japan that has a cedar-y, celerylike flavor. Ground sansho powder is added at the table.

In Japan, there is a pan made specifically for the oyakodon. It's small, resembling a saucer, with gently sloped edges to help slide out the chicken and egg mixture, and it comes with a tight-fitting lid to trap the steam. Oyakodon are typically made in individual servings, but given that you probably want to eat with your dining companions and serve them all at once, I've scaled the recipe to serve four from a single large pan. If you can't find boneless, skin-on chicken thighs, you can either debone them yourself or substitute skinless thighs. If mitsuba is not available, substitute two scallions, cut as described on page 74, adding them as a garnish at the end.

To make the oyakodon tsuyu: In a small saucepan, combine the dashi, mirin, shoyu, and sugar. Bring to a boil over medium-high heat, then remove the pan from the heat and add the katsuobushi. Let the katsuobushi settle, then set the pan aside to cool. Once cool, strain through a fine-mesh sieve lined with a paper towel.

To make the oyakodon: Heat a 12-inch / 30.5 cm skillet over medium heat. Place the chicken pieces in the pan, skin-side down, and salt lightly. Cook until the skin has crisped, about 3 minutes. Scoot the chicken to the side of the pan and add the onion. Cook, stirring, until the onion is soft, 3 to 4 minutes. Evenly distribute the chicken and onion over the bottom of the pan, then add the tsuyu and bring to a low boil.

Crack the eggs into a small bowl and break the yolks but don't beat them. Turn down the heat to medium-low and pour the eggs over the chicken and onion mixture. Add the mitsuba leaves and stems. Cover the pan with a tight-fitting lid and let cook undisturbed for 4 to 5 minutes, until the egg whites are set but the yolks are still runny. Using a spatula, divide the oyakodon into four pieces.

To serve, spoon hot rice into four bowls and top each with a section of oyakodon. Serve immediately, with the sansho alongside.

MABODOFU DON

SPICY TOFU AND PORK OVER RICE

マーボー豆腐丼

- 2 (14-oz / 400 g) packages silken tofu
- 2 tablespoons vegetable or other neutral oil
- 1 tablespoon toasted sesame oil
- 3 tablespoons minced ginger
- 3 tablespoons minced garlic
- 1 to 3 Thai bird chiles, stemmed, seeded, and sliced
- 1 lb / 450 g ground pork
- ½ medium yellow onion, finely chopped
- 8 tablespoons / 167 g red miso
- 2 tablespoons sugar
- 2 tablespoons tobanjan
- ½ teaspoon ground black pepper
- 2½ cups / 590ml chicken stock
- 2 tablespoons potato starch

FOR SERVING:

Hot rice
Ground sansho pepper
Sliced scallions

MAKES 6 TO 8 SERVINGS

Mabodofu, like gyoza, is another Japanese version of a Chinese dish and was something my mother made frequently when I was a kid. Like curry, it's a dish that's incomplete without the accompanying rice. I've always found mabodofu deeply satisfying, and of all the foods we make at the restaurant, it's the one I eat the most. Almost every night when I'm on the line, I'll sneak over to the rice station to make a small taster portion for myself. The mabodofu I make at the restaurant is based on a taste memory from childhood. Although the ratio of meat to tofu and the consistency is the same, I've made a few changes to the seasoning, replacing the fermented black beans my mother used to use with tobanjan, a Japanese-made Sichuan-style paste of fermented broad beans and chile peppers. I also add black pepper and ground sansho pepper to give it a multidimensional spiciness.

Tobanjan is readily available in most Japanese grocery stores. And you should choose the best ground pork you can find. Although you can make mabodofu with medium or firm tofu, I prefer the lush texture of the silken variety. It's very delicate, though, and if you're not gentle in your handling of it, you'll end up with a tofu scramble.

Cut the tofu into 1-inch / 2.5 cm cubes and gently place in a bowl; add hot tap water to cover.

Heat the vegetable and sesame oils in a wok, 12-inch / 30 cm cast-iron pan, or large Dutch oven over high heat until the oil starts to shimmer. Add the ginger, garlic, and chiles and sauté for a few seconds until fragrant. Add the pork, break it up with a wooden spoon, and continue to cook over high heat until the meat has begun to brown. Decrease the heat to medium and add the onion. Cook until the onion becomes soft and translucent, about 7 minutes. Add the miso, sugar, tobanjan, black pepper,

and chicken stock. Bring to a boil, then turn down the heat and simmer for 8 to 10 minutes, or until the pork is tender. Gently add the cut tofu to the meat sauce and return to a simmer.

In a small bowl, mix the potato starch with ¼ cup / 60ml cold water, and gently stir it into the mabodofu. Cook for another minute, until the sauce has thickened.

To serve, spoon hot rice into a large serving bowl and then gently add the mabodofu. Top with a pinch of ground sansho pepper and a mound of thinly sliced scallions.

VARIATION:

For a secret crunch, mound 1 tablespoon tenkasu tenpura bits (see page 225) under the scallions.

BIFU KARE RAISU

BEEF CURRY RICE

ビーフカレーライス

3 tablespoons
 vegetable or other
 neutral oil

2 lb / 900 g beef chuck,
 cut into ¾-inch / 2 cm
 pieces

2 tablespoons kurozato
 black sugar or dark
 brown sugar

1 tablespoon finely
 minced ginger

2 garlic cloves, finely
 chopped

3 medium onions,
 chopped

1 apple, grated

¼ cup / 60 g S&B brand
 curry powder

3 tablespoons mirin

2 tablespoons shoyu

1 qt / 950ml chicken
 stock

Sea salt to taste

2 tablespoons
 konbucha, kelp tea
 powder (optional)

1 large Yukon Gold
 potato, scrubbed
 and cut into ½-inch /
 12 mm pieces

2 large carrots, cut
 into ½-inch / 12 mm
 pieces

1 tablespoon potato
 starch

FOR SERVING:

Hot rice

Yogurt Raita (page 223)

**Store-bought
 fukujinzuke pickles
 (optional)**

MAKES 6 SERVINGS

In high school, curry rice was the first dish I made to sell as part of my senior project pop-up restaurant. I used packaged cubes of S&B curry to flavor it, which were available in the "oriental" section at the country market where I grew up. In college, I made curry for myself, for my girlfriend (now wife and editor), and for my friends and roommates. And even now, when there is a birth or a death, curry is usually what I deliver.

Curry rice was such a big part of my culinary landscape that it wasn't until I was in my twenties, when it struck me how odd it is that Japan has its own national version. It's one of Japan's most popular dishes, a dish that on average is eaten almost once a week. Like many *yoshoku* (Western food) dishes, it was introduced during the Meiji era in the late 1800s, when Japan was finally opening to the world. Curry came to Japan via the British Navy, who in turn had adapted it from India during the Raj. As with almost everything the Japanese borrowed from the outside world, curry rice was quickly transformed into a uniquely Japanese dish. The Japanese version is quite sweet, not particularly spicy, and, because it's thickened with a roux, it has the consistency of gravy.

This recipe is something of an improvement to the curry I ate and cooked while growing up, and it's one that I've been refining for years. I no longer use prepackaged curry cubes, which contain palm oil and an unpronounceable list of preservatives. Instead, I opt for the S&B brand curry powder (and yes, here the specific brand is important) and thicken the stew with a roux. As with any beef stew, much of the success of the dish depends on proper browning and deglazing for a deep, beefy flavor. My version uses kurozato, unrefined black lump sugar, traditionally made in Kagoshima and Okinawa. I caramelize the sugar in the pan after browning the beef; this gives it a nice depth of flavor and deep color. The onions play a crucial role as well. By weight, the amount of onion equals that of the beef. The onion forms the structure of the curry, and with the addition of the apple, lends most of the sweetness. I cook the onions over low heat, combined with the apple, spices, and seasoning, until they are melting and almost jammy, then I blend the mixture with chicken stock into a silky sauce. If this step seems too fussy, however, you can skip it; the finished curry will just have a more rustic texture. Curry rice almost always includes potatoes and carrots. Use a waxy potato like Yukon Gold; russets or other starchy varieties disintegrate too easily and add too much starch to the sauce.

In Japan, curry rice is served in a shallow bowl or on a plate. And perhaps, given its status as a "Western food," it's eaten with a spoon rather than chopsticks. I grew up eating curry rice with raita, a tribute to my mother's interest in Indian food. And although it's definitely not traditional, the cooling cucumber and yogurt go very well with Japanese curry. Fittingly, given the history of the dish, as kids, we ate it with Major Grey's mango chutney, a condiment reputedly created by a 19th-century British officer in British India. This is also not traditional in Japan, where curry is commonly served with a bright red pickle called fukujinzuke. In fact, it's a pickle that is *only* served with curry rice. At Rintaro, we marry national tradition and my own personal tradition and serve the curry with both raita and fukujinzuke. Our in-house pickle expert, Yuko Sato, makes a lovely fukujinzuke with carrot, fennel, turnip, ginger, and beets (for color), but good store-bought fukujinzuke are widely available at Japanese markets.

Heat the oil in a large heavy-bottomed pot over high heat until it starts to smoke. Season the beef with kosher salt. Working in two batches, brown the beef until it's deeply colored on all sides, turning occasionally, and reducing the heat if needed, 6 to 8 minutes per batch. Although you need to color the beef well, you will use the pan drippings to flavor the curry, so take care not to let them burn. With a slotted spoon, transfer the beef to a large bowl, leaving the fat behind. Turn down the heat to medium-high; add the kurozato and a splash of water to deglaze the pan and to help melt the sugar. Continue to cook, stirring, until the water has evaporated and the sugar has started to caramelize (look for a whiff of smoke).

Turn down the heat to low and add the ginger and garlic, and cook, stirring, until fragrant, 15 seconds. Add a splash of water to keep the garlic from burning and then add the onion, apple, curry powder, mirin, and shoyu. Cook, stirring occasionally, until the onion becomes soft and jammy, 15 to 20 minutes. Remove the pot from the heat and stir in the chicken stock.

Transfer the onion and stock mixture to a blender. Working in batches, blend on high speed until smooth, then transfer to a large bowl.

Wipe the pot clean and return the mixture to the pot. (You can omit this step if you'd like a more rustic texture.) Bring the mixture to a boil over medium-high heat, then turn down the heat to medium-low and simmer for 20 minutes, until slightly thickened and glossy. Taste for seasoning, adding the salt and the konbucha (if using) to taste.

Add the beef and any accumulated juices to the curry sauce and simmer, uncovered, stirring frequently, until the beef is almost tender, 30 to 40 minutes. Add the potato and carrots, cover, and cook until tender, 20 to 30 minutes.

In a small bowl whisk together the potato starch with ⅓ cup / 80ml cold water to combine (the starch settles as it sits) and slowly pour into the curry, stirring constantly to avoid starchy lumps. Return the curry to a boil and stir until thickened, about 1 minute.

The curry can be served immediately or made ahead and reheated. It will keep in an airtight container in the refrigerator for up to 3 days. I don't recommend freezing it, since the potatoes and carrots will suffer.

When ready to serve, spoon the curry into a large bowl. Serve with rice, yogurt raita, and the pickles (if using).

YOGURT RAITA

1 Japanese cucumber

½ teaspoon sea salt

1 garlic clove

2 cups / 480 g plain whole milk Greek yogurt

MAKES ABOUT 2 CUPS / 480 G

Using a mandoline or a sharp knife, thinly slice the cucumber. Place the slices in a small bowl and toss with the salt. Let stand until the salt begins to draw out water from the cucumbers, about 5 minutes. Massage the cucumber slices to release their liquid, gently at first to keep them from breaking, then more vigorously as they start to expel water. Gently squeeze out as much liquid as you can from the cucumbers, wipe the bowl dry, and return the squeezed cucumbers to the bowl.

Using a mortar and pestle, pound the garlic with a pinch of salt into a smooth paste (or grate the garlic on a rasp-style grater). Stir the garlic into the cucumbers and add the yogurt. Season to taste with additional salt.

Serve right away or store in an airtight container in the refrigerator for up to 1 day.

VARIATIONS

This curry can be made with chicken instead of beef. Use an equal amount of boneless, skin-on chicken thighs, browning them skin-side down as you would the beef, or with an assortment of chicken parts (though if you use white meat, you want to pull those pieces from the curry sauce sooner, so they don't dry out). Whole boiled eggs are also a good addition to a chicken version, making it another *Oyako*, "mother and child" dish (see page 217 for oyakodon). As for vegetables, kabocha squash is a nice addition, although its cooking time is shorter, so you'll want to add it just 10 minutes before the curry is finished. If you want a lighter dish, broccoli florets, orange or purple cauliflower, and green beans can be blanched in salted water, then arranged over the rice before scooping the curry over.

KAKIAGE DON

MIXED TENPURA OVER RICE

かきあげ丼

Kaisen Kakiage Tenpura
(page 171)
Mori Tsuyu (page 248)

FOR SERVING:
Hot rice
Grated daikon
Grated ginger
Ground sansho pepper
(optional)

MAKES 4 SERVINGS

While all of the elements of this recipe are explained separately in different parts of the book, put together, the kakiage tenpura, rice, and mori tsuyu become something greater than their parts. The mori tsuyu is the secret ingredient. Not only does this highly seasoned dashi mixture flavor the kakiage, but it seeps through into the rice, seasoning that as well. When you've eaten the kakiage, the rice remaining at the bottom of the bowl, flecked with tenpura bits, is delicious. This recipe is a bit of a juggling act. The rice must be hot from the pot, the kakiage straight from the oil, and the mori tsuyu, which you'll pour over it, also heated to a boil. You'll know you're successful if you achieve a sizzle as you pour the mori tsuyu over the tenpura. At first I cringed at the idea of ruining the perfect crunch of the kakiage by pouring liquid over it, but I love the almost silken texture that the formerly crunchy batter develops when doused in mori tsuyu. I'm of the pouring-over camp, but there are also some famous tenpura donburi (of which kakiage don is a subset) restaurants in Japan, where the chef will dunk the kakiage in the tsuyu before laying it atop a bowl of rice. In either case, crunchiness is not the point; rather, it's the marriage of the rice and tenpura, brought together by tsuyu.

Mix the kakiage batter as directed on page 172 and prepare to fry the kakiage. When you're ready to serve, bring the tsuyu to a gentle simmer in a small saucepan over medium heat. Fry the kakiage as directed on page 172.

Spoon the rice into four bowls, place a kakiage on top, and pour ½ cup / 120ml of the hot tsuyu over the top. Serve with the grated daikon and ginger on top and a sprinkle of sansho pepper (if using).

TENKASU

TENPURA BITS

2 cups / 480ml cold water
1 whole egg
1 cup / 175 g pastry or
   cake flour
Canola oil, for frying

MAKES ABOUT 4 CUPS / 945ML

Tenkasu or tenpura bits, as we call them in the restaurant, are the excess bits that you skim from the oil as you are frying tenpura. At Soba Ra, my mentor, Kanji Nakatani, never used them. He said that they are "kasu"—the dregs. But I like the bit of richness and crispiness that they give to a dish.

Mix the egg and water and measure 1 cup / 236ml of egg water into a bowl. Discard the rest. Sift the flour over the water and mix until just combined. You want to do everything you can to minimize gluten formation, so don't overmix it and keep it cold. It'll hold for 30 minutes.

Heat the canola oil in a pan, at least 3 inches / 7.5 cm deep, to 330°F / 165°C.

Transfer half of the batter into a measuring cup with a spout. Very slowly dribble the batter into the hot oil, careful not to let the oil bubble up and overflow. Allow to fry until they are crisp, about 5 minutes per batch; they should only take on a little color. Scoop the bits out with a fine mesh strainer or slotted spoon and let drain in a fine-mesh strainer over a bowl (to catch excess oil). Repeat with the remaining batter, allowing the oil to return to temperature between batches. Once they are cool, store in a sealed container for a day or two.

UDON うどん

I LEARNED TO MAKE UDON at a restaurant about an hour north of Tokyo called Soba Ro from its chef/owner Kanji Nakatani. As the name suggests, Soba Ro is not an udon restaurant. It's known for its soba, toothsome, flavorful buckwheat noodles that Nakatani makes by hand and serves in dozens of different ways. I loved them and Kanji-san offered to show me how to make them—provided I could commit three years to the training. The soba-making craft is notoriously difficult to perfect. As much as I might have liked to spend three years learning to make soba, I had recently married, and I had only planned to spend six months in Japan. So instead, I asked if he could show me how to make udon, which I also loved and which are also easier to learn how to make. Kanji-san always had udon on the menu, mostly for kids and for feeding the staff, and he agreed to teach me. For months, I made udon alongside him, until the staff grew tired of eating my misshapen noodles.

When I returned to California, I started making udon in my garage-turned-catering kitchen. The first challenge was finding the right flour in America, and my early experiments using all-purpose and bread flours resulted in rough noodles without udon's distinctive texture. I finally got my hands on kyorikiko flour, which has a gluten percentage similar to all-purpose but is much more finely milled, and that was the key that unlocked the recipe for me. After more months of practice, I began to make udon similar to what Kanji served at Soba Ro. When I opened Rintaro, udon became one of our signature items, with a whole section of the menu devoted to them.

A couple of years after the restaurant opened, I took a research trip to Takamatsu in Kagawa Prefecture, the udon capital of the world (think what Naples is to pizza) and the birthplace of sanuki udon, the most ubiquitous and popular style. In Takamatsu, most udon restaurants are set up cafeteria-style, with a big open kitchen and counter service. I was shocked by how cheap their dishes were—less than $3 a bowl for a basic kake udon (hot udon with broth), topped with as many scallions and tenpura bits as you wanted. (They are so inexpensive, in fact, that there are nearly no fast-food restaurants in Takamatsu, because they can't compete on price!) I ate udon for breakfast, lunch, and dinner for several days and spent an afternoon working at a new restaurant owned by a friend of a friend. Here, I learned some of the finer points of making and kneading udon dough and how to season the udon soup.

As I have for almost the last decade, I still roll and cut almost all the udon noodles served at the restaurant myself. Early in the morning, before I arrive, one of my cooks will knead the dough underfoot to develop strong gluten, then, in the early afternoon the dough will be re-formed and kneaded again. And just before service, I set up a large board in our back dining room for the final cutting. I don't know if I'll ever consider myself an udon master, even after years of practice, but I have learned that with a few pieces of equipment, the right ingredients, and some time and patience, it's possible to make excellent udon at home. In this chapter, I'll introduce you to the pleasures of udon, both the practice of making the noodles by hand and the deeply satisfying dishes you can create using your own udon noodles.

UDON MEN

UDON NOODLES

---

2 cups less 1 tablespoon / 457ml water

Scant 4 tablespoons / 54 g fine sea salt

8 cups plus 2 tablespoons / 1kg kyorikiko flour

3 to 4 cups / 570 to 760 g potato starch, for dusting

MAKES 3 TO 3½ LB UDON (1.5KG); SERVES 8 TO 10

To be successful with this recipe, you'll need to use Japanese kyorikiko flour. It has a gluten content similar to American all-purpose flour but is more finely milled and includes less of the wheat germ. This results in a silky, pliable dough that, when properly kneaded, has the texture of an earlobe. When I first started making udon after returning from Japan, I tried all sorts of different flours: Italian 00, bleached all-purpose, unbleached all-purpose, bread flours of every stripe—and none of them were right. I'll never forget one of my early attempts at udon at a pop-up I hosted at a friend's store. A Japanese guy from Takamatsu, the center of the udon universe, came in. He tasted my udon and said, "I really enjoyed your *homemade* noodles." It was so subtle but such a burn.

In addition to the flour, which can be purchased online, you'll need several pieces of inexpensive equipment to make udon: a very large bowl, at least 16 inches / 40 cm in diameter; a 3 ft by 1½-inch / 91 by 4 cm wooden rolling pin, or a comparably sized dowel from a hardware store; a 4 by 3-ft / 122 by 91 cm rolling surface, such as an extra-large cutting board or a piece of birch plywood; a ruler; an udon knife (or a cleaver or other heavy, straight-edge knife), and two 3 by-3 ft / 91 by 91 cm pieces of oilcloth or heavy-duty painter's plastic, for covering the udon while you knead it underfoot. Speaking of that: you'll also need to wear clean socks. This dough becomes very stiff, and in order to develop the gluten that gives udon its signature texture, you'll be kneading it underfoot with the whole weight of your body.

Good udon is all about texture. The phrase in Japanese is *suru suru*, *koshi ga aru*, which means "slippery but with a chewy texture." By using the correct flour and building the gluten through vigorous kneading underfoot, the udon can cook for a long time without disintegrating. The surface of the udon noodle becomes soft, but the core remains intact, and during those last few minutes of boiling time, the noodles almost puff up. After boiling, the udon are washed in several changes of water and then rinsed in ice water. This icy soak is what makes the udon texture special: it tightens the udon, a process called *shimeru* in Japanese. *Shimeru* roughly translates to "to close" or "to tighten something up." (The concept of *shime* applies to sashimi, too; there we use either ice or salt to tighten the fish.) With udon, the interior of the noodle remains chewy, but the outside stays quite soft. This recipe makes a large quantity of noodles, but the process is enough work that I think it's sensible to make a big batch and freeze what you don't plan to eat within a few days. To freeze the noodles, lay them in resealable storage bags, squeeze the air from the bags, and then seal them. They'll keep, frozen, for up to 3 months. When ready to use, boil the frozen noodles without thawing.

TO MAKE THE DOUGH

Combine the water and salt in a medium bowl and whisk vigorously until the salt is dissolved.

Sift the flour into a large bowl.

Set a damp towel on a work surface and set the bowl on top of the towel. (This will help keep the bowl from wobbling while you're mixing the dough.) Make sure the work surface and the bowl are at a height that is ergonomically convenient, so you don't strain your back.

Pour about 80 percent of the salted water over the sifted mound of flour in a circular motion, distributing it as evenly as possible. It's important to incorporate the water into the flour quickly so the flour is saturated evenly.

To combine the flour and water, first use your hands like scoops, with your fingers extended and your palms facing up, lifting the flour and letting it fall through your fingers. When the flour is damp, turn your hands palm down and move each hand rapidly in a circular motion, fingers loosely extended, as though you're vigorously wiping a table. You want to create a cornmeal consistency (similar to the consistency of pie dough after you cut the butter into the flour) and you want to avoid lumps. Scrape the sides and the bottom of the bowl with your fingers as needed to mix in any dry patches of flour. Rub any clumps of dough off your fingers into the bowl.

Add the remaining water-salt mixture. Again, mix quickly to evenly incorporate the water with the flour. With the second addition of water, the flour-water mixture will begin to clump. Once again, sweep the bottom and the sides of the bowl with your fingers to make sure any dry flour is mixed in. Continue to work the mixture until it starts to form a dough.

Knead the dough aggressively in the bowl, pressing with the full weight of your body, for 5 minutes or until it is quite firm. (The dough will still be pretty shaggy and rough.) Shape into a lump, then flatten into a rough flat disk.

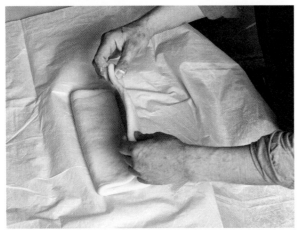

TO KNEAD THE DOUGH

Spread out the oilcloth (shiny side up) on your work surface. Place the dough in the middle of the oilcloth. Fold up the bottom third of the cloth over the dough, then the top third down over it. Then fold the left and right sides of the cloth over the center to create a crisply wrapped package that's 12 inches / 30 cm square.

Lay the dough package on a tatami mat or a clean piece of cardboard on the floor. Remove your shoes and using your stocking feet, step firmly on the package, pressing the dough from the center to the edges of the oilcloth. Use your heels and the outer edges of your feet to push the dough into the corners of the oilcloth packet and continue working the dough with your feet until it has been flattened enough to fill the oilcloth packet and is evenly pressed into all sides and corners.

Unwrap the dough and fold it in thirds, like a business letter. Rewrap in the oilcloth, again creating a wrapped package that's 12 inches square, taking care that the edges of the oilcloth parcel aren't crinkled. Repeat the kneading by foot, until the dough again fills the oilcloth packet. After each kneading, the dough will become firmer and the color more uniform. Unwrap the dough, fold into thirds again, rewrap, and knead underfoot for a third time.

For the fourth and final kneading, you'll change the shape of your package. Fold the dough in half and form a 6 by 12-inch / 15 by 30 cm package. For this final kneading, it's important that the oilcloth be very crisply folded. If the packet becomes crinkled or unwrapped as you knead, stop kneading, rewrap, and continue. Continue kneading underfoot, until you have a very even 6 by 12-inch rectangle. Let the dough rest in its wrapper at room temperature for at least two hours and up to a day.

TO FORM THE DANGO

Using a scale, divide the dough crosswise into two equal pieces, each about 26 oz / 750 g. Working with one piece of dough at a time, lightly moisten one side of the square of dough with water, then orient the dough so that the moistened side is facing you.

Begin by folding the top right corner of the piece of dough into the center and then continue around the entire piece of dough, stretching the edges and three other corners toward the center to form what is known as a dango.

Through this process, you're transforming a rectangle of dough into an even round ball of dough. If you're familiar with bread making, this process is similar to making a boule, albeit with dough that's much stiffer. Once you have a ball, arrange it seam side down on a work surface. Cup your hands around the ball. Your non-dominant hand will remain steady, anchoring the dough. With your dominant hand, cup the top of the ball of dough (so the back of your hand is facing you), then rotate your hand toward the work surface, tucking the dough, which will help develop some surface tension.

Continue this tucking motion, until the top surface is perfectly rounded and smooth and until there's a skinny "neck" where the ball meets your work surface.

With gentle, even pressure, press down on the ball, pressing the neck into the ball of dough and forming a chubby disk. Repeat with the second piece of dough.

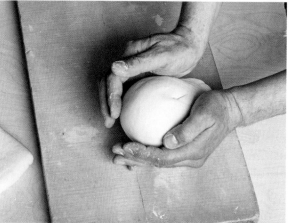

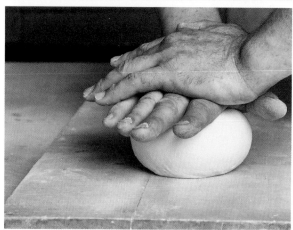

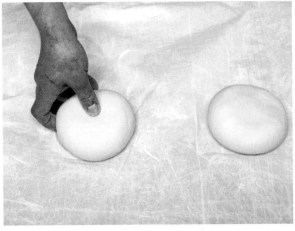

TO FORM THE ZABUTON

Place the two dango side by side on the shiny side of the oilcloth and dust lightly with potato starch. Cover with a second piece of oilcloth, shiny side down, and stepping gingerly, squish each ball into a nearly perfect round circle.

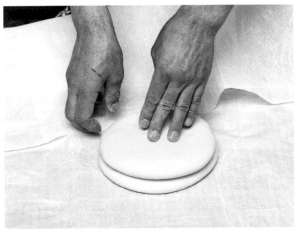

Uncover, stack the rounds of dough, one on top of the other, and re-cover with the second sheet of oilcloth. In stocking feet, step onto the stack with both feet and knead underfoot as you turn your body around twice. Pull back the oilcloth, move the top dough round to the bottom position, re-cover, and repeat. Repeat four more times for a total of six turns underfoot, moving the top round of dough to the bottom each time.

The dough should retain its nearly perfect circular shape, just becoming wider and thinner with each knead underfoot. After six turns underfoot, the circles of dough should be around 11 inches / 28 cm in diameter.

These flat disks of dough are called zabuton. Wrap in a large resealable bag and let rest at room temperature for at least an hour and up to a day.

TO ROLL OUT THE UDON

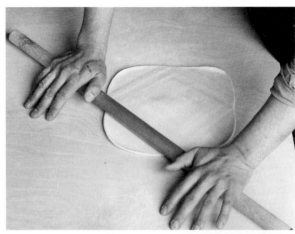

To roll out the udon: Place one of the zabuton in the middle of a large rolling surface. The first step will be to turn the circle into a square. Dust the zabuton very lightly with potato starch. Using a dowel and light pressure, begin by rolling the top third of the dough away from you, flattening and extending it by about 2 inches / 15 cm to form a corner. Turn the dough 90 degrees clockwise, and repeat the process of flattening and extending it by about 2 inches to make a second corner. Repeat with the last 2 corners to make a rough square.

To extend the square, lay the dough with one corner near the bottom of the rolling surface. Wrap the dough around the dowel, starting with the bottom corner. Bring the dowel close to you, then roll the dowel (with the dough still wrapped around it) away from you, applying medium pressure downwards onto the center of the dough with your palms. Repeat this step five more times for a total of six rolls. Unfurl the dough from the dowel and rotate it 90 degrees clockwise. Once again, starting with the corner closest to you, roll the dough around the dowel, and repeat with five rolls. Unfurl, rotate, and roll again four times. And finally, unfurl, rotate, and roll the dough three final times. At this point, the dough should have stretched and thinned into a larger square.

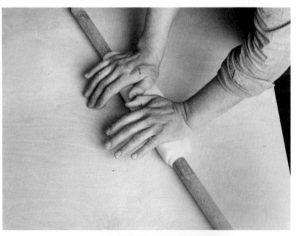

Now you can begin the process of lengthening and flattening. Lay the dough with one of the square's sides parallel to the bottom of the rolling surface. Roll the dough around the dowel and, using medium, even pressure, roll it away from you eight times. Unfurl the dough, rotate it 180 degrees. Roll it back onto the rolling pin and repeat with another eight rolls.

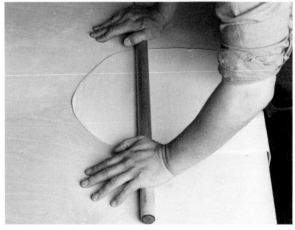

Unroll the dough and, beginning at the center, roll the dowel away from you, until the dough is about 3/16-inch / 5 mm thick. Rotate the dough 180 degrees and again, beginning in the center, continue rolling the dough away from you until the entire sheet of dough is an even 3/16-inch thick and measures 24 by 15 inches / 60 by 38 cm (if you need to, you can pull half the dough off the edge of your work surface so you have more leverage for rolling).

Spread the dough out flat on the rolling surface and sweep your hand over the dough to feel for thick spots. Do a final pass with the dowel.

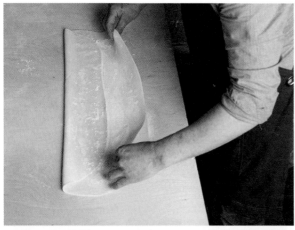

TO CUT THE UDON

Lightly dust the udon dough with potato starch. Fold the dough in thirds, like a business letter, top down first and then bottom up. Sift a small amount of potato starch over the top.

Prepare your cutting board. Choose one that is long enough to accommodate the udon dough, or, cut directly on your rolling surface. Before placing the dough on the cutting surface, cover the surface with a generous, even layer of potato starch. The starch will act as a cushion under the dough and when you cut each noodle, it will prevent them from sticking to one another. Set the dough, long side facing you, on top of the potato starch.

Using an udon knife, cleaver, or other straight-edge knife and beginning at one end of the dough, cut the dough into $3/16$-inch- / 5 mm-wide noodles; use a ruler to measure the first few cuts, continuing until all the dough has been cut.

Grab a handful of the cut noodles by their ends, lift them off the work surface, and shake them to knock off excess potato starch. Take the handful of noodles by both ends and gently whack them on the work surface to shake off even more of the starch, then gather the noodles into a neat hank and set on a sheet pan. Repeat the process with the remaining noodles. With a pastry scraper, scrape up the potato starch from your work surface and transfer to a storage container; it can be reused.

At this stage, you can either cook the udon or store them for a day or two in an airtight container in the refrigerator.

TO COOK THE UDON

Fill a large bowl with cold water and set aside.

Bring a large pot of unsalted water to a boil over high heat. Cook the udon for 15 minutes; this may seem like a long time, and if you were to taste a noodle before the 15-minute mark, it might taste pleasingly al dente, but continue cooking the noodles for the full 15 minutes. In the last few minutes of cooking, the noodles puff up, increasing in volume, and acquire their distinctive soft-but-chewy texture.

With a large strainer, scoop the udon from the pot. (If you will be serving the udon hot, make sure to reserve the cooking water to preheat your serving bowls and reheat the udon.)

Immediately plunge the udon into the prepared cold-water bath. Rub them vigorously between your hands to remove the potato starch. Drain the udon in a colander, refill the bowl with cold water, and wash again. Dump the water one more time, then refill the bowl with cold water, add a handful of ice, and rinse the udon one last time. Strain and proceed as instructed with your udon recipe.

Be sure to serve the udon right away (ideally within 10 minutes of cooking); any longer and the noodles will lose their distinctive and delicious texture.

UDON DASHI

UDON BROTH

8½ cups / 2L water

1½ cups / 40 g cleaned iriko

1 (4 by 3-inch / 10 by 7.5 cm) piece konbu

1 dried shiitake mushroom

2½ cups / 40 g shaved katsuobushi

MAKES 7½ CUPS / 1.8L

When I started making udon, I used our standard katsuobushi dashi for the udon soup (page 238). But on an udon research trip to Takamatsu in Kagawa Prefecture, I learned about a dashi specific to udon. This udon dashi uses a combination of dried anchovies, known as iriko (or niboshi), konbu, dried shiitake mushrooms, and katsuobushi. The dashi is light but deeply flavored and complex. The shiitake add just the right amount of funk.

The iriko we use at the restaurant come from the Seto Inland Sea near Kagawa Prefecture (which also happens to be the prefecture best known for its udon). To clean them, snap off the heads. Use your thumbnail to split the backs of the fish in half lengthwise. Remove the dried black innards. Feed the heads and guts to your cat or compost them. Iriko can be stored in an airtight container in a cool, dark place for several months. You can purchase good-quality iriko online. If your tap water is tasty to drink, there's no need to use bottled water for the dashi.

Pour the water into a large pot and add the iriko, konbu, and shiitake. Let soak overnight refrigerated.

The following day, bring the contents of the pot to a simmer over low heat. When bubbles start to form along the sides of the pot but long before it comes to a boil (the temperature should register around 150°F / 66°C on an instant-read thermometer), use a spider to remove the iriko, konbu, and shiitake. Your goal is to extract the savory flavors without bringing out the strong fishy taste that will result from a hard boil.

Increase the heat to high and bring the dashi to a full boil. Add the katsuobushi,

stirring so the flakes are submerged. Quickly return the pot to a boil, turn down the heat to a simmer, and simmer for 3 minutes. Remove the pot from the heat. Allow the katsuobushi to settle.

Line a fine-mesh strainer or a colander with a clean damp kitchen towel.

Strain the broth into a clean pot, discarding the solids. The broth should be fragrant with a lovely golden color. It's best to use the dashi right away. If you have leftovers, let the dashi cool to room temperature, then pour into resealable freezer bags and freeze for up to 3 months.

UDON KAESHI

UDON SEASONING BASE

うどんかえし

2 cups plus 2
tablespoons / 502ml
mirin

1 cup plus 1 tablespoon
/ 250ml shiro shoyu

¾ cup / 177ml usukushi
(light-colored shoyu)

2 cups / 32 g shaved
katsuobushi

**MAKES 1¾ CUPS
/ 413ML**

This udon kaeshi, together with udon dashi, are the two components in udon tsuyu, the soup base for udon noodles. The kaeshi is essentially a seasoning base, and although it may seem aggravating to make a whole separate seasoning base if you're only making a few bowls of kake udon (page 240), the kaeshi adds incredible depth of flavor to the soup, rounding out the flavors of the dashi and adding sweetness. Beyond using it in udon soup, we also use it to season dressings, liven up mabodofu (page 216); basically, we use it whenever we need to add that certain je ne sais quoi to almost anything. It also lasts forever, well, at least for months, and longer if refrigerated.

Pour the mirin into a large saucepan and bring to a boil over high heat. Boil until all the alcohol has cooked off, about 6 minutes. (The best way to see if the alcohol has burned off is to put your face over the pot; alcohol vapor will curl your eyelashes and sting your nostrils.) Add the shiro and usukushi shoyu and return to a boil. Using a slotted spoon, skim and discard the scum that rises to the surface. Add the katsuobushi, turn down the heat so the liquid is simmering, and simmer for 10 minutes. Turn off the heat and let rest for 1 hour.

Strain the kaeshi through a fine-mesh strainer lined with a layer of damp paper towels into a clean bowl. The kaeshi can be used right away or transferred to an airtight container and stored somewhere cool and dark. It will keep for several months.

SHOYU

Over the years, I've settled on four different types of shoyu to use in my kitchen. The one that's used most is koikuchi shoyu, usually simply called shoyu. It's made with soybeans and wheat, and the one we buy comes from a producer in Saitama called Yamaki Jozu. It's dark and salty, and the most commonly used variety.

The second type is usukuchi shoyu, or light shoyu. Its lightness refers to the color, which is due to a higher ratio of wheat to soybeans than in regular shoyu. While just as salty as regular shoyu it's used for seasoning dishes where you want to preserve the color of the ingredient you're seasoning.

The third type is called shiro shoyu, or white shoyu. It's made completely from wheat, without any soybeans. The color is even lighter, more of a caramel color, and it has a distinctive malty smell. Shiro shoyu is relatively rare and can be quite expensive. We use it in our udon kaeshi seasoning base as well as in the dashimaki tamago base (page 100), where it's extremely important to keep the color bright and light.

The final type is tamari or tamarijoyu. It's usually made with no wheat at all, and tends to be both darker and thicker than standard shoyu. Most often it's used as a condiment for rich sashimi. In the United States, it's favored by the gluten averse.

KAKE UDON

UDON IN HOT BROTH

かけうどん

1 recipe Udon Noodles
(page 230)

UDON TSUYU

1 recipe Udon Dashi
(page 238)

1 cup / 236ml Udon
Kaeshi (page 239)

Fine sea salt to taste

Finely sliced scallions,
for serving

Shichimi, for serving

**MAKES 8 TO 10
SERVINGS**

This is our basic udon, but it's the one I'm most proud of, because the noodles and soup are themselves the stars. When the texture of the udon and the flavor of the soup are just right, this really can be a magnificent meal. Tsuyu, also sometimes written as Mentsuyu, is the soup base used in udon and soba dishes. For kake udon, the tsuyu is made with a combination of udon dashi and udon kaeshi; the combination yields a light but deeply flavored soup. Make sure every component is hot; preheat the bowls, reheat the udon fully, and bring the soup to a boil before serving. It should be served hot enough to (nearly) burn your mouth.

To cook the udon: Bring a large pot of unsalted water to a boil over high heat. Have ready a large bowl of cold water. Cook the udon for 15 minutes. Using a large strainer, scoop the udon from the pot. Reserve the cooking water. Immediately plunge the udon into the cold water bath. Rub the noodles vigorously between your hands to remove the potato starch. Drain the udon in a colander, refill the bowl with cold water, and wash again. Dump the water one more time, then refill the bowl with cold water, add a handful of ice, and rinse the udon one last time. Strain and set aside.

To make the tsuyu: In a large pot over high heat, combine the dashi and kaeshi and bring to a boil; taste for salt, adding as needed. Skim off and discard any

scum that rises to the surface.

Return the pot of water to a boil and heat your serving bowls by filling them with some of the boiling water used to cook the udon. Let them sit for 30 seconds, then pour out the water from the bowls and wipe dry.

Place a quarter of the cooked udon noodles in a large wire strainer and submerge them in the boiling udon water for 10 seconds, then shake dry with a couple of flicks of your wrist. Transfer the udon to two of the heated bowls and repeat with the remaining udon. Top each serving of udon with 1 cup / 236ml of the tsuyu. Top each bowl with a heaping tablespoon of scallions and serve immediately with the shichimi alongside.

VARIATIONS:

Add a warm Onsen Tamago (hot spring egg; page 96).

Add tenkasu tenpura bits (see page 225) and nori.

Add an Oden Satsumaage (fish cake; page 193).

Add Kaisen Kakiage Tenpura (mixed seafood tempura; page 171).

KAMO NANBAN UDON

DUCK AND MUSHROOM UDON

鴨南蛮うどん

---

18 oz / 500 g Udon
   Noodles (page 230)

About 3 oz / 90 g gobo

5 scallions

4 cups / 950ml Udon
   Dashi (page 238)

¾ cup plus 1 tablespoon
   / 190ml Udon Kaeshi
   (page 239)

1 (10 to 12-oz / 240
   to 280 g) skin-on
   duck breast, cut into
   ½-inch / 12 mm cubes

5 oz / 140 g maitake
   mushroom

Grated ginger, for
   serving

Sliced Kamo Yaki (page
   142; optional)

MAKES 4 SERVINGS

Kamo udon is one of my favorite winter dishes. Unsurprisingly, the duck adds a meaty and fatty richness to the udon soup. A bit more surprising is how important the gobo, also known as burdock root, is to the dish—its distinctive earthy flavor positively sings in the soup with the duck. Gobo is a long, skinny root vegetable that's commonly included in simmered dishes or sautéed with carrots or fried in kakiage tempura (page 171). To prepare it, rinse the outside of the root well, then, using the back of your knife, scrape off the skin. It oxidizes quickly, so keep it submerged in water once peeled. With the addition of the duck, gobo, and mushrooms, the udon soup needs a little extra udon kaeshi (in addition to the amount in the tsuyu), since the noodles soak up salt. If you'd like, add a few slices of Kamo Yaki (grilled duck breast, page 142) as a final touch.

To cook the udon: Bring a large pot of unsalted water to a boil over high heat. Have ready a large bowl of cold water. Cook the udon for 15 minutes. Using a large strainer, scoop the udon from the pot. Reserve the cooking water. Immediately plunge the udon into the cold water bath. Rub the noodles vigorously between your hands to remove the potato starch. Drain the udon in a colander, refill the bowl with cold water, and wash again. Dump the water one more time, then refill the bowl with cold water, add a handful of ice, and rinse the udon one last time. Drain and set aside.

Scrape the skin off the gobo with the back of a knife and rinse. Using a y-peeler, shave ¾-inch / 2 cm shavings from the end, rotating as you go as though you were sharpening a pencil. Rinse and set aside. Trim the roots and outer papery layer from the scallions and cut in half crosswise.

Heat a small cast-iron or other heavy-bottomed frying pan over high heat until smoking hot. Add the scallion bottoms and char on two sides (if the

scallions are thin, char only on one side).

In a large saucepan over medium heat, combine the dashi, kaeshi, duck, mushroom, gobo, and charred scallions and bring to a boil. Skim and discard any scum that rises to the surface. Add the scallion tops and remove from the heat.

When you're ready to serve the udon, return the pot of water to a boil and heat your serving bowls by filling them with some of the boiling water used to cook the udon. Let them sit for 30 seconds, then pour out the water from the bowls and wipe dry.

Place a quarter of the udon in a large wire strainer and submerge in the boiling udon water for 10 seconds, then shake dry with a couple of flicks of your wrist. Transfer to one of the heated bowls and repeat with the remaining udon. Pour some broth into each bowl, distributing the duck, gobo, mushrooms, and scallions evenly. Top with a few slices of sliced Kamo Yaki, if using. Serve immediately with the grated ginger on the side.

KAMA TAMA UDON

UDON "CARBONARA"

釜玉うどん

18 oz / 500 g Udon
  Noodles (page 230)

4 tablespoons / 55 g
  salted butter

4 large egg yolks

2 teaspoons shoyu

2 teaspoons Udon
  Kaeshi (page 239)

1 cup / 16 g finely
  shaved katsuobushi

4 teaspoons finely
  sliced scallions

4 teaspoons grated
  ginger

MAKES 4 SERVINGS

I describe this udon as "carbonara" on the Rintaro menu. Tommaso Cristiani, a cook at Rintaro, is from Rome and grudgingly acknowledges there is a similarity to Italian pasta alla carbonara.

It's a variation of the kama tama that's ubiquitous on udon menus in Takamatsu (the udon capital of the world). The original is made by simply putting hot udon directly into a serving bowl, cracking a raw egg over it, and seasoning it with shoyu, ginger, and scallions. I've modified the recipe, using an egg yolk instead of a whole egg; adding butter, which gives it richness; and seasoning the noodles with both shoyu and udon kaeshi to give it some depth.

I replaced the guanciale (cured pork jowl), which is traditionally used in Italian carbonara, with very thinly sliced katsuobushi that adds a similar smoky savoriness to the noodles. The thinly sliced katsuobushi is called *hana katsuo*, which translates as "flower bonito flakes." The slices are very thin, like flower petals, and tender enough to eat without cooking. They are often used as a garnish, and when they're placed on something hot, the thin flakes dance with the heat.

I like to serve this in individual bowls and let people mix their own directly in the bowl. Not only is the presentation more beautiful, it's also more fun.

To cook the udon: Bring a large pot of unsalted water to a boil over high heat. Have ready a large bowl of cold water. Cook the udon for 15 minutes. Using a large strainer, scoop the udon from the pot. Reserve the cooking water. Immediately plunge the udon into the cold water bath. Rub the noodles vigorously between your hands to remove the potato starch. Drain the udon in a colander, refill the bowl with cold water, and wash again. Dump the water one more time, then refill the bowl with cold water, add a handful of ice, and rinse the udon one last time. Drain and set aside.

When you're ready to serve the udon, return the pot of water to a boil and heat your serving bowls by filling them with some of the boiling water used to cook the udon. Let them sit for 30 seconds, then pour out the water from the bowls and wipe dry.

Place a quarter of the udon in a large wire strainer and submerge in the boiling udon water for 10 seconds, then shake dry with a couple of flicks of your wrist. Repeat for each serving. Transfer the udon into the heated bowls and top each with 1 tablespoon of the butter, an egg yolk, and 1/2 teaspoon each of the shoyu and kaeshi. Top with some of the katsuobushi, distributing it evenly among the bowls.

Serve immediately with the scallions and ginger alongside. Before eating, mix vigorously to combine.

BUKKAKE UDON

CHILLED UDON WITH DAIKON AND GINGER ぶっかけうどん

---

18 oz / 500 g Udon
Noodles (page 230)

1 recipe Mori Tsuyu
(recipe follows)

1 (8-oz / 225 g) piece
daikon

1 teaspoon grated
ginger

¾ cup / 40 g tenkasu
tenpura bits (see
page 225)

¼ cup / 40 g thinly
sliced scallions

Lemon wedges, for
serving

MAKES 4 SERVINGS

This chilled udon is especially good during the hot, muggy Japanese summers. The recipe below is a starting point. Add thinly sliced summer vegetables to your taste—carrots, peppers, cucumbers, corn, and cherry tomatoes all work well. The lemon adds a great brightness and really makes the dish. Nestle a wedge in each bowl and allow your guests to squeeze lemon juice over the udon as they eat.

Chill your serving bowls.

To cook the udon: Bring a large pot of unsalted water to a boil over high heat. Have ready a large bowl of cold water. Cook the udon for 15 minutes. Using a large strainer, scoop the udon from the pot. Reserve the cooking water. Immediately plunge the udon into the cold water bath. Rub the noodles vigorously between your hands to remove the potato starch. Drain the udon in a colander, refill the bowl with cold water, and wash again. Dump the water one more time, then refill the bowl with cold water, add a handful of ice, and rinse the udon one last time. Drain and set aside.

Arrange a quarter of the chilled udon in each bowl and add ¼ cup / 60ml of the tsuyu to each.

Peel the daikon and finely grate it with a daikon grater or the punch-hole side of a box grater. Transfer the daikon to a fine-mesh strainer and press it gently to squeeze out some of the liquid. Make small mounds of the daikon on top of the udon in each bowl in a triangular mountain shape, then place the ginger on top of the daikon so it resembles a tiny snow-capped Mount Fuji. Top with the tenpura bits and scallions and tuck a lemon wedge into each bowl.

VARIATIONS

Halve twenty ripe cherry tomatoes, such as Sungold or Sweet 100s, through the stem and toss them in a few tablespoons of the kaeshi. Top each bowl of udon with some of the cherry tomatoes and a small pile of cucumbers, dividing them evenly among the bowls. Finely slice two shiso leaves and garnish each bowl with some.

For a heartier version, add one hot Onsen Tamago (hot spring egg; page 96) on top of the udon in each bowl, then top with nori.

MORI TSUYU

1 cup plus 1 tablespoon / 255ml Katsuobushi Dashi (page 19) or Udon Dashi (page 238)

6 tablespoons / 90ml Udon Kaeshi (page 239)

½ cup / 8 g shaved katsuobushi

MAKES 1 CUP / 236ML

The ingredients for both the mori and udon tsuyu are the same—dashi and kaeshi (a combination of mirin, soy, and katsuobushi). But the mori tsuyu is much more heavily seasoned with each of these ingredients than the udon tsuyu and its classic use is as a dipping sauce for chilled soba. It's quite salty, and at a good soba restaurant, the server will bring you a small pitcher of the soba cooking water at the end of your meal. You add this hot water to the mori tsuyu to your taste and drink the resulting broth.

As I learned at Soba Ro, the restaurant I trained at in Saitama, mori tsuyu is a versatile ingredient, and I use it in lots of different ways at Rintaro. In addition to serving it with chilled udon, I use it to cure fresh salmon roe in the Ikura Don recipe (page 209), and to douse the tempura in the Kakiage Don (page 224). Mori tsuyu, as with most dashi-based tsuyu, is best used the same day it's made, although it will keep in the refrigerator for a day or two.

In a large saucepan over high heat, combine the dashi and kaeshi and bring to a boil. Skim and discard the scum that rises to the top. Add the katsuobushi and remove from the heat. Let stand 5 minutes, then strain through a fine-mesh strainer lined with heavy-duty paper towels. Lightly squeeze the katsuobushi to release more liquid and discard the solids. Use right away or let cool, then transfer to an airtight container and refrigerate for up to 2 days.

NEGI

SLICED SCALLIONS

Cutting scallions is one of the rites of passage for a new cook at Rintaro. We use them on many dishes on the menu, often going through several cases of scallions every week. To successfully slice scallions, you will need a razor-sharp knife, a bit of patience, and the willingness to nick yourself a few times.

The scallion most commonly used in Japan is called *naganegi* ("long scallion"), and they are three to four times the size of the standard scallions you find in the United States. Unfortunately, they're not common in the States, and while I used to have a steady supply for the restaurant, the one California farmer who grew them tired of the heavy labor required to produce them, so we now use standard scallions.

Start by cutting off the root end. Peel away any dried or discolored leaves and rinse. When you're first perfecting your technique, it's best to cut a few scallions at a time. It's useful to bunch them together with a rubber band. Using a VERY sharp knife and your pointer finger as a guide, start at the root end, slice them as thinly as possible, and take care to cut all the way through. Take your time. We usually cut to just above the "shoulder," just past where the white bottom turns to green leaves.

Almost as important as the cutting is the rinsing. You want to wash away the mucilaginous gel inside the scallion without washing away the flavor. Put the sliced scallions in a fine-mesh wire strainer nested in a bowl and, using a faucet sprayer if you have one, spray them with cold water until they are submerged (if you do not have a sprayer, you can just run cold water over them until submerged). Dump the water and repeat twice more. You can dry them on a paper towel, or even better, spin them in a salad spinner. They should be gel-free and crunchy but still taste like green onions.

One bunch of scallions yields about ¾ cup / 112 g sliced scallions.

HIYASHI UDON

CHILLED UDON WITH SESAME SAUCE

GOMA DARE (SESAME SAUCE)

½ cup / 125ml Katsuobushi Dashi (page 19)

7 tablespoons / 100 g neri goma (sesame paste)

⅓ cup / 75ml shoyu, plus more as needed

¼ cup / 60ml rice vinegar, plus more as needed

¼ cup / 50 g sugar

1 tablespoon toasted sesame seeds, finely ground

1 tablespoon saikyo (sweet white) miso

1 tablespoon lemon juice

1½ teaspoons toasted sesame oil

¼ lb / 115 g haricots verts, stemmed

1 red gypsy or small red bell pepper, stemmed and seeded

1 Japanese cucumber, or ½ English cucumber, peeled in alternating stripes

1 large carrot, peeled

18 oz / 500 g Udon Noodles (page 230)

FOR SERVING:

1 recipe Kinshi Tamago (ribbon eggs, page 99)

Pickled red ginger (page 252)

MAKES 4 TO 6 SERVINGS

This cold summertime udon is another nostalgic recipe for me. While growing up, my mother usually served it for lunch, although it also makes a perfectly refreshing dinner. It's kind of like the gazpacho of udon—cold, fresh, and light but deeply flavored. This dish is most often seen in Japanese homes in its "Chinese" version, made with chilled ramen noodles rather than with udon, and sliced ham is often added, but I think it's better with fat, slippery, chewy udon. At the restaurant, we serve the dish in individual portions, but a large platter is a simpler and more festive way to serve this at home. Use this recipe as a guide, but feel free to improvise by adding different vegetables, like snap peas or asparagus in the spring; tomatoes or corn in the summer; poached, shredded chicken breast; or even sliced ham. Don't skip the ribbon eggs, though—they are easy to make and add terrific texture.

To make the goma dare: In a large bowl, whisk together the dashi, sesame paste, shoyu, vinegar, sugar, sesame seeds, miso, lemon juice, and sesame oil. Taste for seasoning and add more vinegar or shoyu as needed. Set aside.

To prepare the vegetables: Bring a medium saucepan of salted water to a boil and prepare an ice water bath. Add the haricots verts and cook until just tender, 5 to 6 minutes. Drain and immediately plunge the beans into the ice water bath. Once cold, remove and dry the beans on paper towels.

Cut the pepper, cucumber, and carrot into 2½ by ⅛-inch / 6 cm by 4 mm batons (if using an English cucumber, cut in half lengthwise and scoop out the seeds with a spoon before slicing). Transfer the vegetables to a plate and cover with a damp paper towel. Refrigerate until ready to serve, up to 2 hours.

To cook the udon: Bring a large pot of unsalted water to a boil over high heat. Have ready a large bowl of cold water. Cook the udon for 15 minutes. Using a large strainer, scoop the udon from the pot. Reserve the cooking water. Immediately plunge the udon into the cold water bath. Rub the noodles vigorously between your hands to remove the potato starch. Drain the udon in a colander, refill the bowl with cold water, and wash again. Dump the water one more time, then refill the bowl with cold water, add a handful of ice, and rinse the udon one last time. Drain well and transfer to a large serving platter.

To serve, garnish the udon with the vegetables, ribbon eggs, and pickled ginger, arranging them in an attractive color-blocked pattern. Serve with a pitcher of sauce on the side or pour the dressing over the udon.

BENI SHOGA

RED PICKLED GINGER

1 small red beet

5 oz / 142 g young ginger

¼ cup / 60ml rice wine vinegar

1 tablespoon sea salt

MAKES ¾ CUP / 120 G

Boil the beet, skin on, until tender. Remove and rub off the skin. Slice in quarters.

Peel the ginger with a spoon. Cut the ginger lengthwise by hand or on a Benriner mandoline into slightly less than ⅛-inch / 4 mm slices. Stack the slices and cut lengthwise again into slightly less than ⅛-inch / 4 mm strips.

Put the sliced ginger in a pot and cover with 2 inches / 5 cm of cold water. Bring to a simmer. Drain the water and repeat. Taste the ginger. It should have a strong ginger taste, but not be too spicy. Blanch again, if necessary.

Combine the salt and vinegar with 1 cup / 236ml of water. Add the ginger and beet and let sit for 1 day.

KAISEN NABEYAKI UDON

SEAFOOD UDON CLAY POT 海鮮鍋焼きうどん

Sea salt

20 mussels

20 Manila clams

8 raw jumbo shrimp (U10)

18 oz / 500 g Udon Noodles (page 230)

4½ cups / 1,065ml Udon Dashi (page 238)

¾ cup plus 1 tablespoon / 190ml Udon Kaeshi (page 239)

½ cup / 118ml cooking sake

4 tablespoons / 55 g unsalted butter

1 small bunch (about 6 oz / 85 g) chrysanthemum greens, pea shoots, or mustard greens

Shichimi, for serving (optional)

MAKES 4 TO 6 SERVINGS

As a kid, in the snowy wintertime (yes, it snows in California, particularly in the Sierra Nevada mountains, where I grew up), one of my favorite meals was nabeyaki udon. *Nabe* means pot, and my mother would either use individual cast-iron pots with wooden lids or a donut-shaped Mongolian hot pot that we heated with coals from the woodstove. It was always served at the table, with the lid in place, and I appreciated the drama of the reveal and the cloud of fragrant steam. There are endless versions of nabeyaki udon, with assorted add-ins, including eggs or toasted mochi. This version takes advantage of some of the seafoods available here in California. The butter used to cook the clams and mussels is a nontraditional but very tasty addition. I always like to add some greens at the end of the cooking process. Here in the Bay Area, I have access to chrysanthemum greens, which are tender and have a distinctive, slightly astringent flavor. Pea shoots, young mustard greens, or even spinach could be used instead.

Fill two large bowls with cold water and add enough salt so the water is as salty as the sea.

Using your fingers, grab each beard of a mussel and pull it toward the hinge to remove it. Put the mussels in one of the bowls of cold water and the clams in the other. Let them soak for 30 minutes, then drain the clams and mussels and rinse with cold tap water. Set aside.

Peel the shrimp, leaving the tail on. Using a toothpick, remove and discard the vein that runs down the center of the back of each shrimp. Rinse the shrimp in cold water, dry on a paper towel, and set aside.

To cook the udon: Bring a large pot of unsalted water to a boil over high heat. Have ready a large bowl of cold water. Cook the udon for 10 minutes. Using a large strainer, scoop the udon from

the pot. Reserve the cooking water. Immediately plunge the udon into the cold water bath. Rub the noodles vigorously between your hands to remove the potato starch. Drain the udon in a colander, refill the bowl with cold water, and wash again. Dump the water one more time, then refill the bowl with cold water, add a handful of ice, and rinse the udon one last time. Drain and set aside.

In a large clay pot or a Dutch oven with a lid over high heat, combine 4 cups / 950ml of the dashi with the kaeshi and bring to a boil. Skim off and discard any scum. Set aside.

In a large saucepan, bring the sake, the remaining ½ cup / 118ml dashi, final 2 tablespoons kaeshi, and the butter to a boil. Add the clams, mussels, and shrimp. Cover and boil for 3 minutes, until the shellfish have opened and the shrimp are cooked through (discard any shellfish that haven't opened).

Return the liquid in the clay pot to a boil. Add the udon and return to a boil. Add the greens, then place the shellfish and shrimp on top of the greens. Pour the liquid from the pan in which you cooked the seafood through a fine-mesh strainer into the clay pot, over the seafood. Bring it all to a roaring boil, cover with a lid, and bring to the table. At the table, uncover the pot, and ladle the mixture into individual bowls. Serve with the shichimi alongside (if using).

VARIATIONS

In place of some or all of the seafood, add fish cakes and eggs. Add four satsumaage fish cakes (page 193) when you add the udon noodles. Crack four eggs into the pot just before you bring the pot to the table; they'll poach in the residual heat. Serve once the whites are set and the yolks are still runny.

DEZATO デザート

DESSERTS

LONG BEFORE I WANTED TO become a chef, I wanted to become a pastry chef. I may have been in eighth grade when I made the decision. Inspired by the cream puffs that my father would buy at the old-time bakery on trips to town, there seemed to be no more worthwhile job. My early desserts were terrible. I made a brick of a cake for my father's birthday, with sandy frosting that he politely choked down. I delivered achingly sweet, crackerlike Napoleons to the carpenters up at my father's workshop that they nibbled at while draining their coffee thermoses. But I did have some limited success, usually when assisted by my mother, making more humble desserts like rhubarb crisp and wild blackberry trifle.

My first restaurant job at seventeen, the summer before college, was as an assistant to the pastry assistant at a big new restaurant that was opening under the TransAmerica building in San Francisco. I learned a lot that summer. I was put in charge of biscuit production. I made crème anglaise, ice cream base, and raspberry coulis. And eventually, I watched as the 300-seat restaurant with its excellent ingredients, talented cooks, and charming servers imploded, tearing apart the dreams and marriage of the chef who had so kindly allowed me to work with him for the summer. Becoming a pastry chef seemed a lot more serious an undertaking than I had imagined as a thirteen-year-old.

After working through college in other pastry assistant positions, learning about pie dough and choux puffs and how to spin ice cream, I eventually drifted out of the pastry kitchen. I still love desserts, though, and although our dessert menu is small—usually only two or three items—it is mighty. This is mostly due to a dedicated pastry chef, Junko Yamada Schwesig, during the early days at Rintaro. A Japanese woman with a design background, she came to work with me when I had a catering company based out of my garage. At the time, she didn't have any formal training in pastry, but she had (and has) excellent taste, patience, a very precise working style, and a sophisticated understanding of sweets. The desserts she made were some of the most beautiful dishes on the menu. She left Rintaro to work in other kitchens and eventually started a pop-up, Oyatsuya, serving her sweets paired with tea. During this time, I would often commission special orders to serve at the restaurant. Her soufflé cheesecake, mochi-wrapped strawberries, or her light-as-air roll cake would usually sell out by the middle of service. Although Junko has since moved to Berlin with her husband, it seemed only natural to ask her to contribute some of my favorites of her dessert recipes to this chapter.

Many of the traditional sweets in Japan are associated with formal matcha tea culture. There is a universe of delicate wagashi made with bean paste, mochi, agar, and fruits. They are quite small, just a few bites each, and can be extraordinarily beautiful and texturally interesting. Although I admire the skill that goes into making them, as they are meant to be eaten with tea, they don't quite hit the spot as an after-dinner dessert. But there is more to sweets in Japan than wagashi, and in the last 150 years, French desserts have become common, especially with the rise of domestic butter and cream production. As you'd imagine, Western classics like tender cakes and choux puffs, parfaits, and custards have been transformed into their own thing in Japan. These Franco-Japanese desserts, sometimes melding wagashi culture with modern pastry, are my favorite, and I'm always impressed by the finesse of Japanese pastry chefs.

HOJICHA PANNA COTTA

ほうじ茶パンナコッタ

ROASTED GREEN TEA PANNA COTTA

PANNA COTTA

3 tablespoons water

1 tablespoon powdered gelatin

2½ cups / 600ml heavy cream

1½ cups / 355ml whole milk

5 tablespoons / 60 g sugar

1½ teaspoons / 6 g hojicha tea

SYRUP

1 cup / 200 g sugar

½ cup / 118ml water

2 tablespoons / 24 g hojicha tea

Almond Cookies (page 263), for serving

MAKES 8 SERVINGS

There is nothing at all *green* about this green tea panna cotta. That's because the tea leaves have first been roasted, transforming them from bright green to chestnut brown. I was surprised to learn that hojicha tea has only been around for 100 years or so, a baby compared to the centuries-old history of matcha tea. But hojicha's distinctive earthy, nutty flavor works particularly well in a panna cotta. And while the pudding itself has a light tea flavor and is not particularly sweet, the hojicha syrup served alongside is highly sweetened, with a very concentrated tea flavor. The caramelized almond wafer cookies we serve alongside (page 263) are a crunchy counterpoint to the silky custard.

Just before we opened the restaurant, our then–pastry chef, Junko, spent some time interning in the Chez Panisse pastry kitchen. The addition of hojicha in the custard and syrup are hers, but she tells me the basic panna cotta recipe was adapted from the Chez Panisse recipe. That was news to me, but I'm happy for this connection back to the mother ship.

To make the panna cotta: Put the water in a small bowl and sprinkle the gelatin over. Let it stand for 5 minutes.

In a 2-qt / 1.9L saucepan over medium-low heat, combine the cream, milk, sugar, and tea. Heat the mixture until it registers 160°F / 71°C on an instant-read thermometer, stirring occasionally to prevent the cream from scalding (don't overheat the cream mixture; it will cause the butterfat to separate). Remove the pan from the heat and whisk in the gelatin mixture. Let stand until it's at room temperature, then divide evenly among eight 6-oz / 177 ml ramekins. Transfer the dishes to the refrigerator, lightly covered with plastic wrap, and chill for at least 4 hours or

overnight. The panna cotta will keep, refrigerated, for up to 3 days.

To make the syrup: In a medium sauce-pan over high heat, bring the sugar, water, and tea to a boil. Turn down the heat to medium-low and cook for 35 minutes, until the syrup has thickened and turned chestnut brown. It should have the consistency of warm maple syrup. Strain through a fine-mesh strainer into a clean bowl and let it cool to room temperature. The syrup will keep, refrigerated, for up to a month.

Serve the panna cotta cold with a small pitcher of the syrup for pouring and the almond cookies alongside.

ALMOND COOKIES
アーモンドクッキー

3 cups / 325 g pastry
   flour

¼ teaspoon baking soda

1 stick / 113 g unsalted
   butter, cut into pieces

5½ tablespoons / 80ml
   water

1 cup / 85 g sliced
   almonds

1½ cups / 300 g
   demerara sugar or
   light brown sugar

**MAKES ABOUT
100 COOKIES**

The melted butter and pastry flour give these cookies a tender, snappy texture.
At the restaurant, we serve them with our panna cotta, but they're great
accompanying a cup of tea or as a garnish for a bowl of ice cream.

Line an 8-inch / 20 cm square pan with parchment paper. Sift the flour and baking soda together in a large bowl. In a large saucepan over medium heat, melt the butter with the water. Remove the pan from the heat, add the almonds, and mix to combine. Add the sugar and mix to combine, then stir in the flour mixture and mix until a smooth dough forms. Let cool slightly, until the dough is beginning to firm up a bit.

Transfer the dough to the prepared pan and spread into an even 8-inch / 20 cm by 6-inch / 15 cm rectangle. Transfer the pan to the freezer and freeze for 90 minutes, until the dough is completely frozen.

Preheat the oven to 350°F / 175°C. Line two baking sheets with parchment paper.

Remove the pan from the freezer and transfer the frozen dough to a cutting board. Peel off the parchment paper, then cut into two 8 by 3-inch / 20 by 7.5 cm rectangles. Return one rectangle of dough to the pan, then put in the freezer.

Slice the remaining rectangle of dough into wafer-thin cookies, aiming for a thickness of about 1/16 inch / 2 mm. Place the cookies on the prepared baking sheet, spacing them about ½ inch / 12 mm apart. Bake until the cookies are golden brown, 13 to 15 minutes, rotating the pan halfway through the baking time. Remove the pan from the oven and let the cookies cool on the pan; they'll continue to crisp as they cool. Repeat with the remaining dough. Store any leftover cookies in an airtight container for up to 1 week. The dough will also keep frozen, well-wrapped in plastic wrap, for up to 2 months.

GUREPUFURUTSU ZERI

RUBY GRAPEFRUIT KANTEN JELLY　グレープフルーツゼリー

---

4 ruby red grapefruits

6 tablespoons / 75 g sugar, plus more as needed

Pinch of sea salt

1 oz / 30ml Umeshu (page 283; optional)

2½ teaspoons / 3 g powdered kanten (see page 266)

MAKES 4 SERVINGS

This ruby grapefruit jelly is one of the first kanten jellies I learned to make. Once I process the juice, I pour the jelly back into the rind of the fruit, where it sets, making for a dramatic presentation. If you have some good umeshu (plum brandy) on hand, I suggest adding a few tablespoons to the grapefruit juice. It's a magical ingredient that will amplify the flavor of the grapefruit juice, making the jelly taste almost like candy. One useful tip is to make sure the juice you are adding is at room temperature. If you add very cold juice, you risk the jelly setting up in the pan, before you can pour it into your grapefruit shells. If you do not have an electric citrus juicer, you can squeeze the juice from the grapefruit with a reamer; avoid citrus squeezers, which will damage the rind.

Cut the grapefruit in half along the equator. Using an electric citrus juicer, juice the grapefruits, being careful not to damage the rind. Place the empty grapefruit rinds, cut side down, on a moist towel, to keep the cut surface from drying out and wrinkling. Pass the juice through a fine-mesh strainer, pressing hard on the solids. Discard the solids and strain the juice twice more. Line the strainer with damp paper towels or a damp cotton kitchen towel and strain a final time. The juice should be absolutely clear; you should have about 2 cups / 472ml strained juice.

Season the juice with the sugar, adding it gradually and tasting as you go (you may not need it all). Add the salt and the umeshu (if using). You should have about 2⅓ cups / 550ml seasoned juice.

Using a soup spoon, carefully peel the inner white membrane and pith from the grapefruit rinds, leaving just the shells. Rinse the shells under tap water and dry with a clean towel. Choose the four most attractive grapefruit cups, avoiding any that have a hole at the bottom where the stem has become dislodged (the liquid will leak through); discard the remaining four rinds.

Arrange the grapefruit shells, cut side up, on top of four water glasses (this will hold them steady) set on a baking sheet to catch the drips.

In a medium saucepan over medium heat, whisk a quarter of the seasoned juice with the kanten, whisking constantly. When the juice boils, remove the pan from the heat and whisk in the remaining juice. Transfer the juice to a spouted measuring cup and immediately pour the juice into the prepared grapefruit shells. The jelly will contract a bit as it cools, so pour the shells as full as possible. Use your finger to run some of the liquid along the cut rim of the grapefruit shell. Pop any bubbles that form at the surface with your fingertip. Let cool to room temperature, undisturbed, until the liquid sets. Once firm, the grapefruit can be stored in an airtight container in the refrigerator for a day or two.

KANTEN JELLIES

VARIATION

If you have ume (plums) from a batch of Umeshu (page 283), you can make a tiny ume-flavored jelly to float in the center of your grapefruit jelly. Prepare these tiny jellies before making the grapefruit jelly. To make the jellies: Pit enough ume to make ⅓ cup of fruit. In a blender or food processor, combine the fruit, 3 tablespoons umeshu, 3 tablespoons water, and 3 tablespoons sugar and blend or process until smooth. Strain through a fine-mesh strainer; you should have about 4¼ oz / 125ml. Transfer to a small saucepan over high heat and add 1 teaspoon kanten. Bring to a full boil, then remove from the heat. Pour 1 tablespoon portions into champagne flutes or white wine glasses. Chill until firm. Using a long spoon, slip the jellies out of the glasses and set aside in the refrigerator. Pour the grapefruit juice back into the shells, as described above, and let cool for 5 to 10 minutes, until the juice has just started to set. Place an ume jelly in the center of each grapefruit, pushing it down into the grapefruit juice until it's suspended just below the surface. Let stand at room temperature until the liquid sets. Once firm, the grapefruit can be stored in an airtight container in the refrigerator for a day or two. Serve chilled, sliced in wedges.

When I worked at Chez Panisse, there was no more divisive a dish on the menu than the nightly fruit bowl. It might consist of a few figs and a peach or some dates with mandarins or a pear and some grapes. How could you possibly charge real money for a small bowl of fruit? After a few years of working there, it became clear to me. Chez Panisse has a long relationship with the most skilled farmers in California. They select the best of the best to send to the restaurant, and the pastry cooks then sort the fruit to choose the very best of what they receive to include in the nightly fruit bowl. The cooks will let the fruit ripen for a day, or maybe two or five, until they're at their prime. Suddenly, $15 for one of the best Faye Elberta peaches (or Pixie tangerines or Comice pears) in California, if not the country, doesn't seem so absurd.

Good fruit is relatively rare. At Chez Panisse, the magic of that fruit bowl is that the cooks see no need to manipulate a perfect ingredient. In Japan, a similar ethos applies, and kanten jellies are another way of capturing the ephemeral flavor and fragrance of ripe, beautiful fruit.

Kanten jellies, so named because they are set with kanten, a natural gelatin derived from seaweed, are one of the best ways of capturing the ephemeral flavor and fragrance of ripe, beautiful fruit. You can make the jellies from almost any juicy fruit, from strawberries to grapes to citrus. The specific technique varies from fruit to fruit, but generally speaking, you begin with fruit juice, strain the juice until it's crystal clear, sweeten it with sugar and maybe sharpen the flavor with lemon, and then cook it as little as possible. That last point is important, because the delicate nuanced aromas and the flavor of the fruit can be lost when cooked.

To extract the juice from fleshy fruit like strawberries, peaches, grapes, or apricots, I typically slice them, macerate them with sugar overnight (the amount I use depends on how sweet the fruit is, sometimes adding a little lemon juice to protect the fruit from oxidizing), and then, on the following day, I cook them gently to no more than 165°F / 75°C to coax out as much juice as possible. For citrus, I only need to squeeze them before adding sugar. And for melons, I scoop the flesh from the rind, blend it into a liquid, and then strain it multiple times.

The ratio of kanten to juice that works the best for all sorts of thin juices, like citrus or melon, is 4½ teaspoons / 6 g powdered kanten to 2 cups / 472 ml of seasoned juice. For thicker juices, like that from strawberries or peaches, I reduce the ratio to a scant 1 tablespoon / 4 g powdered kanten per 2 cups / 472ml. Kanten is clear when melted and has no discernible taste of its own. Unlike gelatin, which melts at body temperature, kanten requires full boiling to activate. To avoid destroying the flavor of the juice, I melt the kanten into a quarter of the total quantity of the juice. Once it's at a rolling boil, I remove the pan from the heat and add the remaining fresh juice.

You can pour the juice into individual molds or into a larger pan and then cut the jelly into cubes once it has set. Or, in the case of citrus jellies, you can pour the mixture back into the citrus rind for an especially striking presentation. To remove the bubbles that form on the surface of the jelly, use your finger or wooden skewer. If you'd like, you can remove any fine foam that forms at the surface with a crisply folded paper towel, cut to the width of the pan, gently scraped along the surface to capture the foam.

MELON PARFAIT

GREEN MELON ICE CREAM PARFAIT

メロンパフェ

MELON JUICE

1 medium Piel de Sapo or similarly fragrant green or orange melon (about 3½ lb / 1.5kg)

5 tablespoons / 74 g granulated sugar

2 tablespoons lemon juice

Pinch of sea salt

1½ teaspoons / 2 g powdered kanten

SAUCE

½ cup / 120 ml seasoned juice

¼ teaspoon powdered gelatin

½ cup / 120 ml heavy cream

2 tablespoons confectioners' sugar

Vanilla ice cream, for serving

Wafer cookies, store-bought (optional), for serving

MAKES 4 PARFAITS

My grandmother Fumie Mishima was from a different world. Although she had never spoken to me or even to my mother directly about it, I gathered that she had lost her first family during the Second World War. For years following the end of the war, she, like much of the nation, often didn't have enough to eat; this later translated into extreme thriftiness when it came to food. As a kid, I was appalled at how she would fetch half of a mealy apple from a dish in the refrigerator, cut a few slices for dinner, and then return it to the refrigerator for the next meal. I swear, she could make one sad apple last a week. She refused to waste food. This created a problem when, in my early twenties, I presented her with a foil-wrapped "gift" melon, which had cost me, even twenty years ago, about $70. It was one of those Yubari green melons that are grown with just several to a vine so as to concentrate their flavor and sweetness. Clearly, for my grandmother, something so expensive and rare was too special to eat. So, there it sat in the refrigerator, getting riper and riper. When I finally insisted we cut it open, it was impossibly fragrant and sweet but also nearly liquid inside. She had let it go too long! I had started working as a pastry assistant and had the clever idea of turning the juice into a granita to salvage what was a near catastrophe. That batch of melon granita, too, lasted for a week, coming in and out of the freezer to be eaten a couple of spoonfuls at a time.

If I were to go back in time, knowing what I know now, I probably would have transformed that fancy melon into jelly. In Japan, fruit jellies, made with actual fruit juice, are incredibly popular and often served layered in a parfait glass with whipped cream or ice cream.

Throughout the year, parfaits appear on the menu at Rintaro, showcasing jellies made from the best seasonal fruit. But my favorite is green melon parfait. I use a variety of melon called Piel de Sapo. It's similar to a honeydew, but when they are good, they are intensely fragrant with a flavor that reminds me of that melon I had given to my grandmother. If you can't find Piel de Sapo, use the most fragrant melon you can find. Charentais, similar to a cantaloupe, work well, as do muskmelon and canary melons. While sweetness can be an indication of flavor, remember you can always add more sugar. It is the strong flavor you're after. If you can't find a green melon that's overwhelmingly fragrant but you really want to make this parfait, it's not terrible to add a couple of tablespoons of artificially green Midori, the Japanese liquor made from the famous Yubari King and muskmelon.

To make the juice: Cut the melon in half lengthwise. Scrape out the seeds with a large spoon into a wire-mesh strainer, set over a medium bowl, to catch the juices.

Cut one of the melon halves in half again lengthwise and set aside a quarter for garnish. Scoop out the melon flesh from the remaining three quarters into the bowl, using a spoon to scrape close to the rind, where the flesh is deeper in color (this will improve the color of the jellies).

Transfer the flesh to a food processor and process until liquefied. Pour the pureed fruit through the strainer into a clean medium bowl. Use a spoon to gently stir the puree and encourage the juice to strain but don't push any of the fibers through the strainer. Discard the solids, then pass the liquid through the strainer again into a clean bowl and then back again into the original bowl.

Line the strainer with damp paper towels and strain a final time. The juice should be absolutely clear; you should have at least 1 cup / 236ml of clear juice.

To season the juice: Add 3 tablespoons of the granulated sugar, 1½ teaspoons of the lemon juice, and a very small pinch of salt to the bowl with the juice. Since the sweetness of every melon is different, you will have to taste carefully for seasoning. The seasoned juice should be as sweet as a soft drink; the lemon should balance the sweetness and enhance the flavor of the melon with its acidity, but it shouldn't taste lemony. Add the remaining sugar and lemon juice, if necessary. You should have about 1½ cups / 354ml of seasoned juice.

To make the jellies: In a small saucepan over medium heat, whisk ¼ cup / 60ml of the seasoned juice with the kanten. Bring to a boil, whisking constantly. When the juice boils, remove the pan from the heat and whisk in ¾ cup / 177ml of the seasoned juice. Immediately pour the mixture into a 4 by 4-inch / 10 by 10 cm pan; the liquid should be about 1-inch / 2.5 cm deep. Pop any bubbles that form at the surface. Let cool to room temperature, undisturbed; the jelly will set. Cover and refrigerate until cold or for up to 1 day.

To make the sauce: In a small saucepan over low heat, whisk the remaining ½ cup / 120ml of seasoned juice with the gelatin. Warm gently, just until the gelatin dissolves and the mixture registers around 110° to 120°F / 43° to 49°C on an instant-read thermometer (the temperature of a very hot bath). Be careful not to overheat the juice, since its flavor will quickly deteriorate. Pour the juice into a bowl and chill in the refrigerator for about an hour until thickened; it should be the consistency of cold maple syrup.

To assemble: Chill four parfait glasses. Remove the jellies from the refrigerator and cut them into sixteen pieces, each 1-inch / 2.5 cm square.

Pour the heavy cream into a chilled bowl, add the confectioners' sugar, and whisk until medium peaks form.

Slice the remaining quarter of the melon widthwise into ¼-inch / 6 mm slices.

Place a cube of melon jelly at the base of each dish. Spoon in 1 tablespoon of the sauce. Layer with a spoonful of whipped cream and a small scoop of vanilla ice cream. Arrange three cubes of melon jelly around the ice cream. Stack a second small scoop of ice cream on top. Spoon on 1 more tablespoon of sauce and top with a small dollop of whipped cream. Garnish with the melon slices and a few cookies. Serve immediately.

ICHIGO DAIFUKU

MOCHI-WRAPPED STRAWBERRIES

6 oz / 165 g sweet bean paste (shiro koshian) homemade, recipe follows, or store bought

8 medium strawberries

MOCHI

5 tablespoons / 74ml hot water (from the tap is fine)

½ cup plus 1 tablespoon / 110 g sugar

Potato starch for dusting

1⅓ cups / 210 g mochiko sweet rice flour

¾ cup / 177ml cold water

MAKES 8 STRAWBERRIES

There is a bit of alchemy to ichigo daifuku. Rice, beans, and strawberries are transformed into snowy white balls with just the tips of the bright red strawberries showing through a semi-translucent skin of mochi. They look like a spirit from a Hayao Miyazaki movie. The mochi act as a blanket, trapping and intensifying the aroma of the strawberries. When you bite into a daifuku, the pent-up strawberry flavor is so strong that it almost tastes artificial. They are sensational. But wait to make them until you have glorious in-season strawberries. Look for ones that are red nearly all the way through and that you can smell from across the room.

Traditionally, the layer of bean paste between the strawberry and the mochi is made with dark red azuki beans. But Rintaro's former Pastry Chef Junko prefers a sweet white bean paste called shiro koshian. It's lighter in flavor, allowing the taste of the strawberry to shine, and she prefers the color, as well. While making shiro koshian is not difficult, it is time-consuming. I've included store-bought sweet bean paste in the recipe below, but if you'd like to make it yourself, that recipe follows.

The trickiest part of making these is working with the super sticky mochi. To make it easier, generously dust the baking sheet and your hands with potato starch while you work.

If the bean paste is so wet that you can't shape it into a ball by hand, place it in a saucepan over medium heat and cook it for a few minutes, stirring constantly to prevent burning, to evaporate some of the excess water. Then spread the paste on a baking sheet and let it cool to room temperature. Cover with plastic wrap and refrigerate until cold before using.

Rinse and dry the strawberries. Cut the stem flush with the top of the berry, but be careful not to cut into the strawberry itself. Once the flesh of the strawberry is cut, its juices will run, making the bean paste and mochi soggy.

Divide the paste into eight even pieces; lightly moisten your hands and roll each piece into a ball. Flatten each ball into a 2½-inch / 6 cm disk between

your palms, remoistening your palms as needed to prevent sticking. Place a strawberry on top of each disk, stem side down. Push the bean paste up and around the strawberry, leaving just the tip exposed, then again shape into a ball. Transfer to a plate, tips up, and cover and refrigerate while you prepare the mochi.

To make the mochi: Bring a large saucepan of water to a boil over high heat.

In a small bowl, combine the hot water with the sugar and stir until the sugar dissolves. Set aside. Sift a generous layer of potato starch onto a rimmed sheet pan.

In a medium bowl, combine the rice flour and ¾ cup / 177ml cold water and knead well by hand until a smooth

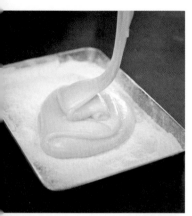

dough forms. Using your hands, divide the dough into four equal pieces; roll each piece into a ball. Flatten the balls into thin disks and punch a hole with your finger though the center of each disk so the mochi will cook more quickly and evenly. Add the disks of dough to the boiling water. When they float, use a slotted spoon to transfer to a medium saucepan (nonstick, if you have it). Mix well with a rubber spatula until you have a completely smooth dough.

Add one-third of the sugar water to the dough and use the spatula to lift the dough so the syrup runs beneath the dough (this will help prevent it from sticking to the pot). Set the pot over low heat and cook, stirring constantly. Keep mixing vigorously, scraping down the sides of the pan until the dough absorbs all the syrup and the texture is smooth and bouncy. Repeat this process three times until you've used all the syrup; the dough will remain very sticky but will become bouncier. Continue to cook over low heat, stirring vigorously, for 7 minutes. Use the spatula to scrape the mochi dough onto the prepared sheet pan, then sift more potato starch over the surface of the dough. Let cool to room temperature. Once the mochi has cooled, you need to work quickly, since it will soon become too hard to handle. Use a plastic bench scraper to divide

the dough into eight equal pieces, each about 1¼ oz / 40 g.

To assemble: Remove the bean paste–covered strawberries from the refrigerator. Dust a work surface and your hands with potato starch (it's crucial to handle the sticky mochi with starch-dusted hands). Working with one piece of mochi dough at a time, stretch it into a 2½ to 3-inch / 6 to 7.5 cm disk. Hold the mochi dough in one palm and place the strawberry ball, tip side down, into the center of the mochi. Cup the mochi and the strawberry ball with one hand, as if you were holding a tennis ball. Use your other hand to stretch the mochi dough from all sides toward the center, then pinch to close the gap and pinch off any excess dough. Place the ichigo daifuku pinched side down on the starch-dusted work surface, then use both hands to shape into a ball, gently stretching the mochi down toward the bottom, as if you were forming a loaf of bread. Brush off any starch from the ball. The daifuku are now ready to serve, and are best eaten the same day they're made.

If you don't plan to eat the daifuku immediately, dust them with potato starch and store in an airtight container. Keep the container in a cool spot; if the weather is hot, keep the container in the refrigerator.

SHIRO KOSHIAN

SWEET BEAN PASTE

3½ oz / 100 g dried
    white beans, such as
    cannellini
7 tablespoons / 85 g
    sugar
2 tablespoons water

MAKES 6 OZ / 165 G

To make your own shiro koshian: Put the beans in a large bowl and add cold water to cover by several inches. Soak the beans at room temperature overnight. The next day, drain and transfer the beans to a medium heavy-bottomed saucepan and add enough water to cover the beans by 1 inch / 2.5 cm.

Bring to a boil over high heat and reduce to a simmer. After 15 minutes, when the beans are no longer wrinkled, drain and rinse them again in fresh water. Along with preparing the beans for even cooking, this parboiling step washes away some of the stronger flavors and helps reduce the "beaniness" of the final paste.

Return the washed beans to the pot and add enough water to cover by a couple of inches. Bring to a boil over high heat, then reduce the heat to simmer. Cook for 1 to 1½ hours, until the beans are tender enough to easily crush between your fingers, adding cold water periodically as needed to keep them submerged.

Once the beans are cooked, remove from the heat and cool the beans in their liquid to room temperature. Save the bean water to make the paste.

Working in batches, pass the beans and bean water through a food mill into a large bowl. Discard the skins. After it's been strained once, pass the bean starch liquid a second time through a sieve into a large clean bowl. Work in batches and use a spatula or plastic bench scraper to help pass the bean starch through the fine sieve. Let stand, undisturbed, for 5 minutes, until the solids have sunk to the bottom of the bowl.

Carefully pour off most of the cloudy water, leaving the bean starch on the bottom of the bowl. Fill the bowl with cold tap water, stir, and let stand again for a few minutes, until the solids settle. Pour off the water. Repeat this process with two more changes of water or until the water becomes clear enough to see the bean starch at the bottom of the bowl.

Line the fine-mesh sieve with a clean cotton kitchen towel or cheesecloth, then strain the mixture. Squeeze the cloth to remove all the liquid from the bean paste. If your sieve is small, work in batches.

Add the sugar and the 2 tablespoons of water to a small saucepan and cook over medium-high heat until the sugar dissolves. Add half of the bean paste to the saucepan and, stirring with a rubber spatula, bring to a low simmer.

Add the remaining bean paste to the saucepan and continue cooking, stirring, over medium-high heat. Make sure the paste doesn't start to brown, especially at the edges. It's ready when the bean paste has thickened and starts to hold sharp edges, about 10 minutes.

Remove the pan from the heat and spread the paste on a rimmed sheet pan or plate in an even layer. Let cool to room temperature, then cover with plastic wrap and refrigerate for about 30 minutes or up to a day.

Or you can transfer the bean paste to a resealable storage bag and freeze for up to 1 month; thaw before using.

ROLL CAKE

ロールケーキ

SPONGE

3 large eggs

6 tablespoons / 75 g sugar

6 tablespoons / 45 g cake flour, sifted

WHIPPED CREAM FILLING

½ cup plus 2 tablespoons / 150ml heavy cream

1¼ tablespoons sugar

Sliced peaches, for serving (optional)

MAKES 1 (9-INCH / 23CM) CAKE; SERVES 4 TO 6

For better or worse, if there is one characteristic that defines the Japanese baking aesthetic, it might be "softness." This manifests itself in the fluffy milk bread "melon pan," crustless katsu and egg sandwiches, and, in its purest form, the Japanese roll cake. After a few months in Japan, I started to lose my patience with mild, tender, and sweet baked goods and began to crave a properly chewy and crunchy loaf of bread (although, admittedly, some good French bakeries—with excellent bread—have opened in Japan in the last decade). That said, when I'm back in San Francisco, with all the hard edges of city life, a slice of Japanese roll cake takes me away; it's so soft, gentle, and pleasing.

Pastry Chef Junko's recipe is for a tender genoise cake, simply filled with lightly sweetened whipped cream. It's delicious served with fresh sliced peaches (if you want to lean into the aesthetic, use white peaches). Once you are comfortable with the basic recipe, you can vary the flavor of the cream and, of course, the fruit you serve with the cake.

To make the sponge: Line the bottom and sides of a 9 by 13-inch / 23 by 33 cm rimmed sheet pan with parchment paper. The paper should not overhang more than ⅜ inch / 1cm. Preheat the oven to 350°F / 175°C.

Combine the eggs and sugar in a large bowl and whisk together. Set the bowl over a saucepan of hot water (about 140°F / 60°C as registered on an instant-read thermometer), taking care that the bottom of the bowl does not touch the water. Cook, whisking constantly to warm the egg mixture, until it reaches 96°F / 36°C (about 30 seconds). Remove the bowl from the saucepan. Beat with a hand mixer on high speed until the egg foam becomes very thick and airy, about 4 minutes.

Decrease the speed to low and beat for 2 more minutes to break down any large air bubbles; you should see a smooth foam without visible bubbles.

Add the cake flour all at once, then use a rubber spatula to fold the flour into the beaten eggs, about 60 strokes. To retain the air in the egg mixture and to prevent the sponge from becoming too dense, do not overmix.

Pour the cake mixture into the center of the prepared pan. Using an offset spatula or a bench scraper, spread the batter evenly and efficiently, pushing it to the corners. Try not to work the batter too much, since this will deflate it. Tap the pan once on your flat work surface to release any large air pockets.

Bake for 10 to 11 minutes, until the surface looks dry and golden.

Remove the cake pan from the oven. To release steam and to prevent the sponge from shrinking, hold the pan about 4 inches / 10 cm above your counter or work surface and drop it. You can put down a kitchen towel to protect the counter if you'd like.

Remove the sponge from the pan and place it on a wire rack with the parchment paper still attached to the bottom of the sponge. Let cool for about 15 minutes.

To make the whipped cream: In a large bowl, combine the cream and sugar. Beat with a whisk until stiff peaks form. Refrigerate until ready to use.

Once the sponge is cool, cover it with a second piece of parchment paper (slightly larger than the sponge cake) and gently invert the sponge onto the paper. Peel off and discard the parchment paper from the bottom (now the top) of the sponge, then flip it again, top side up.

Remove the whipped cream from the fridge and orient the cake (still on its parchment) so a short side is facing you. With an offset spatula, spread the cream onto the sponge. To ensure a good amount of filling at the core of the cake, the cream should be spread thicker on the half of the cake closest to you. Using the parchment paper to aid you, begin rolling the cake away from you. At the start, you'll need to push down the edge of the sponge with your fingers so that the cake curls easily; continue until the entire cake has been rolled.

Carefully move the cake to the center of the sheet of parchment paper. Grab the ends of the sheet of parchment and hold them in your hand, then use a long ruler to push the top layer of paper under the roll cake. Gently pull on the bottom layer of paper to tighten the roll.

After tightening the roll, wrap the parchment paper around the cake and refrigerate, seam side down, for at least 15 minutes or up to one day.

When ready to serve, unwrap the cake and cut it into thick slices using a warm knife. Junko likes to serve this cake garnished with sliced peaches.

VARIATIONS

- Condensed milk cream and strawberries: Substitute 1 tablespoon of sweetened condensed milk for the sugar in the whipped cream filling. Beat the cream with a whisk until soft peaks form, then stir in the sweetened condensed milk and beat until stiff peaks form. Fill the cake as described above. Serve with fresh strawberries that have been hulled, halved, seasoned to taste with sugar and lemon juice, and macerated for 30 minutes.

- Apricot noyaux cream and stone fruit: Beat the cream with a whisk until stiff peaks form, then stir in a drop of almond extract. Serve with fresh stone fruits (peaches, nectarines, or plums) that have been sliced, seasoned to taste with sugar and lemon juice, and macerated for 30 minutes.

- Lemon verbena cream and melon: In a small saucepan, combine the cream and a very small handful of fresh lemon verbena leaves. Bring to a simmer, remove from the heat, cover and let steep for 15 minutes, then strain. Chill until cold, then add the sugar and beat with a whisk until stiff peaks form. Serve with small cubes of melon that have been seasoned to taste with sugar and lemon juice and macerated for 30 minutes.

- Earl Grey tea cream and figs: Increase the cream amount to ½ cup plus 3 tablespoons / 165ml. In a small saucepan, heat the cream to a simmer, remove from the heat, add ¾ teaspoon / 3 g Earl Grey tea leaves, and let steep for 15 minutes, then strain. Chill until cold, then add the sugar and beat with a whisk until stiff peaks form. Serve with quartered fresh figs that have been seasoned to taste with sugar and lemon juice and macerated for 30 minutes.

SOUFFLÉ CHEESECAKE

スフレチーズケーキ

10 oz / 280 g cream cheese, at room temperature

3 tablespoons unsalted butter, at room temperature

½ cup plus 2 tablespoons / 150ml whole milk

3 large eggs, separated

6 tablespoons / 75 g sugar

2 tablespoons cornstarch

Seasonal fresh fruits, for serving

MAKES 1 (7-INCH / 17 CM) CAKE; SERVES 6 TO 8

Like many of Pastry Chef Junko's desserts, her soufflé cheesecake is distinguished not only by its flavor, but also by its lovely texture. It is soft and velvety, not very sweet, and unlike the creamy, dense cheesecakes I loved as a kid, it's lighter than air. Her cheesecake really is a soufflé, with carefully beaten egg whites folded into the cream cheese base. And like a soufflé, the cake is cooked in a water bath to maintain a steady gentle heat. Junko recommends aging the cheesecake overnight before serving. During this time, the cheesecake firms up, and its flavor develops.

Serve the cheesecake with sugar-macerated berries (strawberries, raspberries, wild blackberries, blueberries, and lemon zest), or, as Junko prefers, with a spoonful of Meyer lemon marmalade.

Place an oven rack in the upper third of the oven. Preheat the oven to 375°F / 190°C. Line the bottom and sides of a 7-inch / 17 cm springform pan with parchment paper. The parchment paper should not extend more than ⅜ inch / 1 cm above the edge of the pan. Completely wrap the bottom of the pan with aluminum foil.

Fill a large saucepan partway up with water and bring to a simmer.

Put the cream cheese in a large heatproof bowl and mix with a spatula to soften. If the cream cheese is too cold and hard to mix, hold the bowl over the saucepan of simmering water for 10 seconds. Mix and repeat as needed; the cream cheese should be creamy and easy to mix but not as liquid as mayonnaise. Add the butter to the softened cream cheese, mix well with a spatula to combine, and set aside.

In a small saucepan, heat the milk until it's warm to the touch (about 96°F / 36°C).

In a medium heatproof bowl, combine the egg yolks and 2 tablespoons of the sugar and mix well until the sugar dissolves completely. Add the cornstarch and mix well to combine, then add the warm milk and mix until homogeneous.

Set the bowl over the saucepan of simmering water, taking care that the bottom of the bowl does not touch the simmering water. Hold the bowl with a dry kitchen towel or an oven mitt and cook, whisking continuously, until the mixture thickens slightly, about 4 to 5 minutes. Do not overcook the custard; aim for a loose texture, since it will continue to cook even after it's removed from the heat. As soon as it begins to thicken, immediately remove the bowl from the saucepan and add the custard to the bowl with the cream cheese. Mix well to combine.

With a hand mixer on medium speed (or in a stand mixer fitted with the whisk attachment), beat the egg whites on medium speed for about 30 seconds, until foamy. Add half of the remaining

4 tablespoons / 50 g sugar and beat on high speed for 90 seconds. Add the remaining 2 tablespoons sugar and beat for about another 90 seconds, until the whites hold soft peaks.

Whisk one quarter of the beaten egg whites into the cream cheese mixture to lighten, then gently fold in half of the remaining egg white mixture with a rubber spatula. Fold in the remaining egg whites until just combined; do not overmix. Pour the mixture into the prepared pan. Shake the pan a little bit to make the surface flat. If you see any air bubbles, poke them.

Position the pan in a larger baking dish and pour hot water into the baking dish so it comes about ½ inch / 12 mm up the side of the pan. Bake for 12 minutes, open the oven door for 10 seconds, then decrease the oven temperature to

275°F / 135°C and bake for another 30 minutes, until golden brown (quickly open the oven door to check, then immediately shut it again).

Turn off the oven and leave the cake in the oven for 1 hour (this will prevent any sudden temperature changes that could cause the cake to sink). After an hour, remove the cake from the oven, remove the pan from the water bath, and let the cake cool to room temperature in its pan, then cover and refrigerate overnight.

When ready to serve, remove the cake from the pan, peel the parchment paper from its sides, and slice the cake into wedges with a hot knife, wiping it clean and rewarming it between slices for the cleanest cut. Serve cold, garnished with seasonal fresh or preserved fruits.

MONT BLANC モンブラン

MERINGUES

3 tablespoons confectioners' sugar, plus more for dusting

2 tablespoons almond flour

2 tablespoons hazelnut flour

1 large egg white, cold

Pinch cream of tartar

¾ teaspoon granulated sugar

CHESTNUT CREAM

9 oz / 250 g cooked, peeled chestnuts

¼ cup / 50 g granulated sugar

¼ cup plus 3 tablespoons / 100ml water

2 teaspoons whole milk

WHIPPED CREAM

½ cup plus 3 tablespoons / 162ml heavy cream

4 tablespoons / 52 g mascarpone cheese

Scant tablespoons granulated sugar

MAKES 6 SERVINGS

Like many of my favorite Japanese sweets, the Mont Blanc has European roots. Named for the famous alpine mountain, this chestnut dessert has existed in some form or other in France for a couple hundred years. It wasn't until after World War II, though, that the Mont Blanc became a Japanese obsession. Particularly in the fall, when chestnuts come into season, you'll see the dessert in higher-end pastry shops and at confectionary kiosks in fancy department stores. It is a layered dessert with a base of meringue and a center of whipped cream, covered with a piped swirl of sweetened chestnut vermicelli. Although long considered heavy and old-fashioned in France, the Japanese version, and Pastry Chef Junko's specifically, is delightfully light.

When Junko was working with us at the restaurant, we'd serve Mont Blanc in October, when the first California chestnuts are harvested. This dish is time-consuming to make, especially when starting with raw chestnuts. However, unsweetened, peeled cooked chestnuts are a reasonable compromise. We have also included the method for peeling chestnuts below if you are feeling ambitious. Apart from the chestnuts themselves, the recipe is fairly straightforward. If you don't have hazelnut flour, you can double the quantity of almond flour.

To make the meringues: Preheat the oven to 275°F / 135°C. Line a sheet pan with parchment paper.

In a small bowl, sift together the confectioners' sugar and almond and hazelnut flours.

Put the egg white and cream of tartar in a medium bowl. With a hand mixer at medium-high speed or with a whisk, beat the egg white for about 30 seconds, until foamy. Add a third of the granulated sugar and continue beating, until it starts increasing in volume. Add half of the remaining granulated sugar and continue beating or whisking until the mixture begins to form peaks that hold their shape. Add the remaining granulated sugar and beat or whisk until the peaks hold their shape when the beater or whisk is lifted.

With a rubber spatula, gently fold the dry ingredients into the beaten egg white until just combined; do not overmix.

Spoon the mixture onto the prepared pan into disks about 2½ inches / 6 cm in diameter, spacing them about 1-inch / 2.5 cm apart. You need six disks for this recipe, but you may have enough batter to pipe seven—cook's treat!

Sift a light blanket of confectioners' sugar over each disk, then transfer to the oven and bake for 45 minutes, or until golden. Remove from the oven and set aside to cool completely.

To make the chestnut cream: In a medium saucepan over high heat, combine the chestnuts, granulated sugar, and water. Bring to a boil, then turn down the heat until the mixture

is simmering. Using a slotted spoon, skim and discard any scum that rises to the top. Cook for 10 minutes, until the chestnut pieces are very soft and almost all the liquid is gone. Add the milk and mix to combine. Transfer to a food processor and process into a paste, adding additional water by the tablespoonful, as needed, to aid the processing. Let cool to room temperature, then press the mixture through a fine-mesh sieve into a clean bowl. Refrigerate for 20 minutes.

To make the whipped cream: In the bowl of a stand mixer fitted with the whisk attachment or in a large bowl and using a hand mixer or a whisk, combine the cream, mascarpone, and sugar and beat until stiff peaks form.

Remove the chestnut cream from the refrigerator and fold a generous third of the whipped cream into the chestnut puree in three additions. Transfer to a piping bag fitted with the Mont Blanc tip (see note below). Transfer the remaining whipped cream to a second piping bag fitted with a plain tip.

To assemble: Arrange the meringues on a small tray or serving plate. Pipe a small ball of whipped cream into the center of each meringue, then transfer the meringue and cream to the freezer and freeze for 20 minutes.

Remove the meringues from the freezer.

To pipe the chestnut cream, you will need good pressure. Squeezing firmly and working in a circular motion pipe the chestnut cream over the whipped cream in concentric circles; it should resemble a small mountain and should now completely cover the cream filling

and meringue. Repeat with the remaining meringues and chestnut cream. Tidy up any stray noodles at the base of each meringue and refrigerate for at least 15 minutes.

Just before serving, lightly dust each meringue with confectioners' sugar.

Notes:

If you're starting with fresh chestnuts, you'll need 14 oz / 400 g chestnuts in their shells to yield enough for this recipe. Wash the chestnuts, then transfer to a large pot and add 4 ¼ cups / 1L water; the chestnuts should be submerged. Add ½ teaspoon salt, then cook over low to medium heat until the water boils, 10 to 15 minutes (if the water hasn't boiled in that time, nudge the heat up a bit and continue to cook until boiling). Once the water boils, turn down the heat so the water is simmering and continue to cook, covered, for 40 to 50 minutes (smaller chestnuts will take less time). Turn off the heat and leave the chestnuts in the pot until the water cools down enough that you can comfortably put your hands in it. Drain the chestnuts and carefully cut each one in half (take caution—they can be slippery!). Scoop out the chestnut meat with a spoon and transfer to a bowl; discard the shells. Weigh the chestnut meat; you should have about 9 oz / 250 g for the chestnut cream.

One special piece of equipment that you'll need is the Mont Blanc piping tip for your pastry bag. It has eight to ten holes, and it pipes the distinctive noodlelike cream. If you don't have a Mont Blanc piping tip, you can use a small round tip or cut off a very small tip of a disposable pastry bag to make a small single hole.

UMESHU
梅酒

PLUM BRANDY

7½ lb / 3.25kg rock, raw, or granulated sugar

14 lb / 6.3kg unripe ume plums

3 gal plus 3 cups / 12L vodka

MAKES ABOUT 4 GAL / 15L

After returning from Japan, the first ingredient that I set myself to finding in California was the Japanese ume plum. Related to apricots, they are a small, hard fruit. Although they are too sour to eat fresh, they have a distinctive and very strong fragrance that make them indispensable in umeshu, often marketed as "plum wine" in the US. When made with good fruit, homemade umeshu is a world apart from the store brands, which I find both too sweet and lacking in ume flavor. However, with good fruit, it's a magical elixir made by combining the plums with vodka and sugar, then letting it mellow until the fragrance of the fruit perfumes the liquid and colors it a golden hue.

For the first couple of years, through word of mouth, I found small quantities of ume from backyard trees in Berkeley, which Japanese American families had planted generations ago. However, my determination to find a significant quantity finally paid off when Maya Shiroyama, the owner of Kitazawa seed company, introduced me to her father-in-law, a retired UC Davis botany professor. He had consulted on an ume farm in Winters, near Sacramento, in the 1970s. Together, with only his memory as guide, we spent hours on the road searching for the farm. When we found it, it was like I'd discovered El Dorado. My jaw dropped to see acres and acres of ume trees, thousands of them, laden with fruit. The air was thick with the smell of ume. Now, every year, we order 500 to 600 pounds of the fruit, picked to my specifications: color breaking from green to yellow and extremely fragrant.

Every spring, we make around 150 gal / 568L of umeshu. As you have to wait nearly a year for the spirit to be ready to drink, and the ume harvest comes but once a year, we make enough for the duration. In late May you can often find ume at Japanese markets, although they tend to sell the ones that have been picked when totally green and rock hard. I've been told countless times that that is the "way it's done in Japan," but I assure you that the riper fruit make an infinitely more fragrant and delicious umeshu. If you find good fruit, I recommend you buy a lot. This recipe is for a large batch, but since sourcing the ume is the hardest part, and you have to wait so long for it to be ready, it makes sense to really go for it.

As the umeshu ages, the taste changes, developing a deeper, almond-y flavor as the essences from the pit of the ume are extracted. We still hold on to a few small reserve bottles of umeshu we made a decade ago.

Most recipes for umeshu in Japan specify rock sugar because it melts slowly, thereby drawing the juice out of the fruit slowly and keeping the ume plums from puckering. At the quantities we use, rock sugar is prohibitively expensive, so I've found that by adding regular white granulated sugar over the course of two additions, I can keep the fruit plump and attractive. If you don't mind wrinkled fruit and you are using granulated sugar, you can add it all at once. Either way, be sure to mix the liquid well as the sugar sinks to the bottom.

One final note: Although most of the umeshu we use is served as a drink, it is also very useful as a seasoning ingredient for fruit jellies, such as the grapefruit jelly (page 264). When used in moderation, it will enhance the flavor while adding a nominal amount of alcohol, making your seasoned fruit juice taste like (very good!) candy.

Wash the ume in two changes of water to remove any dust. Dry on a towel. Remove the stem and calyx from each fruit with a toothpick.

Separate the sugar into two batches. To prevent the fruit from wrinkling, the first batch will be added at the beginning and the second will be added one week later. In a 5-gal / 19L bucket, layer a quarter of the ume, followed by a quarter of the half batch of sugar, repeating until you've used all the ume and half batch of sugar. Pour the vodka over and cover the bucket. Make sure it's sealed tightly so the alcohol doesn't evaporate.

One week later, pour in the second batch of sugar, and give the umeshu a good stir.

Don't worry about dissolving it all.

The umeshu should be stored in a cool dark place for at least 6 months; the flavor will continue to develop for several years. The longer the umeshu cures, the more complex the flavor will become as the almond-y flavor of the pit starts to season the alcohol.

This recipe yields a not-too-sweet umeshu. If you prefer it to be sweeter, stir and taste it after 6 months and add sugar to your taste. At the restaurant, we serve it over a single large cube of ice, garnished with one of the ume from the bucket. You can also add some seltzer if you'd like to make an ume fizz.

ACKNOWLEDGMENTS

This book would not exist without my wife and editor, Jenny Wapner. She is brilliant at her work and with incredible clarity and persistence, helped form something real out of my amorphous ideas. The project was a family affair. My sister, Aya Mishima Brackett, has been taking photos of my cooking long before I had a restaurant. Her acute visual sense comes through clearly on these pages. And a cookbook is only as good as the recipes themselves. For this, I thank my co-writer and recipe tester, Jessica Battilana, who worked though the recipes, painstakingly noting omissions and contradictions. With good humor, she steered me away from my more chef-y inclinations to make sure the recipes can be properly made at home. Thank you to Emily Timberlake who helped jumpstart the book, and to Carolyn Insley who kept all the pieces together. And finally, I'm grateful to Lizzie Allen for her playful design sense and patience as she pulled all the parts of this book together.

And there are also the people who kept the restaurant going while I was off writing. My partner and the General Manager of Rintaro, Virginia Haruna Vaughn, fearlessly lead the team with John Lee. And my sous chefs Mamiko Kobayashi, Brian Ishii and Nelson Hernandez, kept up the standard in the kitchen with Aaron Linenberger and helped work out many of the trickier recipes.

Yuko Sato, who has cooked with me longer than anyone, was invaluable in the photoshoots and provided her handmade ceramics, which have become an important part of the restaurant. And for a number of the recipes that needed a second opinion, I asked for help from my cooks and servers. I'm grateful to old timers, who have been with me through thick and thin: Coco Lim, Aaron Linenberger, Tommaso Cristiani, Izzy Moriyama, Kasumi Suzuki, Gerardo Hernandez, and Natsumi Iimura; as well as the some of the new generation: Ken Mayeda, Taito Nakayama, Rean Taylor, Derek Chan, Kayla Hoffman-Rogers and Claudia Chan.

I feel lucky to include dessert recipes from my opening Pastry Chef, Junko Yamada Schwesig. She cheerfully returned to San Francisco from her new home in Berlin, Germany, for the photoshoots. And my friend and longtime collaborator, Tomoko Tokumaru, who shared the definitive gyoza recipe. And to John Lee for sharing his profound enthusiasm for sake.

And finally, this book is dedicated to my father, Leonard Carpenter Brackett. He showed me how to work and the importance of bringing the best of Japan to the West.

INDEX

INDEX

Hardie Grant North America

2912 Telegraph Ave
Berkeley, CA 94705
hardiegrantbooks.com

Copyright 2023 by Sylvan Mishima Brackett

Photographs copyright © 2023 by Aya Mishima Brackett

Cover illustration by Austin Long

Published in the United States by Hardie Grant North
America, an imprint of Hardie Grant Publishing Pty Ltd.

Library of Congress Cataloging-in-Publication Data is
available upon request.

Hardcover ISBN: 9781958417003

eBook ISBN: 9781958417294

Printed in China

Design by Lizzie Allen

First Edition

SYLVAN MISHIMA BRACKETT is the chef/owner of Rintaro in San Francisco, which was named one of Bon Appétit's Top 10 New Restaurants six months after opening in 2015. Sylvan was born in Kyoto and raised in Northern California. He is the former creative director at Chez Panisse, and trained at Soba Ro in Saitama, and at a Ryotei in Aoyama, Tokyo.

JESSICA BATTILANA is a food writer, recipe developer, and author of *Repertoire: All the Recipes You Need* (Little Brown, 2018) and the co-author of over 6 cookbooks.